THE MILITARY FOUNDATIONS OF THE MODERN POLITICS

THE MILITARY FOUNDATIONS OF THE MODERN POLITICS

G.K. Pagare

CYBER TECH PUBLICATIONS
4264/3, Ansari Road, Daryaganj, New Delhi-110002 (India)
Ph.: 011-23244078, 011-43559448 Fax: 011-23280028
E-Mail: cyberpublicationsdelhi@yahoo.com
Website: www.cybertechpublications.com

THE MILITARY FOUNDATIONS OF THE MODERN POLITICS

G.K. Pagare

First Edition 2010

Published by :

G.S. Rawat for **Cyber Tech Publications**
4264/3, Ansari Road, Daryaganj, New Delhi-110002 (India)
Ph.: 011-23244078, 011-43559448 Fax: 011-23280028
E-Mail: cyberpublicationsdelhi@yahoo.com
Website: www.cybertechpublications.com

Printed at: Asian Offset Printers, Delhi-53

Preface

In war, do mass and materiel matter most? Will states with the largest, best equipped, information-technology-rich militaries invariably win? The prevailing answer today among both scholars and policymakers is yes. But this is to overlook force employment, or the doctrine and tactics by which materiel is actually used. In a landmark reconception of battle and war, this book provides a systematic account of how force employment interacts with materiel to produce real combat outcomes.

This book argues that force employment is central to modern war, becoming increasingly important since 1900 as the key to surviving ever more lethal weaponry. Technological change produces opposite effects depending on how forces are employed; to focus only on materiel is thus to risk major error—with serious consequences for both policy and scholarship.

In clear, fluent prose, it provides a systematic account of force employment's role and shows how this account holds up under rigorous, multimethod testing. The results challenge a wide variety of standard views, from current expectations for a revolution in military affairs to mainstream scholarship in international relations and orthodox interpretations of modern military history.

Military Foundations of the Modern Politics will have a resounding impact on both scholarship in the field and on policy debates over the future of warfare, the size of the military, and the makeup of the defense budget.

—Author

Contents

1

INTRODUCTION

Since the Russian Revolution, most socialists have supported armed struggle to achieve or defend socialism. Yet historical events, including the development of weapons of mass destruction and war-making by socialist states, show the limitations of socialist militarism. Furthermore, there are strong theoretical objections to socialist militarism, including the undemocratic and patriarchal nature of the military. One alternative to socialist militarism is a socialism based on an organised system for popular nonviolent resistance to aggression and repression, called social defence. This alternative is built on popular participation, decentralisation and self-reliance and hence is quite compatible with democratic socialism. Importantly, the nonviolent methods of social defence are compatible with the goal of the defence, unlike military methods. Promotion of social defence seems to be a promising way to aid struggles against systems of domination.

Socialism has both an antimilitarist and a militarist tradition. Martin Shaw points out that antimilitarism was the dominant strand in the fifty years before the Russian Revolution, but since then military methods have been widely used and accepted as a means of furthering socialism. During this latter period, the problem of war received little attention from socialist scholars. It was only the rise of the 1980s peace movements that once again made war into a problematic issue.

Socialists have long attributed the problem of modern war to the workings of international capitalism. The classic work in this vein is Karl Liebknecht's analysis of militarism dating from before World War I. Liebknecht also emphasised that military training serves to make proletarians act against their class interests and that the army is frequently used to repress people "at home," most notably workers.

The success of the Russian Revolution led many socialists to defend or condone socialist militarism to defend the revolution, while attributing the overall problem of war to capitalism.

In addition, the success of armed struggle in a number of Third World countries, notably China and Vietnam, led many socialists to support guerrilla warfare in the name of socialism. Military methods have not generally been seen as a problem in themselves. They have been treated by socialists as a means, either to defend and promote capitalism or to defend and promote socialism. Yet the use of military methods to achieve or sustain socialism can be criticised on both historical and theoretical grounds.

Historical events certainly have shown the limitations of socialist militarism. First, guerrilla struggles have been successful only in Third World countries, usually those seeking independence from colonial rulers. There is no example of guerrilla warfare successfully challenging an established capitalist state.

Second, the development of weapons of mass destruction undermines the view that military means can be an acceptable means to any progressive end. Nuclear weapons may be used to defend socialism only at the potential cost of millions of lives.

Third, socialist states have shown themselves to be just as warlike as capitalist states. Since World War II, there have been no major wars between rich capitalist societies. On the other hand, the socialist world experienced the invasions of Czechoslovakia and Afghanistan, war between China and Vietnam, and continued military confrontation between China and the Soviet Union. Arguably, of course, capitalist societies have at least as bad a record in terms of military interventions and the promotion and propping up of military dictatorships. The point here is that state socialism has not provided any hint of a solution to the problem of war.

A key reason for this is that socialism developed in the mould of states, just like capitalism. Socialist states have relied on military forces to protect themselves internally and externally, just like capitalist states. Liebknecht's analysis of the use of military forces for internal repression seems to apply to socialist states as well as to capitalist ones. In the face of capitalist militarism, "actually existing socialism" failed to challenge the foundations of militarism.

The rise of modern war can be linked to the rise of both capitalism and the modern state, a complex process that can only be summarised schematically here. War under feudalism in Europe was mainly carried out by mercenaries and had only an occasional impact on the peasantry. The decentralised economic system could not sustain large standing armies.

In order for the crown to develop control over recalcitrant nobles, larger and more permanent military forces were required. The developing capitalist economies provided surpluses that could be tapped to supply armies. The extraction of this surplus from the population required tax collectors and other bureaucrats. Militarisation and centralisation of power were central to the rise of the modern state, with its bureaucracy, administrative centralism and close relation to the process of economic extraction. Looked at one way, militarism and the modern state are certainly linked to capitalism, whose surpluses can be tapped for the purposes of the state (and capitalism).

But, from another point of view, capitalism is only one economic system - a convenient one to be sure - that can service the military and the state. The historical development of state socialism involved a challenge to capitalist social relations, but replaced it with another economic system that allowed central extraction to support the military and state.

The course of the Russian Revolution gives an idea of how this happened. The revolution was a largely nonviolent affair made possible by the collapse of discipline and loyalty in the Russian army resulting from the disastrous war with Germany. The early months of the revolution had a strong libertarian flavour, especially in the soviets of workers and soldiers.

Although a peace treaty was soon negotiated with the German government, the fledgling Bolshevik government had to confront an invasion supported by several capitalist states. This war of survival from 1918-1920 was crucial in the militarisation of the revolution. Trotsky took control of the disintegrating army, reappointed former Czarist officers to commands and instituted traditional military discipline.

This same period saw the triumph of a command system in politics. The Bolsheviks moved to smash independent political forces and instituted for themselves the principle of "democratic centralism," an exact analogy to military command. The later development of Stalinism was, according to some commentators, an accentuation of "command politics" rather than a qualitatively new development.

Most other socialist states resulted either from guerrilla wars or from Soviet conquest. In most cases, successful guerrilla leaders became the subsequent political leaders. In this way, the military model of command became the model for socialist development. The net result was that state socialism challenged capitalist social relations but not militarism, the state or the necessity of an extractive economic system at the service of central managers.

Of course, "actually existing socialism" was quite different from a truly democratic socialism, with less hierarchy and bureaucracy and more participation. Is such a socialism compatible with the military? Can military methods be used to promote democratic socialism? Historical examples do not prove the case one way or another. However, there are a number of theoretical reasons why a democratic socialism cannot be based on an authoritarian guardian of society and why, by relying on military methods, socialist struggles are forged in a mould of nationalism, centralism and male domination. It should, then, be no surprise that the result, in terms of propensity to war, is little different from capitalist militarism. The military, as a form of organisation, is the antithesis of democracy. The key principles of the military are hierarchy and command. The most important lesson in military training is obedience to orders. The democratic practice of dialogue and debate is contrary to the structure of the military.

The system of military command is linked to the command economy that is characteristic of state socialism. In both cases the key decisions are made by planners at the top and implemented by workers at the bottom. Bureaucracy, a method of organising work based fundamentally on hierarchy and the division of labour - essentially a command system - is the central organisational form in contemporary industrial society, being especially characteristic of both the state sector and monopoly capital. Bureaucratic organisation is fundamentally antagonistic to participation and equality, and hence to democratic socialism. A bureaucracy, with its hierarchy and command, is not an administrative but a political system, and as such can best be likened to an authoritarian political system - the only difference being that the latter relies ultimately on military force for its survival.

The military is the prototypical bureaucracy. To accept the military is to import bureaucratic principles into society. Indeed, methods of social control developed in Western military forces has been taken up by civilian bureaucracies.

As noted earlier, modern state bureaucracies had their origin in the need to extract resources in order to support military expenditures, as well as the state bureaucracy itself. The state thus has a continuing interest in an economic system that allows extraction of a surplus, both for capitalists and the state itself. This is directly linked to contemporary environmental problems. Methods of organising society based on local self-reliance in food, transport and energy - such as decentralised renewable energy systems, with maximum energy efficiency - do not lend themselves to extraction of a surplus for military or other purposes. Oil supplies can be taxed or commandeered for military purposes; this is not so easy with buildings designed on passive solar principles or towns designed for pedestrians and cyclists.

Another central characteristic of military systems is male domination. Young fit men are the main recruits to most armies, and military commanders are almost always men. Only in a few guerrilla armies do women play much of a combat role, and rarer still are female guerrilla commanders. This pattern persists in modern technological warfare, where brute strength plays little role. In principle, a woman is just as capable as a man of being a jet pilot or working in a nuclear missile silo.

In practice, the power systems of patriarchy and military command mutually reinforce each other. Men use their positions in the military to exclude women and maintain a male chauvinistic psychology to reinforce the military hierarchy. The invariably patriarchal nature of militaries adds weight to the argument that the military as an institution is antagonistic to democratic socialism.

There are, then, a number of reasons why a military is inherently incompatible with democratic socialism: the military form of organisation is itself undemocratic; the economic support for military forces is linked to bureaucracy and to an extractive economy detrimental to the environment; and the military reinforces patriarchy.

But is there any alternative? How can a democratic socialism be defended from its enemies without creating pressures for authoritarian politics? One possible answer is social defence.

SOCIAL DEFENCE

Social defence can be defined as nonviolent community resistance to aggression as an alternative to military defence. It relies on methods such as strikes, boycotts, noncooperation, protests and setting up alternative institutions.

Social defence is founded on the assumption that no regime, however ruthless, can survive without the support or acquiescence of a large proportion of the population (including police and military personnel). If a significant proportion of the population withdraws this support, rule is impossible.

The idea of using nonviolent methods as a method to resist military aggression dates from earlier this century. Gandhi was a key figure, and his campaigns and ideas triggered much of the thinking on this topic. The first full development of social defence as a comprehensive policy was by British ex-officer and writer Stephen King-Hall, for example in his 1958 book *Defence in the Nuclear Age*. King-Hall advocated abandonment of Western military forces and their replacement by organised citizen resistance as a more effective way of countering the communist threat to the British way of life. About the same time, a number of peace researchers began developing the idea of social defence, including Theodor Ebert in West Germany, Johan Galtung and Arne Naess in Norway, and Gene Sharp in the United States. Social defence is also called nonviolent defence, civilian defence, and civilian-based defence.

To many people, the idea of nonviolent resistance to military aggression sounds nice but completely impractical. How could it possibly work? One of the prime tasks of the social defence researchers has been to mobilise both arguments and examples.

Gene Sharp is the most important figure in the study of nonviolent action. He has identified and classified 198 different *types* of nonviolent action, giving historical examples of every one, and has integrated this mass of data with a comprehensive theory. Only some of the historical examples of nonviolent action are relevant to defence against military aggression.

In 1923, French and Belgian military forces occupied the Ruhr due to Germany's failure to pay reparations. Military resistance was impossible, but a number of groups - especially trade unions - advocated nonviolent resistance to the occupiers, and soon the German government supported this. Civil servants, transport workers, shopkeepers, trade unions, the Social Democratic Party, and the press participated in the resistance, which was maintained for many months in spite of bloody repression. Although the German government, due to acute financial crisis, called off the resistance, outrage in France, Belgium and other countries over aspects of the occupation meant that its original aims were not achieved.

In 1961, French generals in Algeria staged a revolt in order to halt French government moves towards Algerian independence, and there was a possibility of an invasion of France. The revolt quickly collapsed in the face of massive nonviolent resistance. In France, ten million workers joined a one-hour general strike demonstrating opposition to the coup. Vehicles were placed in airport runways to block any invading force. Even controlling Algeria became impossible for the generals. Over half the transport planes and many fighters were flown out of Algeria by pilots who disobeyed their officers; others simulated mechanical problems. Many troops resisted simply by staying in their barracks. Other actions included losing orders and files and delaying messages. The rebel forces gave up without a single shot being fired on them.

In Poland in 1981 there was a military coup, staged with the tacit support of the Soviet government, to stem the growing challenge, spearheaded by Solidarity, to bureaucratic rule. In the aftermath of the coup, nonviolent resistance continued in the form of strikes, underground publishing and cultural events, and noncooperation. The continued resistance to military rule contributed to the eventual easing of martial law and to the 1989 changes throughout Eastern Europe.

Historical examples can only point to the potential for nonviolent resistance and certainly cannot prove the case for social defence. It is important in this regard that the popular resistance in every case was spontaneous. Social defence, it can be argued, has never been tried because proper preparations for it have never been undertaken. Nonviolent resistance to an invasion or coup can no more be expected to succeed without preparation than can an improvised army in which the soldiers have no training, no stock of weapons, and no plan.

What, then, would a prepared social defence system look like? It would involve setting up communication systems that would be difficult to shut down, such as a supply of short-wave radios for every member of the population. It would involve constructing factories so that they could be disabled by destruction of difficult-to-replace pieces of equipment (replacements could be kept in another country), so that even torture could not get production going again. It would involve considerable decentralisation and self-reliance in the production of energy, food and transport, so that aggressors could not readily control these vital functions by destroying a few vital facilities. It would involve widespread training in nonviolent techniques, including large-scale simulations. It would involve widespread learning of foreign languages and cultures, in order to facilitate fraternisation. It would involve developing links with opposition groups in countries from which aggression might stem.

A social defence system clearly could involve massive changes. It might well require just as large a social investment as now made in military defence. Thus, historical examples of nonviolent resistance only hint at what might be possible with a fully prepared social defence system.

But could even such a system succeed against the Nazis or against Stalinist repression? It is impossible to know for sure. Nonviolent methods *were* used against the Nazis, especially in Norway, Denmark and the Netherlands, sometimes with success. But more important is the fact that there was a massive degree of collaboration with the Nazis. Resistance, whether violent or nonviolent, was the rare exception until victory by the Allies became a likely prospect. Again it can be said, social defence has not yet been tried. Similar comments apply to Stalinism except that, unlike Nazism, its collapse owed little to military methods.

There are some historical examples that show that nonviolent methods can succeed against severe repression. The Iranian revolution is a good example. The Shah's regime was supported by all the major powers, had a massive military arsenal, and employed secret police and torture on a large scale. Tens of thousands of peaceful protesters were shot dead by troops, but eventually the troops joined the revolution. Needless to say, the subsequent course of the revolution is not a victory for the principles of nonviolence. But the revolution itself shows that severe repression does not always win out against nonviolent methods. The key in this and many other cases is the loyalty of the regime's troops. This loyalty is more likely to be undermined when they are faced by nonviolent protesters than by partisans trying to kill them.

It spite of these arguments, it is natural to have reservations about the effectiveness of social defence. To keep things in perspective, it is useful to make comparisons with the strengths and weaknesses of military defence.

Military defence is basically defence of a territory, and protecting borders is crucial. Social defence, by contrast, is basically defence of the social fabric. It is designed to protect key features of a society, such as freedoms, justice and participation. Social defence is not very good at guarding borders; military defence is not very good at protecting freedoms.

Military forces can be called out by governments; popular participation in military decision making is limited. Social defence depends on popular participation. It can only be effective with widespread popular support, and is difficult to use to support oppressive features of society.

Military preparedness often triggers off military preparedness in other countries, thus justifying itself. Social defence provides no threat, in the traditional sense, to the security of other societies. It may, though, provide a threat to repressive regimes by encouraging nonviolent resistance by their populations.

Military defence provides no protection against nuclear attack; nor does social defence. But there is much less justification for using nuclear weapons against a society without arms.

Military forces are essential for military coups and military regimes. Social defence cannot be used for purposes of repression, but can be used *against* military coups and regimes. Given that military regimes prevail in many countries throughout the world, in open or veiled form, this is a crucial difference. While social defence may have limitations, these must be weighed up against the undoubted disadvantages of military defence.

Whereas the *idea* of social defence has been moderately well developed, there has been less development of cxperience in how to promote the alternative. A good portion of "promotion" has taken the form of raising the idea in various forums. Due to the efforts of committed individuals, several governments - including Sweden, Denmark, Austria, and the Netherlands - have sponsored studies of social defence. But government interest has been difficult to arouse. The Netherlands government planned to fund a series of ten studies into social defence, but ended up funding only one of the proposals made by an expert committee. In the United States, Gene Sharp and associates have made persistent efforts to interest government and military officials in social defence, with some success at the level of individuals but very little at the level of policy.

Another approach is to promote social defence at the grassroots, namely among peace activists, trade unions, community groups, feminists, and so forth. Efforts in this direction have been made in a number of countries, especially in Europe. Unlike the English-speaking countries, social defence has long had considerable salience in most Western European peace movements. For example, social defence is on the platform of the German Green Party. In October 1989, a social defence conference with over one thousand participants was held at Minden, West Germany. In the Netherlands, different groups in the social defence network focus on women, research, government officials and so forth. In Austria, pressure from social defence advocates led to introduction of a social defence component in the alternative service provided for conscientious objectors. In Australia, community-based research projects have been carried out on communication and social defence.

Initiatives so far must be considered small and tentative compared to what is required to bring about a substantial challenge to military methods. Nevertheless, both theoretical developments and practical experience are sufficient to show the radically different implications of social defence for the nature of society.

Social defence is inherently participatory. Unless a substantial fraction of the population joins the nonviolent resistance, it has little chance of success. This is quite different from military methods, which can succeed even without popular support.

All sectors of the population can contribute to social defence, irrespective of gender, age, knowledge or ability. Because the methods used are nonviolent, there is no premium on fitness or masculinity. The participation of groups marginalised by the military increases the total number of those directly involved in the resistance and also increases its effectiveness. It is difficult enough for commanders to get their soldiers to use violence against nonviolent men, and more difficult still against women and children.

A society that makes decisions in a participative manner can offer more effective nonviolent resistance. A society dominated by a set of elites is vulnerable, because the elites may be intimidated or coopted. The first thing an aggressor will do is to undermine leaders, for example by arresting them or winning their cooperation. A social defence system must be able to survive this sort of attack, and this is best done by use of networks, sharing of responsibility and skills, and use of participatory planning.

As noted earlier, nonviolent resistance to aggression will be more effective when workers have greater control over production and when there is greater decentralisation and self-reliance. Factories where workers can shut down production or easily tool up to produce alternative products are much more difficult to use by an aggressor.

Communications are crucial to social defence, both to coordinate resistance, to alert supporters in other countries, and to communicate to the people and soldiers of the country from which the attack stems. The most effective communication system for a military dictatorship is one-directional, and this is why military coups often start with occupation of central television and radio facilities. The most effective communication system for social defence is many to many, with numerous alternative methods of communication and high redundancy. Face-to-face meetings and electronic mail are models. The connection with democratic socialism should be obvious.

In summary, military systems, with their hierarchy, command and limited participation, are most compatible with authoritarian political and economic systems. By contrast, community-based social defence, with wide participation, decentralisation and self-reliance, is highly compatible with egalitarian political and economic systems.

SOCIAL DEFENCE AND LIBERATION

In industrialised capitalist societies, few on the left today even endorse violence, much less plan for serious use of it. The reason is simple: the power of the state is so overwhelming that violent resistance is futile. That is certainly the experience of urban guerrillas, who have been singularly unsuccessful.

One of the reasons for this is the increasing power and sophistication of the technology of repression. Only a couple of centuries ago, the rifle, a technology used to control a population, could also be used to liberate it. It was, in a sense, a people's weapon. Liebknecht pointed out that democracy flourishes when everyone can obtain weapons of equal value. But modern states underwrite research and development of technologies that are essentially weapons for the state alone. It is difficult to imagine liberation via tanks and saturation bombing, not to mention nuclear weapons. These are not people's weapons in any sense. Their main use is inevitably against people, whether in the name of reaction or liberation.

It is partly an awareness of the futility of violence to topple industrialised states that is behind the renunciation of violence by many left groups today. But many still have an emotional attachment to violence. One reason for this is the apparent effectiveness of Third World guerrilla struggles. In considering this issue, it is important to note at the outset that there has never been a systematic comparison of violent and nonviolent liberation struggles in terms of effectiveness or costs and benefits. Indeed, there is not a single comprehensive argument for violence available in the literature: Gene Sharp's classic treatment, *The Politics of Nonviolent Action*, has no equivalent dealing with violent methods. Therefore, it is tempting to conclude that support for violent liberation struggles occurs largely in the absence of rigorous relevant evidence.

Those supporting these struggles can point to undoubted victories in countries such as China, Vietnam, Cuba, Algeria, and Nicaragua. What are often forgotten are the losses such as Malaya, Uruguay, Bolivia, South Africa and Palestine. Also often forgotten are the massive human costs of violent struggles. In Algeria, for example, there were as many as one million deaths in the war for independence from France.

Supporters of nonviolence are not in a position to dictate to others who live under oppression what they should or should not do. Gandhi said that it was better to resist oppression violently than not to resist at all. The key point here is examination of alternatives. Nonviolence deserves just as much attention and development as violence, especially considering the tarnished record of violent liberation struggles and their connection with centralisation and male domination.

It is often said that violence must be used because nonviolence was tried and failed. This claim cannot be sustained. In fact, nonviolent struggle has seldom been tried to its utmost. Unlike military methods, its dynamics are relatively unstudied and undeveloped. No nonviolent struggle has yet been carried to the scale of suffering one million casualties, as in Algeria.

One seldom hears the claim that nonviolence must be used because violence was tried and failed. Yet that is the reality as often as not. In Palestine, the intifada succeeded in a way never achieved by violent methods. The multifaceted unarmed struggle mobilised the entire population. All could participate, women and men, shopkeepers and consumers, teachers and students, young and old. Previous violent actions had been the prerogative of small groups of men, with planning carried out in secret and much greater opportunity for misrepresentation and counterproductive results. The PLO, which was as surprised as everyone else by the intifada, reaped a credibility from its success never achieved through violent methods.

The other thing to remember is that guerrilla struggles are, first and foremost, political struggles. The classic liberation struggles involved many nonviolent methods, including providing services to communities, building of political networks, development of skills, setting up communication systems, and a full range of strikes, boycotts, demonstrations, and other forms of protest. Without these nonviolent methods, and especially the building of support from local communities, guerrillas have little chance of success and are seen simply as terrorists.

It is for this reason that social defence has been called the nonviolent equivalent of guerrilla warfare. Indeed, these two methods of struggle are very similar except for the use of violence. This is, of course, a big difference. The risk with violence is that the social organisation and weapons of liberation will turn into the social organisation and weapons of repression, as in

Cambodia and elsewhere. The possibility of nonviolent liberation struggles is one of a search for alternatives that are participative, effective, and respectful of human life.

In a world in which numerous wars are being fought and in which there continue to be vast arsenals of weapons designed for mass destruction, it is illusory to imagine that violent struggles provide salvation. Violence is not simply a means to an end, but shapes the end. It is associated with secrecy, hierarchy, male domination, and systems of command. In almost every way it is antagonistic to the widespread participation, dialogue, and equality that are central to a democratic socialism.

There *are* nonviolent alternatives to the military, as yet quite undeveloped, but deserving of attention, experimentation, and improvement. The introduction of social defence, arguably, requires complementary changes in the economy, state, communication and technology, all in the direction of greater participation, autonomy, and self-reliance. The promotion of social defence cannot be treated as an isolated campaign, but needs strong links to other campaigns against systems of domination.

Nonviolent struggle has the advantage of being prefigurative: unlike military methods, its ends are embodied in its means. Many pacifists, for example, have emphasised individual resistance to militarism at the expense of structural factors, and this may make some on the left feel uncomfortable. The challenge is to develop nonviolent struggle into a truly revolutionary method.

2

Military-social Politics: Definition of the Concept

The state is a universal system-forming institute that administers all spheres of social life, that is, conducts policy through its power function in a public way. Administration of the social sphere is translated into its social policy designed "to create conditions of dignified existence and free development of people" (Art 7, Constitution of the Russian Federation).

Political science describes social policy as an activity the aim of which is to administer society's development, meet its material and cultural requirements, and regulate social differentiation. A balanced, stable, integral, and dynamically developing society based on ample material resources, adequate political forces and social system are the basic alms of such policy. It is closely connected with the most important sphere of interests of all members of society and therefore should be treated as a political priority. Regulation of social relationships within a special state institute, the military organization, is one of most important elements of social policy.

At the present stage of a military-technological revolution an all-round, scientifically substantiated, and balanced military-social policy is the key to the reforms in the military organization of the Russian Federation. This is explained, first and foremost, by an enhanced role of the principle of humanization of military development designed to create the best possible conditions for man as the main subject of armed struggle, for reproduction of his natural-biological and spiritual potential and for creating adequate conditions for his existence in the system of military-social relationships.

The following factors make it possible to regard the military-social policy as a relatively independent structural element of the entire system of the state's social policy.

First, a special nature of the military's activity: they are duty bound to be always ready to defend the state and its citizens with the force of arms, to carry out any tasks without questioning them under any conditions even at the peril of life. This explains why they are granted privileges, guarantees, and compensations that should be regarded as the form of realization of the state's military-social policy. It was A. Dobrovolskiy, A. Gradovskiy, and A. Grekov who at the turn of the 20th century first scientifically substantiated the special legal status of the military as compared with other citizens. They were convinced that the state "should create special norms designed to identify the legal position of the military within which their civil rights can be limited or the military can get privileges unknown to other citizens."

Second, the high state and public significance of what the military do, namely protection of the state in the military sphere, a direct cause-and-effect connection between the state's defense capability and the degree of social protection of the military, the quality of the military-social policy carried out by the state and its structures.

Third, presence in the general legislative system of a vast and varied system of normative legal acts regulating the sphere of social protection and insurance of the military, retired military and their families.

Fourth, the presence in the RF of a vast group involved in the military social sphere (the military, their families that enjoy certain additional guarantees and compensations connected with the family head's professional activity, retired military whose pensions and other types of social insurance are determined by their former military service, war veterans, etc.).

So far the term "military-social policy" has not yet been widely accepted and is not used as often as the term "social policy." At the same time, academics, journalists, public and military leaders have been more and more often discussing the state's policy in the military-social sphere as a special field of social policy.

The above suggests that the military-social policy can be regarded as a special social institution the existence of which is objectively stipulated by the practice of the military and social reforms going on in Russia.

The following factors are steadily increasing the importance of the military-social policy in carrying out the tasks of military development and reforms of the state military organization.

First. The earlier social problems became more acute. There are new no less acute problems such as unemployment, wage arrears, de facto paid education and medicine, loss of certain social guarantees. The consumer market has changed a lot: on the one hand, the market relations extended the supply of commodities and services. On the other, purchasing power of the absolute majority (including the military and their families) dropped considerably. As an inalienable part of society the Armed Forces are inevitably affected by the same problems as the rest of society.

What is more, due to the military organization's specific features (strict regimentation of everyday life and duties connected with risk of life and health as well as legal limitations of certain civil rights and freedoms, etc.) the army more keenly feels many of the social problems.

Second. The reforms now underway in the Russian Federation (in the pension system, in the municipal services system, and the system of privileges to certain social categories). They are intended to gradually abandon the policy of state guarantees that in the past relieved people of the duty to look after themselves by the same token depriving them of any desire to fight for existence and self-realization. The state is embracing the liberal policy in the social sphere designed to limit the state's involvement in the citizens' personal affairs and giving them more freedom. It is expected that the citizens will learn to rely on their own forces and not to expect help from outside. If one takes into account that the law bans the military to undertake any other paid jobs (with the exception of scientific, teaching and creative endeavors) the military and their families totally depend on the level of state security. This explains why the current reforms should introduce additional measures to improve the content, a lms and directions of the military-social policy.

Third. A complex military reform was caused by the radical military-political changes and new tasks, and conditions in which the Russian Federation ensures its military security. The reform is an important part and a priority task at the present stage of military development in Russia. All components of the state's military organization, including the military-social sphere, are reformed within the current military reform in a balanced and well-coordinated way.

Fourth. An active involvement of the servicemen in the armed conflicts, peacekeeping and counter-terrorist operations that took place in the last decade. This added urgency to the problem of additional measures designed to protect those who fought, those who were left crippled and the families of those who died in action.

To better understand the meaning of military-social policy one has to regard it as an element of the state's military policy. This will deepen one's understanding of the role and place of the social factors in the development of the state's military organization and in the course and results of armed struggle. The military doctrine of the Russian Federation as a specific expression of the state's military policy proclaimed the principle of realization of the rights and freedoms of the servicemen, their better social protection, adequate social status and the standard of living as one of the principles according to which the military organization of Russia will develop. The state identified the following tasks as the key goals of its military-economic policy: higher standard of living and social security of the servicemen and civilian employees of the Armed Forces and other troops and realization of the social guarantees under the federal laws. From this it follows that while being a part of the state's social policy and an inalienable part of the state's military policy military-social policy is a relatively independent social institution objectively needed to maintain domestic stability and the stability of the military socium. It can be described in the following way.

The military-social policy is based on a sum-total of special normative legal acts and is a relatively independent component of the social and military policy of the state. It is designed to govern social development of the state's military organization, to meet the material and cultural requirements of the servicemen and their families so that to ensure reproduction of their moral-psychological and physiological potential, to preserve the inner balance, stability, and battle worthiness of the military organization.

The structure of military-social policy is rather complicated. The following are its key structural elements: politics in the sphere of payment; pensions to retired servicemen, and families of servicemen that lost their breadwinners; politics in the sphere of rations, clothing, lodging and other types of material allowances; politics in the sphere of medical services of the military, retired military, and families; politics in the sphere of housing accommodation; politics in the sphere of compulsory state insurance; social insurance for the most vulnerable groups of servicemen, retired military and family members (disabled, senior citizens, families of the military killed in action, families with many children, those who took part in liquidating the effects of the Chernobyl disaster, etc.); social policy in relation to the servicemen with special merits (those who took part in hostilities, veterans of wars and service in the army); policy in the sphere of social adaptation, retraining and job placement of those who left the service and civilian employees.

The objects of military-social policy are citizens connected in any way with the functioning and development of the military organization; the citizens who were transferred to the reserves who receive pensions and other material allowances from the RF Defense Ministry, other structures of the federal executive branch that have troops of their own; family members of retired military; civilian employees of the RF Armed forces, other troops, military formations, and structures.

Subjects of military-social policy in the contemporary conditions are: the state as a whole and its structures, departments, and agencies; organs of state administration; organs of local self-administration; public, charity, religious and other nongovernmental organizations and funds.

The problem of criteria of efficiency of military-social policy is equally important. In many respects the problem is reduced to the question of which level of social security for all members of military organization can be regarded as sufficient to ensure the state's military security. Experience has taught us that the answer to this question lies within the moral-psychological and social sphere. The main thing is not an absolute level of family income but the step on the hierarchical ladder on which the military find themselves (according to the objectively assessed income level and self-assessment of the military themselves). It is the objective index of the place and role the state allocates to the military organization in the system of its priorities and values.

One should bear in mind that military-social policy resolves the most important strategic tasks in the sphere of national security closely associated with the process of reproduction of intellectual, moral-psychological, and physical potential of those working in the military sphere, with preventing social conflicts with unpredictable results among the military. The content and direction of the military-social sphere has come to the fore in the military service and is determining the moral and psychological state of the servicemen and, in the final analysis, Russia's national security.

MILITARY SCIENCE AND NEW SECURITY THREATS

If we take a critical look at the situation with ensuring the state's military security, we will see, among many other problems, the ineffectively tapped intellectual potential of the domestic military science. As a result, we have yet to hear coherent, clear-cut answers to these questions: What kind of war against Russia is possible in principle, considering the evolution of and the current status of the military sphere and the character of international relations? In this context, how should the country's defense be organized? And, what are the reasons for the prevailing situation?

On the one hand, public opinion tends to ignore the knowledge about the nature, essence, and substance of modern warfare. Many Russian politicians, who have rapidly risen to prominence (oftentimes riding on the crest of criticism against the military), failed to competently assess the military-political and military-strategic situation and organize the country's force development in compliance with the requirements of science, not propaganda slogans. They saw any argument by military experts in defense of Russia's security as a manifestation of the corporate survival instinct. The character of the ongoing polemics around military reform is indicative in this respect. Remember Kozma Prutkov's comment to the effect that an ignoramus feels absolutely at home in any sphere unknown to him.

Politicians who have little knowledge of the military or who have a personal agenda, are heavily influenced by the U.S. simplistic ("stand-off"), high-tech vision of warfare, forgetting the essential, marked difference between U.S. and Russian military policy, predetermined by the specifics of the geopolitical situation, history, development, and values of these states. Blind projection, transplantation of the U.S. worldview and methodology in the defense sphere to Russian soil naturally leads to their rejection, and will never ensure the American standard of quality in defense here.

Russia is a special country and it needs its own, specific defense and security (by all parameters). They say that "aliens" during the era of Peter the Great and Catherine II greatly benefited Russia. Indeed that was the case because their influence was offset by a powerful counterbalance within the country, comprising various restrictions on their will and the clearly defined limits on manifestation of their creative activity in Russian land. Foreign experience did not replace but supplemented Russia's capabilities. Today, however, we are witnessing attempts to replace the national defense system with another, based on a different worldview, other principles and methods of organization. Furthermore, what is disregarded is the great difference in the resource capabilities of Russia and the United States at present, as is the danger of ending up completely dependent on powerful "assistants" (once a foreign worldview, methodology, and principles of practical operation have been adopted, foreign specialists take charge of the defense sphere).

On the other hand, our military scientists have lost a unified scientific-methodological basis for analysis of warfare—a view thereof as a complex, integrated, systemic phenomenon, connected, through a multitude of threads, with various spheres of life. So, in their majority, they generate sound, good-quality fragments of knowledge that are easy to manipulate at will.

This fragmentation and one-sidedness is especially manifest in analysis and summarization of combat experience, in particular, in the Persian Gulf area, Afghanistan, the Balkans, on the Tajik-Afghan border, and in Chechnya.

Granted, scientific analysis is necessary in any particular event, but it should not be made a fetish of and extrapolated to entirely different situations. Say, it is wrong to build the entire personnel combat training system exclusively on the experience in mountain terrain warfare. After all, tomorrow it could be flatland or forest terrain.

What then? The fact is that for all the importance of the combat experience in the counterterrorist operation in Chechnya, it is inexpedient to use it as the basic component of the state's military organizational development. This also applies to the choice of weapons and military hardware and the correlation of precision and traditional and nuclear and conventional weapons. Otherwise we will have to keep acquiring new knowledge about warfare in the process of warfare itself. The cost of this kind of education is well known from history.

Experience, history and present-day reality show beyond any doubt that there has never been, nor will there ever be, a "pure" war, conducted according an "armchair" scenario. The very outbreak of any war brings in a multitude of new circumstances that can substantially change its course. Remember World War I. No one had ever especially planned it. It was simply that the political situation went out of control, and the war began to follow its own logic, producing so many unexpected twists and turns that baffled the collective brain power of the smartest of general staffs.

Today, in order to attain their objectives, Russia's opponents will seek an assortment of methods to exert pressure, special operations, and weapons (above all precision guided weapons). "Decisive intentions" against Russia could arise from the instability of its domestic situation, criminalization of society, and concern about the security of nuclear facilities or of the environment. The aforementioned circumstances are, essentially, but an excuse, not a real cause of war, because the latter lies in the sphere of vital interests of states, resulting in acute contradictions between them. These include the struggle for natural resources, material values, means of communication, land and subsoil, and water and air space; elimination of competition (obstacles) in the way to world and regional leadership (including the establishment of amenable political regimes in other countries); the aspiration by multinationals in developed countries to promote their products, and so forth.

Deterrents against any forms of ag gression against Russia are: the progressive character of its development, pro-active diplomacy, the stability and effectiveness of state administration, constant protection of state interests both at home and on the international arena, and military power (the quantitative and qualitative characteristics of military organization).

Proceeding from the logic of the evolution of the present-day military-political situation and the specifics of the country's geopolitical status, it is essential to single out, among the possible kinds of wars, first of all, wars against Russia, the aims of military aggression by one or several states being the country's population, its material and spiritual values, natural and scientific-production resources, and change of the sociopolitical system; second of all, wars into which Russia could get involved for various reasons.

In that event its military power, international authority, and leverage over other countries could become a means (instrument) of the military policy of other states or coalitions thereof. Russia's entry into World War I is indicative in this respect. There was no pressing need for Russia to participate in it; there was no evidence of large-scale military aggression, but there were excessive military-political ambitions and heavy dependence on the allies.

Here is what the military historian A.A. Kersnovskiy wrote: "For all its mediocrity, the Russian strategy in the Great War was not so bad as it might seem judging by its results. But it was tied hand and foot by the most deplorable of policies.

Russia unquestioningly followed even the most absurd demands of its allies, readily sacrificing its vital interests to their petty, mercantile designs (under the guise of the 'allied cause'). We never knew how to deal with foreigners, and in the Great War, in particular, were unable to take a fitting place, failing to use our highly advantageous political situation. We should have been selling our assistance to them just as they were selling their to us." (1) History repeated itself in 1945.

The Red Army, having reached the Wisla, was unprepared for a new strike. Yet, in response to a request from its allies, it precipitated, to the degree possible, the preparation of an offensive operation to rout the Nazis deployed between the Wisla and the Order. Soviet troops save d the allies from routing in the Ardennes, but at the cost of several hundred thousand lives. Meanwhile, when celebrating the 50th anniversary of their landing in Normandy, the "greateful" allies did not even invite those who had saved them in the winter of 1945. Why is it that no historical lessons are being learned? Why it is that the dialectics of international politics and the military sphere are not being studied while important state decisions concerning the country's defense interests are made without the necessary substantiation? These also are questions for the military science.

There is yet another peculiar method of warfare—the arms race. The moral, intellectual and financial costs of the arms race are huge and can be compared to the economic damage caused by a real war. The entirely different character of the aforementioned types of war dictates different priorities in ensuring the state's military security. Thus, the main brunt in the arms race is borne by the national economy, the defense complex, and the high-tech branches of industry. Participation in a war as an ally requires strenuous efforts by politicians and diplomats while in the event of outright armed aggression, the main burden will be borne by the state's military organization,. primarily its Armed Forces.

Forms of armed aggression will be predicated on the war's political objectives and the capabilities and methods of the employment of weapons and military hardware. The form of war against Russia will to a very large extent be contingent on the experience and achievements in the military sphere of states and coalitions intending to use force to destroy us or to impose their will on us. They will above all use strategy and tactics enabling them to use precision guided weapons and weapons based on new physical principles, delivering massed strikes in a stand-off mode. These strikes will be accompanied by strong EW and psychological impacts and acts of sabotage.

The experience in antiterrorist operations in Chechnya points to the reality of non-classic (unconventional) wars. In these wars, the Armed Forces have to act according to the laws of unconventional warfare. Furthermore, it needs to be borne in mind that the scale of such wars is contingent on support from the outside.

Hence their complexity. Armed forces have to deal not only with the actual perpetrators of various terrorist and criminal acts, but also with their economic, political, and military sponsors, who cover up and hide their activities from the public and are based far away from the area of operations. So it is wrong, say, to compare the effectiveness of combat operations by Soviet troops in Afghanistan with U.S. strikes on Taliban bases. In the first instance, a limited contingent had to deal not simply with mujahedin guerrillas but with a well organized opposition to the Soviet Union on the part of the United States, Pakistan, and other states. In their operations against international terrorism i n Afghanistan, however, the Americans were objectively assisted by the Northern Alliance, supported by other countries. This problem is of principal importance to Russia as long as there are forces that intend to resort to a strategy of dismembering this country to prevent it from emerging as a strong competitor, especially a superpower.

A new approach to ensuring military security is based on the premise that the main threat in the future will originate not from the regular militaries of various countries, but from all sorts of terrorist, criminal, and other organizations whose participants are united into the so-called network structures. The latter are known as SPINs, or Segmented, Polycentric, Ideologically Integrated Networks. In this set-up, the main thrust is placed on what is known as operations other than war. A new term has even been coined: "network warfare."

There are several key characteristics that distinguish "network warfare" from conventional warfare. The first is the use of geographically distributed force. The second is that forces involved in "network warfare" are highly intellectual. By using knowledge acquired as a result of comprehensive surveillance over the battle area and an in-depth penetration of command plans, these forces are able to synchronize their actions while operating more effectively in an independent mode. The third is the availability of diversified and reliable communication channels (links) between their elements in a combat area, enabling them to carry Out joint operations, quickly adapting to the situation on the ground.

By relying on the laws of dialectics, we have every reason to believe that owing to the specifics of its geopolitical position, the complexity of the internal situation and the fact that Russia has yet to complete the building of a modern defense system, a whole spectrum of forms of warfare and operations other than war, including special operations, could be used against it. Everything will hinge on the wisdom of the country's military-political leadership, its reliance on the constructive sections of society, the dynamic development of the national economy, and the state of its Armed Forces.

The army and the navy have always been the most effective political instrument of the state. There are three main tasks in the structure of state policy: acquisition of power, the exercise of state power in a particular sphere (for the military, in ensuring defense of the state), and maintenance of power, The principle of depoliticization prohibits the Armed Forces from engaging in the fulfillment of the first and the third task. But this does not applied to the second. Furthermore, any evasion (including by the military science) of problems confronting the state in the defense sphere that are essentially political, has to do not with depoliticization but inaction, which should be judged on an entirely different set of standards. Virtually all matters pertaining to force development are of great state and, therefore, political significance. So an oversimplified approach to the principle of depoliticization can provide fertile soil for the emergence of irresponsible people in the military, unable to prepare o bjective, well substantiated material for decision-making on the state level.

Military operations are complex in many respects. Here, it is impossible to do without expert opinion. This is especially important when it is war that is at issue. There is a view that war is too responsible a matter to be entrusted to the military. Yet it is even more irresponsible to prepare for and conduct a war without the military, whose ultimate mission is in fact to strengthen the country's security.

So, what needs to be done to fulfill this paramount state task?

First, it is critical to understand that just like all countries, Russia has its own interests whose realization is designed to ensure the existence and development as an independent and sovereign state. The population, the territory, the mineral resources and production assets, transport communications and facilities and installations beyond its boundaries-all of this must be protected (there is no shortage of those wanting to appropriate "no-one's" or poorly protected facilities). It is essential to declare national interests in a fitting and utterly comprehensible manner. They should be reflected in the Russian Constitution and other laws and regulations.

Second, establish at the top state level exactly what Russia should have and what resources and instruments it actually has to uphold its interests. To this end, a program and technology to advance state interests should be worked out.

Third, define the priorities of military organizational development and identify the resources to meet this need. Here, well substantiated proposals and calculations should be presented by the military since state security is at stake. It is perfectly clear that if a target is 1,000 kilometers away, it is senseless to fill a bomber with fuel to last only for 500 kilometers, invoking considerations of economy.

Either the fuel should be provided in full or the mission should be canceled. Until recently, things in the military sphere have been done exactly in reverse. Development of the military-industrial complex and the Armed Forces was planned not in terms of what they should be in accordance with the logic of the evolution of the military-political situation but what we could afford them to be, proceeding from considerations of economic expediency, which tended to decline with crises.

Furthermore, there were attempts to mechanically downsize the military and reduce the number of enterprises in the defense i ndustry as a means to address economic and social problems although it has long been known that when security and defense become hostage to other interests, a country sooner or later turns into a military camp, paying a very high price for negligence—in the lives of its citizens. Unfortunately, with regard to this country, history has been repeating itself with striking regularity. Chechnya is a good case in point.

Fourth, it is critical to drastically review the attitude of state structures as well as individuals toward defense, toward those who defend the country's interests with weapons in hand. Unfortunately, it has yet to be fully appreciated that the armed forces of any state are not only a major institution, not only a highly complex system with state-of-the-an weapons and equipment at their disposal, but also a specially organized, large mass of people designed for action under extreme conditions.

Not only many individuals but even politicians have yet to understand military service as a specific, special state service. What is even more important is the military's attitude to society which is apparently ignored by the majority of politicians, presumably believing that people in uniforms should have endless patience, be like robots, denied civil right and isolated from society and ongoing processes. The fact is that after all is said and done, a military serviceman, just like any other person, needs a clear-cut answer to the question why he should risk his life. The military itself always stays out of politics. It is being pushed into political battles by short-sighted politicians—through humiliation, disregard for the military, and abuse of its patience and organization.

If Russia is to advance and prosper, preserving its independence in a less-than-favorable external environment, it ought to realize that military science is not simply necessary—it is objectively the state's highest priority. It is not time-serving politicians but above all scientists who should provide clear-cut answers to topical questions in the practical sphere and make appropriate recommendations to the country's political leadership.

3

Military-first Politics and Building a Powerful and Prosperous Nation

INTRODUCTION

Byung Chul Koh, Professor Emeritus at the University of Illinois, Chicago, writes: "In sum, whether or not Kim Jong Il can continue to make progress, however small, in building a "powerful and prosperous nation" utilizing "military-first politics" will hinge to a striking extent on his ability to make pragmatic tactical adjustments to the changing strategic environment, thus helping to bring about a peaceful resolution of the nuclear standoff."

The views expressed in this article are those of the author and do not necessarily reflect the official policy or position of the Nautilus Institute. Readers should note that Nautilus seeks a diversity of views and opinions on contentious topics in order to identify common ground.

Essay by Byung Chul Koh

"Military-First Politics" And Building A "Powerful And Prosperous Nation" In North Korea

If a single phrase can characterize North Korea under Kim Jong Il, it is most probably songun chongch'i (military- first politics). If one were allowed to add another phrase, the best candidate would be kangsong taeguk (powerful and prosperous nation). These two phrases, moreover, are closely intertwined, for "military-first politics" is touted as a key instrument for building a "powerful and prosperous nation."

Within the limits of available information, then, I shall explore the origins and aims of (1) "military-first politics" and (2) "powerful and prosperous nation" as well as the linkage between the two—that is, the role of the Korean People's Army (KPA) in building the latter. I shall conclude my analysis with a tentative assessment.

ORIGINS AND AIMS OF "MILITARY-FIRST POLITICS"

Stripped to its essentials, "military-first politics" refers to the elevation of the military in its dual sense of organization and function to the highest position in the North's priority list. When the term is construed in that fashion, then one can trace its origins to the early 1960s. The North's pursuit of a "four-fold military line" (4-dae kunsa noson) bespoke the high priority Pyongyang placed on fortifying its military capability in the face of what it perceived as a hostile strategic environment. The "four- fold military line" consisted of (1) arming the entire nation, (2) training all KPA soldiers to assume higher responsibilities than their rank and position would dictate, (3) turning the entire country into a fortress, and (4) modernizing the KPA.

Although the military continued to receive a preferential treatment in terms of resource allocation, however, it did not emerge as the dominant force in the North's political arena until after Kim Il Sung died in July 1994. The seeds of the military ascendancy in North Korea under Kim Jong Il, nonetheless, were sown by Kim Il Sung, who had paid extraordinary attention to political succession.

After giving Kim Jong Il top positions in the Workers' Party of Korea (WPK)—notably, secretary (September 1973), politburo member (February 1974), and member of the politburo standing committee (October 1980)—, Kim Il Sung decided to hand over control of the military to his eldest son as well. First, Kim Jong Il was appointed the First Deputy Chairman of the National Defense Commission (NDC) in May 1990. Six months later he became the Supreme Commander of the KPA. In April 1992 he was awarded the rank of "marshal of the Republic" (konghwaguk wonsu), which made him the second highest-ranking person in the KPA, next to his father who held the rank of "grand marshal" (tae wonsu). In April 1993 Kim Jong Il was promoted to the chairman of the NDC. Since the DPRK constitution had just been amended to transfer control over the KPA from the state president (chusok) to the NDC chairman, Kim Jong Il now controlled the North Korean military in a legal sense.

Efforts to enhance his de facto control had been under way since the early 1980s, when he began visiting military bases, giving presents to division commanders, and receiving reports on key developments in the military on a regular basis. Since assuming official positions in the military in the early 1990s, Kim Jong Il invariably presided over promotion ceremonies for general officers, personally pinning stars on their shoulders. By the end of the decade, several hundred KPA general officers "owed" their promotions to their supreme commander.

The ascendancy of the military in the post-Kim Il Sung North was accentuated by a relative decline, and in a few cases, abolition, of other institutions. Elections for delegates to the Supreme People's Assembly (SPA), whose term expired in April 1995, were not held until July 1998. The SPA, in fact, failed to convene for four years following Kim Il Sung's death. Nor was there any sign that the WPK Central Committee held any plenary meetings. Abolished altogether were two key institutions—the Central People's Committee (CPC), which had functioned as a kind of "super-cabinet" since 1972, and the state presidency. All but invisible for three years was the DPRK Administration Council.

None of this meant, however, that the WPK has been downgraded relative to the KPA. Kim Jong Il's decision to assume the top WPK post—that of the General Secretary (ch'ongbiso)—is noteworthy in this connection. For it is the only position not directly related to the military he has chosen to occupy. The manner in which he assumed the top party position, however, is revealing. Bypassing the WPK constitution, which empowers the WPK Central Committee to elect the General Secretary, the party organ, Nodong sinmun, published a "special press report" on October 9, 1997 announcing that Kim Jong Il had assumed the post in accordance with resolutions adopted unanimously in a series of meetings of representatives from WPK branches in nine provinces, three cities, major government organizations, and the KPA. The special report was released jointly by the WPK Central Committee and the WPK Central Military Affairs Committee.

Before the phrase "military-first politics" made its debut in Pyongyang's official rhetoric, Nodong sinmun served notice that the KPA's stature had reached the highest position ever. In an editorial commemorating the 65th anniversary of the KPA's founding in April 1997, the party organ noted: "Never before have the status and role of the People's Army been so extraordinarily elevated as today when it is being led energetically by the Respected and Beloved Comrade Supreme Commander." The editorial added that in North Korea the People's Army was synonymous with the people, the state, and the party. It pointed out that because the People's Army and Kim Jong Il shared both aspirations and destinies when Kim Il Sung was alive, the KPA was able to protect Kim Jong Il after the demise of the elder Kim. The editorial characterized having Kim Jong Il as its top leader the "greatest accomplishment of the People's Army in its 65-year history" as well as the source of its "infinite pride."

It was not until January 1999, however, that the word, songun (military-first), appeared in the North. In a New Year's Day editorial published jointly by the daily organs of the WPK, the KPA, and the Kim Il Sung Socialist Youth League, Kim Jong Il's leadership style was labeled one of "military-first"—one in which the People's Army serves as the main force of the revolution and in which the unity of the army and the people helps to safeguard as well as build socialism. In January 2000 the expression, "military- first politics," made its way into a joint New Year's Day editorial for the first time. In elaborating on the novel concept, the editorial noted that Kim Jong Il had devoted much time throughout the preceding year to the tasks of "inspecting the front-line, safeguarding the fatherland with the People's Army, and leading socialist construction." "The Comrade Kim Jong Il's military-first politics," it added, "depends on the People's Army as a pillar of our revolution, enabling the entire people, including workers and peasants, to wage their struggle armed with revolutionary army spirit; this is a powerful and refined socialist political method that radiates brilliantly." Finally, in January 2003 the phrase, "songun sasang" (military-first ideology), entered Pyongyang's political lexicon, signaling that Kim Jong Il's "military-first" method of leadership has now attained the lofty status of ideology. Although the joint New Year's Day editorial mentioned "military-first ideology" three times, however, it did not explain why "military-first politics" could be viewed as embodying a new ideology. That explanation would come later in the year.

A lengthy exposition entitled "Essential Attributes of Military-First Politics" that appeared in Nodong sinmun in December 2003 asserted that the originality of "military- first politics" stemmed from its "fresh clarification of the theory on the main force of revolution:" Whereas the theory on proletarian revolution posited the proletariat as the main force of revolution, "our Party's military-first politics" assigns that role to the People's Army. For only the latter meets the stringent criteria of loyalty, revolutionary spirit, cohesiveness, and esprit de corps. All these, Nodong sinmun noted, are prerequisite to the fulfillment of the "mission of preserving with rifles and lives the security of our party, revolution, fatherland, and people." Additionally, the party organ underscored the importance of the unity of the military and the people as well as "revolutionary military spirit," which empowers the people to carry out all the tasks of socialist construction as if they were engaged in revolution and combat.

In the joint New Year's Day editorial of 2004 the word songun is mentioned more frequently than any other words-a stunning 40 times. In most cases, however, it is used not as a noun but as an adjective—such as "military-first politics," "military-first ideology," "military-first leadership," and even "military-first Korea."

"POWERFUL AND PROSPEROUS NATION:" THE RHETORIC

The phrase kangsong taeguk (powerful and prosperous nation) made its debut in North Korea in January 1999. That year's joint New Year's Day editorial was entitled "Let Us Make This Year a Great Turning Point in Building a Powerful and Prosperous Nation." The preceding four and a half years since Kim Il Sung's death had been exceedingly difficult for North Korea. Barely had Kim Jong Il overseen the solemn funeral of his late father when he found his country plunge into the worst food crisis in its history. Faced with the threat of imminent and widespread famine, Kim Jong Il was compelled to seek aid from Seoul, Tokyo, Washington, and the international community as a whole. With its entire economy tottering on the brink of collapse, the North embarked on what it called an "arduous march" (konanui hanggun). Not until 1998 did it manage to stabilize the situation a little. Elections for the tenth Supreme People's Assembly (SPA) were finally held, and its first session convened in September to revise the state constitution and re-elect Kim Jong Il as the chairman of the National Defense Commission (NDC), which, with the abolition of the state presidency, now became the "highest post of the state that involves overall leadership and control of the country's political, military, and economic capabilities."

It was in large part to commemorate the latter event that on August 31, 1998 North Korea launched a three-stage rocket from its east coast that flew over Japan and landed off the coast of the Sanriku in the Pacific Ocean. Even though Tokyo and Washington saw the incident as a failed attempt to launch a satellite into orbit, Pyongyang claimed that it had actually succeeded and that a satellite was orbiting the earth beaming patriotic songs.

This was the backdrop against which North Korea unveiled the lofty goal of building a "powerful and prosperous nation." As the 1999 New Year's Day editorial put it, "the past year was a proud year in which the national power of Socialist Korea was forcefully displayed. By successfully launching our first earth satellite 'Kwangmyongson 1-ho' [Bright Star Number One], we demonstrated to the entire world our Republic's greatness and might. For our country to join the ranks of those who possess satellites in the midst of a severe ordeal is a miracle in history."

Kim Jong Il's vision of a kangsong taeguk, the editorial points out, aims to turn North Korea into a "socialist powerhouse embodying the most potent capabilities in ideology, politics, military affairs, economy in the near future." Ideologically, the entire country must be armed with Kim Jong Il's ideas as well as absolute loyalty in the sense of a willingness to defend the supreme leader with one's life. The "first pillar" of a militarily strong socialist country, the editorial stresses, is the People's Army, which also serves as the suicide squad for the defense of the supreme leader.

To build an economically strong country, "production needs to be normalized in all sectors of the people's economy" and the people's daily life stabilized and improved. To solve the problem of food shortages, the editorial underscores the importance of "improving the structure of agriculture," double-cropping, "revolutionizing seeds," and land leveling and rezoning.

The goal of building a "powerful and prosperous nation" would reappear in the title of a New Year's Day joint editorial in 2002 and 2004. The 2002 editorial was entitled "Let Us Glorify This Year, the 90th Anniversary of the Great Leader's Birth, As a Year of a New Leap in Building a Powerful and Prosperous Nation." In addition to the usual emphasis on the role of ideology and the People's Army, the editorial was notable for highlighting the "pressing demand for improving and perfecting economic management stemming from the changed environment." It called for "maximizing practical gains, while firmly adhering to socialist principles" and for encouraging innovation at lower units, while maintaining the state's centralized and unified guidance.

The 2004 joint editorial featuring kangsong taeguk for a third time in five years was entitled "Under Party Leadership Let Us Glorify This Year as a Year of Proud Victory Through Revolutionary Offensive on All Fronts of Building a Powerful and Prosperous Nation."

The editorial asserts that the preceding year saw the DPRK defend its pride and dignity, display its resilience, and safeguard its sovereignty and socialism under extraordinary adversity; in a word, it was a year of "proud victory." It was a year in which the DPRK marked its 55th birthday in a "great victory celebration," consolidated its unique ("our own style") socialist political system embodying "army- first" principles, and opened the way for a new leap in building a kangsong taeguk.

The main goal North Korea will strive to attain in the New Year, the editorial states, is to pave the way for a "fresh victory" in building a "powerful and prosperous nation." This, it adds, can be accomplished by conducting a "revolutionary offensive" on three fronts—(1) politics and ideology, (2) anti-imperialism and military affairs, and (3) economy and science.

Kangsong taeguk, then, is the distant destination the Kim Jong Il regime ardently hopes to reach eventually. It is a term that is being utilized in political indoctrination, which remains a key instrument of regime maintenance and economic development. Let us now turn to the linkage between songun chongch'i and kangsong taeguk—that is, the role played by the KPA in building a "powerful and prosperous nation."

THE KOREAN PEOPLE'S ARMY AND KANGSONG TAEGUK

The two components of kangsong taeguk are (1) becoming "powerful" (kang) and (2) becoming "prosperous" (song). Although the two are closely intertwined, they are nonetheless distinct, both analytically and empirically. Analytically, military and economic capabilities are clearly distinguishable. Empirically, one can find examples of countries that have awesome military capabilities that are not matched by economic capabilities as measured in per capita terms, notably the former Soviet Union and present- day China. More numerous are countries that are economically advanced but militarily weak, of which Japan, Singapore, and Scandinavian countries are conspicuous examples.

North Korea, however, aims to become both powerful and prosperous, and the KPA has a pivotal role to play in what is certain to be a long and arduous journey to make the dream come true. The goal of becoming a "powerful nation" requires strengthening the KPA both quantitatively and qualitatively. "With 1.17 million personnel," according to General Leon J. LaPorte, Commander of the ROK-U.S. Combined Forces Command and U.S. Forces Korea, the KPA "is the fifth largest active duty military force in the world." Additionally, the "North Korean air force has over 1,700 aircraft and the navy has more than 800 ships, including a large submarine fleet." When one adds "an estimated six million reserves" to the above, North Korea's "ground force is the world's third largest."

What is more, "about 70 percent of the [KPA] is deployed south of Pyongyang, where they are capable of attacking with very little tactical warning. The preponderance of the North Korean long range artillery force can strike Seoul from its current position." LaPorte adds that in addition to pursuing programs to develop nuclear weapons, North Korea "maintains a substantial chemical weapons stockpile and production capability" and "has the capability to develop, produce, and potentially weaponize biological warfare agents." Estimating that Pyongyang's "ballistic missile inventory includes over 500 SCUD missile variants that can threaten the entire peninsula," LaPorte points out that North Korea continues "to produce and deploy medium- range No Dong missiles capable of striking cities and United States bases in Japan."

LaPorte warns that "North Korea's 122,000-man special operations forces are the world's largest and pose a significant threat. We consider them a tough, dedicated, and profoundly loyal force During wartime, these forces would attack to disrupt command facilities of the Republic of Korea-United States Combined Forces Command and seek to destroy our force generation capability. The North will concentrate their special operations forces against our critical war fighting nodes while seeking to deny reinforcement from the continental United States."

Finally, LaPorte underscores the adaptability of the KPA. "They concentrate their efforts against the combined surveillance, precision attack, and force generation capability of the Republic of Korea and the United States." North Korea, he adds, "continues to improve their command, control, communications and intelligence systems, harden and bury their facilities, improve lines of communication, disperse forces, and improve camouflage, concealment, and deception measures. These efforts increase the survivability of North Korean combat power, and complicate our attack warning capability."

If North Korea's claim that it already possesses and is continuing to strengthen a "nuclear deterrent force" is true, then it may be a step closer to becoming a "militarily strong country" than ever before.

Inasmuch as a qualitative upgrading of the KPA necessitates the acquisition of ultra-modern weapons from external sources, however, the North needs to increase its revenue base; hence military power goes hand in hand with economic ability. Efforts to make the DPRK a prosperous nation, in other words, cannot be divorced from its ambition to become a militarily strong nation as well.

The linkage between the two goals, however, is reciprocal. That is to say, the KPA can contribute to the North's economic development both directly and indirectly. Directly, the KPA can perform economic tasks such as participating in agricultural and construction projects. Indirectly, the KPA can provide a model and an inspiration to the civilian population engaged in various economic activities.

Examples of the KPA's participation in economic activities include (1) providing labor and materiel to agricultural cooperatives, (2) assisting in land reclamation projects, (3) building roads, (4) building hotels and houses, (5) building power plants, both thermoelectric and hydroelectric, and (6) building mines.

The KPA also serves as a model and an inspiration to the civilian population, who are urged to emulate "the revolutionary spirit, virtues, and fighting style of the People's Army." Only by arming themselves with a "revolutionary military spirit" (hyongmyongjok kunin chongsin), the North Korean people are told, can they hope to make a big leap in building an "economically strong nation" (kyongje kangguk).

CONCLUSION

To what extent does the North Korean rhetoric pertaining to "military-first politics" and "powerful and prosperous nation" jibe with the reality? To what extent has Kim Jong Il attained or is he attaining his goals? What needs stressing is that the gap between rhetoric and reality may arguably be somewhat narrower than is widely assumed. "Military-first politics," in fact, may reflect the reality if one construes the term as encompassing the emergence of the military as the most influential group in the North, the top priority the KPA receives in resource allocation, and the frequency with which the phrase is mentioned in editorials, commentaries, and speeches published in the North Korean press.

Even the phrase "powerful and prosperous nation" is used in such a way as to tone down its connotations. In the editorial cited above, for example, the claims made for the preceding year's accomplishments and the goals enunciated for this year tend to be modest. It says that in 2003 the North merely "opened the way for a new leap" in building a powerful and prosperous nation and that in the New Year the North will strive to "pave the way for a fresh victory" in building a kangsong taeguk.

Notwithstanding the above, the North is much closer to becoming a militarily strong country than it is to becoming a "prosperous" one, no matter how loosely the latter term is defined. For the North is on "life support" insofar as food and energy are concerned, and the prospects for attaining self-sufficiency, in terms of ability to produce and import what is needed, are slim. Even if one were to accept a drastically diluted definition of "prosperous" nation—meaning a country in which production has been stabilized, most economic functions are performed in a normal fashion, and the basic needs of the people are met to a large extent—the North would still need to go a long way. Aiming high, nonetheless, will do no harm but may well do some good. It may help keep hope alive in a desperate situation, and it may also serve as what the regime hopes will be a useful propaganda tool.

To what extent, then, has Kim Jong Il attained his goals in embracing both "military-first politics" and "powerful and prosperous nation"? If, as has been hypothesized above, the major goal of "military-first politics" has been to consolidate his power and perpetuate his regime, then Kim Jong Il appears to have been successful thus far.

If a closely related goal has been to bolster the DPRK's external security, it too may have been achieved to some degree. The strengthening of the KPA's capabilities, including conventional, asymmetric, and weapons of mass destruction, may indeed have enhanced the North's deterrent power at least in the short run. Should six-party talks aimed at resolving the nuclear issue fail, however, the probability that coercive measures may be used would increase. There is, in other words, a chance that Pyongyang's quest for security may turn out to be counter- productive.

In sum, whether or not Kim Jong Il can continue to make progress, however small, in building a "powerful and prosperous nation" utilizing "military-first politics" will hinge to a striking extent on his ability to make pragmatic tactical adjustments to the changing strategic environment, thus helping to bring about a peaceful resolution of the nuclear standoff.

Journal of Libertarian Studies Volume 18, no. 4 (Fall 2004), pp. 29Ð93 ©2004 Ludwig von Mises Institute www.mises.org

SOVEREIGNTY, INTERNATIONAL LAW, AND THE TRIUMPH OF ANGLO-AMERICAN CUNNING

The Peace of Westphalia (1648), which closed out the era of wars "of" or allegedly "about" religion, established what might be called a rule-bound cartel of sovereign, territorial states, conceived as externally equal to one another and internally hierarchical.2 At that moment, we see an end to any effective claim by the Papacy and the Holy Roman (German) Emperor to universal jurisdiction. The state system that displaced those competitors thereby created a rule-following international "society" of civilized, Christian European monarchies and states. International law grew within this framework, and, in time, came to be seen as applicable to all outwardly independent political societies in the world. Coming out of the Late Middle Ages, writers on international relations built upon, radically altered, and ultimately threw aside the Stoic and Roman notions of natural law and jus gentium (the law of nations). Originally, natural law, taken as a sub-field of divine law, overlapped, but did not wholly agree with, jus gentium, the set of general rules deducible from the actual practices of separate political societies.

It was understood that "municipal" law, that is, the laws of separate states, could depart from the underlying foundations in natural law.4 International lawyers accepted the practical necessity of the case, but their work left municipal deviations from the general rules, such as slavery, under something of a moral cloud. Their writings also licensed the sovereigns of the world to make war on one another at their own discretion, there being no common judge or power set over them. International relations scholars refer to this right as "self-help" under conditions of systemic "anarchy." The sources of international law included customary law, the practice of states in their mutual relations, explicit engagements such as treaties, and, absent these, the general principles of law and reason themselves, as embodied in the natural law.5 Since the founding statements of more-or-less modern international law answer exactly to the period of European state building, and equally to a period of European explorations and "discovery," commercial expansion, and empire building in the extra-European world, there was naturally much slippage in how its concepts applied in practice to non-European states and peoples.

Writers on international relations always stress that the state system is a "horizontal" one, involving relations between theoretically independent actors answering to no superior. Thus, international law cannot be legislation handed down by an overall superior with coercive powers of enforcement. There is, therefore, a fluid character to international law, depending as it does on voluntary compliance to sundry rules and practices. The system's rules are enforced, or not, by the "self-help" of each state unit.7 These facts have led to many theoretical disputes within the fields of Political Science and International Relations between neo-realists, liberals, and social constructivists about whether the state system determines the behavior of its units, or the units generate the system.8 We may leave these issues to one side, although Gianfranco Poggi likely has a point when he writes that "states do not presuppose the system, they generate it."9 Malcolm N. Shaw, a noted authority, observes that, contrary to what might be expected, states comply with the known rules most of the time.10 This is comforting since, in the nature of things, regulation of hostile action war or conflicts that could lead to war is perhaps the weightiest issue in international law. Accordingly, rules dealing with the causes and conduct of war form an important part of such law.

Sovereign States in the "State System"

For present purposes, our overriding interest in international iaw arises from the implications of changing doctrines for the actions of sovereign and potentially violent states. We may therefore begin the discussion with sovereignty itself. Many modern writers would ask if the concept still matters. Lately, we hear much about the weakening, modification, and "relativization" of sovereignty, or even its withering-away in favor of a new secular millennium, to be led by the U.N., or with more firepower the United States, as final judge for All Mankind. In fact, as we shall soon see, today's debates within the "western" and U.S. elites focus almost entirely on this rather restrictive choice. Nevertheless, even if sovereignty seems to be, and to have been, nothing more than a useful legal fiction from its beginnings, it has been useful to someone. What, after all, is the point of theories of sovereignty of the sort that sprang up in the sixteenth and seventeenth centuries (and after)? According to French jurist Lon Duguit, such notions are "a way of imposing authority by making people believe it is an authority de jure and not merely de facto." Political scientist Karl Loewenstein calls sovereignty "nothing else, and nothing less, than the legal rationalization of power as the irrational element of politics."

A SUMMARY HISTORY OF CLAIMS FOR SOVEREIGNTY

C.H. McIlwain writes:

In Rome, we have the first actual "sovereign." We should probably have had at the same time a definite theory of sovereignty to account for this fact if the jurists of the Empire had possessed a capacity for political speculation commensurate with their genius in formulating the specific rules of law.

Stromberg Sovereignty, International Law

Relative sovereignties and jurisdictional multiplicity characterized medieval European society. At the level of ideology, the claims of the Papacy and the Holy Roman Emperor worked as practical and theoretical restraints on the power of kings, barons, and other actors in the system. This decentralization, which rested on a "non-event" the lack of an effective empire in the West after the middle of the fifth century A.D. made an opening for freedom and the development of market economies. The German Holy Roman Empire, effectively organized around a kind of feudal federalism, was itself no empire in the Roman sense.15 Quoting Marxist historian Perry Anderson, International Relations theorist John Ruggie observes that medieval Europe was a "patchwork of overlapping and incomplete rights of government," which were "inextricably superimposed and tangled," and in which "different juridical instances were geographically interwoven and stratified, and plural allegiances, asymmetrical suzerainties and anomalous enclaves abounded."

He adds: "The difference between the medieval and modern worlds is striking in this respect." Further, as McIlwain observes, "the main obstacle" to a theory of sovereignty was twofold: the prevalence in the middle ages of the theory of dominion and the absence of any clear notion of legislation. What characterizes the modern "sovereign" is supreme authority to make law.

French political theorist Bertrand de Jouvenel notes that a king enjoyed a "superiority" involving wider lands, more prestige, and so on, but was expected "to live off his own" that is, on the production and rents of personal estates. He did not enjoy an unbounded supremacy, as German historian Friedrich Meinecke complains: Although the "State certainly existed in the Middle Ages . . . it did not rank supreme. The Law was set above it; it was a means for enforcing the law." The downside of European pluralism was competitive warfare by aspirants to regional, or even wider, power. Charles Tilly notes that a deadly struggle began, one that entailed a cycle of extraction, aggression, conquest, and further extraction made possible by successful enlargement of the tax base. Centralized territorial monarchies emerged from this strife, especially from the late fifteenth century on, and these state-building wars increased the felt need for a better, more ironclad theory of royal sovereignty. New formulations of sovereignty, drawing on Roman law and other sources, became very important for the rising territorial monarchs, especially in France, England, and Spain. There were a number of steps along the ideological way. Since Carolingian times, there had grown up the notion of the corpus mysticum the mystical body of the church a body for which it might, at times, be rightful to sacrifice one's life.

The distinguished medievalist Ernst H. Kantorowicz notes that, as early as the campaign in Flanders undertaken by Philip IV (1285-1314), kings began to claim that such a duty was owed to the sovereign ruler. Thus came back to life the classical world's notion of a duty to die for the state as a secular corpus mysticum. Kings had resort, as well, to "organic" or "organological" analogies in which individuals subject to a ruler were parts of a body, whose head was the king.

Such analogies, as developed in detail by medieval writers, are now derided, but are somehow persuasive when deployed by moderns such as Hobbes, Hegel, or Lincoln. The new law of corporations was also taken on board to help give King or state a real, legal "personality." Robert Eccleshall notes "the medieval assimilation of political society to a corporation in which authority was said to reside with the collectivity of the members." Royalist writers readily claimed such corporate authority for the crown. The kingdom, or state, could now be seen as the most inclusive corporate body of all and suddenly, membership in it was no longer optional. Counter-trends to these notions were found in the writings of canonists, civilians, philosophers, and the conciliarist movement, and, as historian Ralph Raico points out, elements of these flowed into early liberalism. The struggles that set royal plunder-seeking statebuilders against traditionalist opponents nobles and townsmen alike are collectively known as the General Crisis of the Seventeenth Century.

Sovereignty Fully Theorized

The partisans of Absolutism and Divine Right Monarchy assembled their case from the elements treated above. These friends of bottomless sovereignty included Bartolus of Sassaferrato, Nicol— Machiavelli, Jean Bodin, and Thomas Hobbes, among others. The general trend was as follows: for Bodin and his successors, a mere agent of the people would not be sovereign. But Jacques Maritain points out that if the people have "divested themselves of their total power," then the king becomes "a separate and transcendental whole," and sovereignty is, thus, a property held by someone, instead of a means to security provision agreed to, on the basis of individual rights, by self-owners. The whole medieval dimension of "vicariousness" or agency disappears. Working in the context of the English Civil War part of the General Crisis of the Seventeenth Century Hobbes adopted the language of "contract," "compact," and "covenant," so as to show original consent, which unites the will of all into the One Sovereign Will of the Leviathan, or Artificial Man, i.e., the state. This onetime-only "contract" is irrevocable unless the state collapses. Hobbes's English contemporaries damned him, but quickly and thoroughly assimilated his ideas to the mainstream of English "liberalism." Anticipating the Chicago School's notion of state licensing of all private property, Hobbes writes: "It is a doctrine that tends to the dissolution of a commonwealth, Ôthat every private man has an absolute propriety in his goods, such as excludeth the sovereign.'" Certain German writers stepped up the claims for unrelieved sovereignty, and their ideas crossed the ocean in time for the American "Civil War." Cary Nederman writes that, for G.W.F. Hegel, war is the essence of the state.

> In a time of war . . . the state comes into its own as a force. . . . The sovereignty of the state is the rallying point for the common defense, which transcends all particular interests and all internal mechanisms of society, since in war the general good is incontestable and unambiguous. The state's sovereignty in its external relations is only really manifested in war. And this "outward" form of sovereignty is present not merely to a foreign state, but also to the populace of one's own state, during periods of war.

Writers like Hegel and Heinrich von Treitschke ratcheted upward the pure theory by detaching it from Hobbes's utilitarian claim that having a sovereign was good for the citizens; now it turned out that the State had its own unique personality and "life," as well as a historical mission to fulfill.31 At the same time, a peculiarly "modern" notion of individualism came into play. Bodin, for one, had "redefined Ôthe people' as being uniquely composed of individuals, equally alienated from sovereign power."32 And sociologist Robert Nisbet notes how "loose individuals" appeared, historically, alongside modern, centralized states.

Was There a North American Exception?

Some writers have denied that any such "sovereignty" grounded on unity of will, "allegiance" owed, and so on, ever existed in British North America. Yet, James Wilson, James Madison, John Marshall, Joseph Story, and others deployed the notion of unified sovereignty fairly early (pace Harry Jaffa34), even if they adopted the dodge of attributing it to an imagined singular "people" of the United States in the aggregate, in whose name all governments, federal and state alike, exercised their respective powers. Only John Taylor of Caroline, perhaps the most gifted theorist of the Virginia Republican movement, wished to sideline the whole rhetoric of sovereignty. Summing up Taylor's views, Yehoshua Arieli writes:

The American Revolution did not . . . transfer political sovereignty from the English to the American people, but rather reduced the political framework to contractual forms of self-government.

Accordingly, the idea of the sovereignty of the state was subversive of the principles of American government, for it presupposed undefined and unlimited power. For better or worse, later Southern critics of centralized power, such as John C. Calhoun, Abel Upshur, Jefferson Davis, and Alexander H. Stephens tended to adopt the language of sovereignty in both its internal and external aspects, but attributed this vast set of claims to the several states. However posed, the Southern critique had great merit in terms of the "feudal/federal" facts of history in British North America. Relatively neglected by the imperial center, the American colonies had thrived in a rather pre-modern, quasimedieval, federal environment. Political scientist Daniel Deudney, developing these institutional facts, contrasts America's "Philadelphian" state system with Europe's Westphalian order.

The original U.S. model rested on a geographical distribution of powers that required no absolute sovereignty in the center or the members. Such an interpretation of the early republic licenses the defensive "sovereignty" of local political societies as against supposed "superiors," and does so in a way meant to keep the international lawyers off the case. But the opposing view had been present from the start. As J. Allen Smith notes: "The apostle to America of the Hobbesian gospel of legislative sovereignty was Sir William Blackstone," one of the writers most widely read in the colonies.

It seems fair to add that many of the American "founders" were practical Hobbesians in Lockean sheep's clothing. And it is significant that Deudney dates the Philadelphian system from 1787 to 1861, suggesting that something else38 took its place upon the success of Mr. Lincoln's educational project.

During and after the "Civil War," sundry paladins of Northern integral nationalism, including Catholic editor Orestes Brownson, legal advisor to Lincoln's War Department Francis Lieber, Senator Charles Sumner, and the subtly influential St. Louis Hegelians, proclaimed the absolute sovereignty of the union. Force of arms confirmed, for them, this dubious claim. In a forecast of things to come, Denton Snider, one of the St. Louis Hegelians, foresaw the American union, lately saved, as the affirmation of all particular states in a larger whole which recreates them and which they in turn continually recreate. Such a process might well end in the development of a world-state corresponding to the World Spirit. The American federal system was to point the way. There is no room here to deal with the ideas of Emerson and Walt Whitman, who demanded a colossal "whole" within which to work out their antinomian individualism.40 The War Against Southern Independence underscored the U.S. government's legal positivism. Frederick O. Bonkovsky writes:

Modern, total warfare by sovereign nation-states seriously undercut proscriptions against violence. Naturalism had built its prohibitions on the foundation of noncombatant and civilian immunity . . . on the assumption that political man could be defined as human being apart from the state. This was an assumption that positivism could not allow. In the positivist schema people have no natural standing. . . . The state determines people's rights and obligations. The opposing nation establishes the rules of combat and civilian exemption.

Whatever may have been true about a late eighteenth and early nineteenth century American exceptionalism in relation to sovereignty, J. Allen Smith concludes that Americans ended up with "governmental supremacy under the guise of popular sovereignty."42 The federal state apparatus established, as of 1865, its sovereignty vis-a-vis its own constituent states and population, but whether the U.S. had ever been a normal member of the larger European state system is another matter. Given U.S. leaders' long-range goals, it seems safe to say that the United States always was and remains a revisionist power. Already with the Monroe Doctrine, the rising empire of the west had issued a challenge to the logic and rules of the state system. For some U.S. statesmen, certainly, noninterference in European affairs represented a mere "stage," pending spread of the North American system over the whole world.

SOVEREIGN, EQUAL, AND INDEPENDENT STATES IN THEIR MUTUAL RELATIONS

So much for theory. How has the European and later global state system operated since its inception, especially in the external realm of state activity?

International Law and Inter-State Warfare

Recall that in the age of feudal war, the king was thought to be under the law divine, customary, and natural. Indeed, there was slippage, but it was usually limited to very specific royal goals. And naturally, kings wished to be out from under such a restrictive notion of law. On the purely practical side, by the late thirteenth century, kings in France and Sicily began instituting routine taxation pro defensione regii ("for defense of the realm"), and other rulers followed suit. Taxation is easily the original "war power." And Georg Schwarzenberger writes that formal declarations of war were instituted precisely as claims to an extraordinary power, that of making public war, an enterprise into which all can and must be roped and with "legal" consequences even for third parties. Competitive state-building and, for the losers, state-destruction picked up considerably with the French invasion of Italy in 1494. The development of public debt, perfected in England at the start of the eighteenth century, added to an ever-upward ratcheting of military competition. As territorial monarchies triumphed over competing political forms like city-states in Italy and city-leagues in northern Europe, a systemic logic set in. Territorial states "recognized" like units, admitting them into the rising system.

States carried on wars, and wars profited the successful states materially as well as in "psychic income," whence the centrality of war and the so-called "laws of war" to international law. Thus, sovereignty the juridical residue of the process sketched out above is Janus-faced, looking both inward and outward at the same time. Friedrich Kratochwil writes: "It denotes internal hierarchy as well as external equality" within the state system. An imperial frontier, such as that of the Roman Empire, represented "a temporary stopping place," whereas in a system of theoretically equal units, boundaries were fixed demarcations between the territories of sovereigns. In recent times, "the universal recognition of territorial sovereignty as the differentiating principle in the international area" comes into conflict with "the erosion of boundaries through the increasing interdependencies of modern economic life." As modern, abstract, bureaucratic states emerged, each one undertook to map its territory and gather factual information regarding resources fit for extraction, such as properties and other economic assets, population, and the like. Soon enough, they replaced the kings themselves as the real wielders of power.

The Rise and Triumph of Positive Law

We have already noted the displacement of natural law by positive law in American war-making. In the seventeenth century, the transition to a new outlook that focused on sovereign states as sources of law and final judges in their own cause was under way, and writers on international law reflected the shift. The trajectory Su‡rez-GrotiusPufendorf-Vattel sums up this development, with each writer more tied into legal positivism than his predecessor.

Schwarzenberger comments that, in their efforts to be realistic and relevant, these writers made "natural law . . . subservient to the reason of state." Thus, the natural lawyers conveniently lent their authority to the thesis that some rather disconcerting passages in the Gospel on war were not to be taken too literally, and that war, provided it was just, was authorized, both by divine and natural law.

Finally: The insistence of naturalist writers on the element of bellum publicum in their definitions of war corresponds to the interests of rising absolutism, as does their postulation for a declaration of war. Therefore, during the period of early absolutism, this part of their doctrine meets with the full approval of State practice.

Nicholas G. Onuf believes that the state was not fully modern until the eighteenth century. While republican writers had appropriated the idea of sovereignty, there was, nonetheless, no impersonal state in republican thought. It was under liberalism and democracy that states became fully modern and sovereign. Now, the territorial monarchs gave way, and were replaced by the rational central bureaucracies which they had called into being. Alain de Benoist comments: "Once the concept of Ôthe nation' was legitimized, the concept of Ôthe people' became an abstraction." As popular, middle class, nationalist movements arose in the nineteenth century, state apparatuses contrived to take them over for state purposes. By the end of the century, conservative parties everywhere were reborn as parties of integral nationalism and absolute, if allegedly popular, sovereignty, having abandoned earlier commitments to feudal legitimacy, particularism, and religion. When more popular forms of government came on the scene, they inherited from kingly states the whole ideological apparatus of unbounded sovereignty and positive law. This inheritance duly passed from republicanism to liberalism and then to mass democracy.54 Perhaps the last serious resistance to the ideological victory of sovereign states was found in the work of Erasmus of Rotterdam in the sixteenth century. Unfortunately, Erasmus was seriously hampered by a belief in the necessity of states. He himself saw the problem:

Once you have granted imperial rule, you have granted at the same time the business of collecting money, the retinue of a tyrant, armed force, spies, horses, mules, trumpets, war, carnage, triumphs, insurrections, treaties, battles, in short everything without which it is not possible to manage the affairs of empire.

"Civilized Warfare" within Positive Law

Some seventeenth- and eighteenth-century exponents of (a reformulated) natural law, like Pufendorf and Thomasius, adopted the language of sovereignty, and took law to be "the command of a superior."59 Nevertheless, much practical and useful work could be done from within this modernist perspective to define laws of war and craft rules for international relations. Hence, these centuries saw the development over time of a body of customary and treaty law seen as the law of nations. In effect, rather than pursue the seemingly futile job of assessing jus ad bellum the justice of a particular war on either side the applied international jurists began focusing on jus in bello: the rightfulness of the means employed by any party, once a war had come into being.60 Edwin M. Borchard, a protŽgŽ of noted international lawyer John Bassett Moore, noted:

Since the Armed Neutralities of 1780 and 1800, in which neutral nations first sought armed organized protection for their rights, steady progress had been made by international agreement in limiting belligerent claims to interfere with neutral rights, and in enabling neutrals to escape ruination from wars in which they had no part or interest.

According to the classic study by F.J.P. Veale, a code of civilized warfare "won general acceptance in Europe from about the beginning of the eighteenth century." Central to this code was the principle . . . that hostilities between civilized peoples must be limited to the armed forces actually engaged. In other words, it drew a distinction between combatants and noncombatants by laying down that the sole business of the combatants is to fight each other and, consequently, that non-combatants must be excluded from the scope of military operations.

Thus, for at least two centuries, European nations broadly accepted restrictions on the methods of war, which bettered the situations of the societies whose states were at war, as well as those of neutral powers.

In 1854, Belgian economist Gustave de Molinari discussed this progress in his essay "Progress Realized in the Usages of War." Economic progress, Molinari wrote, has resulted from the separation of the personnel and materials of war from those of peace, as symbolized by the contrast of open cities and fortified towns. With the growth of peaceful occupations came respect for the productive and commercial sectors and a desire to disrupt their activities as little as possible in war. The utility of this policy had been shown by practice; such practices had been codified in the law of nations. "Unfortunately," writes Molinari, the new practices which the properly understood interest of the belligerents introduced into war in accord with the general interest of civilization did not prevail always during the great struggle of the Revolution and the Empire [1789-1815].

He praised Wellington, the Iron Duke, for adhering strictly to the rules of civilized warfare and treating civilians well. Wellington's forces took nothing from the people for which they did not pay. By contrast, Russian forces in Wallachia and Moldavia paid for their acquisitions in "depreciated paper money!" So far, rules protecting commerce and private property only applied on land. At sea, seizure and destruction of property were normal, and belligerents even menaced neutral shipping. Molinari mentions a 1780 draft treaty between Sweden, Denmark, the U.S., Prussia, Austria, Portugal, and the Two Sicilies intended to rectify matters.65 Murray Rothbard's discussion of U.S. diplomacy under the Confederation provides interesting support for Molinari's account. Rothbard notes that in April 1783, Benjamin Franklin negotiated a treaty with Sweden "based on the Libertarian American Plan of 1776": freedom of trade and the safeguarding of neutrals' rights: in particular, restricting contraband that might be seized by belligerent powers;

the freedom of neutral shipping between belligerent ports; and [the principle that] free ships make free goods. The Swedish treaty made the further liberal addition of agreeing to convoy each other's ships in time of war.

In 1784, Congress appointed a new treaty commission, headed by Thomas Jefferson, to work toward treaties grounded on the logic already adopted. Congress sought agreements "prohibiting privateering between the parties in case of war between them; and restricting the scope of blockades." Further, a new rule should be introduced that now contraband was to be purchased rather than seized. (John Adams, indeed, wished to abolish the contraband category altogether, and thus preserve neutral rights totally.)

A Treaty Negotiated with Prussia in 1785

It is not only provided for neutral convoys, but also for purchase of contraband and abolition of all privateering between the two countries, even if they were at war. Jefferson explained, on behalf of the American commissioners, that these provisions were "for the interest of humanity in general, that the occasions of war, and the inducements to it, should be diminished." The ultimate goals were to be "the total emancipation of commerce and the bringing together of all nations for a free intercommunication of happiness."

These attempts to protect commerce, even during war, did not prevail. Instead, as Molinari noted, the powers had gone beyond the "active" pursuit of plunder at sea to the "passive" policy of injuring an enemy's productive enterprises through general blockades. Of the two, the latter might well be more damaging and counterproductive, having the opposite of the desired effect. Thus, the allied coalition (from 1793) sought to impose a starvation blockade on France. This strengthened the Revolution, delayed peace, and "exasperated national animosities." It was no accident, Molinari wrote, that the coastal regions of France showed the greatest hatred for England. One might well compare the World War I blockade of the Central Powers by the Allies.70 Molinari now turned to the Eastern (Crimean) War, which had begun in March of 1854.

Here, too, was found counterproductive economic warfare. He remarks rather dryly that something was wrong when the Czar, hoping to punish his enemies, prohibited the export of Russian cereals and metals, while England sought to punish Russia by preventing the movement of the same exports! Other misbegotten policies accompanied the Eastern War. English attacks on Finnish private property had driven the normally antiRussian Finns into Russia's arms. Such destruction of property underlay most national hatreds. This made lasting peace more difficult and, implicitly, set the stage for new wars. Molinari recommended a distinction between strategic and commercial blockades. It made sense to blockade an enemy port that was primarily a naval base. However, general commercial blockades were an attack on prosperity and civilization. The problems arising from blockades in the War of 1812, the War for Southern Independence (1861Ð1865), and World War I (1914Ð1919) bear out Molinari's reasoning.

Molinari notes that the real interest of all in respecting commerce and property is "no less real for not being immediately obvious to the eyes."

Balance of Power

Other themes ran alongside the pragmatic development of civilized warfare. One of these was the notion of the "balance of power" a rationalization, it would appear, of British practice from the sixteenth century forward.76 In 1916, German political historian Otto Hintze commented on that policy:

England's conception of the European balance of power was to the effect that it should be the means of increasing and maintaining her maritime ascendancy. It meant that the Continental Powers should destroy each other by constant warfare, in order that England might have a free hand at sea and in the colonies. Throughout the centuries of modern history, it has been the relentless principle of British policy to fight the strongest Power of the Continent by means of the others.

World War I and the Reversion to Barbarism

In the frenzy of World War I, the powers involved increasingly departed from the code of civilized warfare with the British starvation blockade of Germany, unrestricted German submarine warfare, poison gasses, senseless mass slaughter on the Western Front, and the first experiments with air power. The war proved so destructive of life, property, and civilized values that, to many observers, it seemed that only an international system built on totally opposed principles could avert another such disaster. Thus was hatched the notion of a League to Enforce Peace by military means, if necessary. Of course, this was not a new idea. As far back as 1735, Jules Cardinal Alberoni proposed a league of Christian princes to adjudicate their differences, keep the peace, and make war on the Turks! Some contemporary writers even see in Immanuel Kant's essay Perpetual Peace a charter for present-day global democratic crusading. (We shall return to this reading of Kant a bit later.) Distinguished diplomatic historian Roland N. Stromberg has noted an array of problems inherent in the whole notion of a league to "enforce peace" by making war. He notes that the usual reading of the history of the League of Nations is that there were a number of suggestions from 1915 forward, all amounting to the same idealistic package to which the statesmen of the day were unable fully to commit themselves. This is said to have been tragic, but Stromberg disagrees, and writes that there were many plans precisely because the whole idea was riddled with inner contradictions.

The great ideal of a league to enforce peace had grown up in reformist circles well placed at the top of the British Empire. After all, if a league could actually work, it would help preserve the British and other European Empires more cheaply than resorting to general war, as in August 1914. These reformers among them Robert Cecil of the very important Tory Cecils passed the idea along to their allies in Washington. Woodrow Wilson, perhaps the greatest Anglophile of all, was smitten, as were his associates, including Colonel House and a number of his partisan Republican enemies. All could agree it was a jolly good idea. Then they all drew up wildly divergent plans to be put into operation as soon as the terrible Germans were beaten.

Inner Contradictions of the League Ideal

The fundamental question was "whether the League would be in the nature of a world state, or an old-fashioned alliance, or whether there was anything in between."81 The New Republic opined on March 30, 1915:

The League of Peace would either be the old imperialistic alliance under a dishonest name, or else it would be a highly conservative federation which would keep its members in a very straight pacifist jacket. . . . There is no stopping point at a league to prevent war. Such a league would either grow to a world federalism, or it would break up in civil war.

On the conservative end of the pro-league spectrum were those like Nicholas Murray Butler and Elihu Root, who "put their trust in international law and a world court as the slow but sure path toward eventual world government" by the path of "organic growth." Others, less patient, demanded action and plans spelling out the brave new world in detail. In practice, their plans took shape in a kind of muddled middle ground. The war was allegedly being fought on the part of the allies for high ideals, and after U.S. entry, even more was heard of high ideals, since that is an inseparable feature of U.S. wars. Now it was said that the war was being waged for the "national self-determination" of captive peoples specifically, those held captive by the German, Austrian, and Ottoman empires.

Not so much was heard of those held captive by the British, French, Dutch, and other worthy empires. Yet, self-determination for even this self-serving shortlist of wouldbe nations would create more national sovereignties in the world, while the league idea necessarily required renunciation of sovereignty to some unknown degree. How to sort that out? Was the war being fought, at the same time, for and against nationalism and self-determination? This was a contradiction the league planners and theorists could never overcome. Another matter of quaint dispute was whether the league should form before German defeat so as to wage the war better the path actually taken in World War II with the "United Nations." Once the Bolsheviks took power in Russia, late in 1917, Wilson's program of collective security, or cooperative imperialism, took on added importance as an answer to the challenge posed by Lenin's doctrine of worldwide communist revolution.

The League in Practice

As things worked out, the League of Nations had to await the end of World War I. The various Anglo-American drafts of its Charter left the ambiguities in place. Article X spelled out collective guarantees of the independence and existing boundaries of all states. Yet Wilson himself took back this inelastic guarantee, by saying that it did not rule out boundary changes or constitute a status quo imprisonment.

But existing boundaries themselves rested on earlier successful warfare, and the League looked more and more like an agreement among the victors to hold onto what they had grabbed. The Treaty of Versailles, of which the League formed a part, created enough new grievances for a series of new wars. Given all this, it was quite mad to think that the League could be a force for "peace" even a peace to be enforced by "sanctions," or a blockade, as more honest generations put it (and itself an act of war), or full-scale war. The most the League accomplished was to give the appearance of international cooperation the cause of all mankind to some policies adopted by certain powers against other powers in the aftermath of the unfinished disaster called World War I. Where the League could not be used, it was largely ignored. League enthusiasts saw in it the germ of a new world order.

But, as we previously noted, the New Republic warned that "such a league would either grow to a world federalism, or it would break up in civil war." Actually, we may remove the "or": a league, world federalism, whatever we may call it, would necessarily be oppressive and lead to the result mentioned.

The worst part is that, under such an arrangement, enemies who would otherwise be foreign powers with some rights under the laws of war become "rebels" with no rights at all. There were many League enthusiasts in the U.S.: Americans are often sentimental about setting up and preserving wider unions to guarantee peace. This has to do with the way they learn American history. For some, world federation would work just as well as the American confederation did after 1789, provided you don't count that big war between 1861 and 1865 with the 620,000 military deaths on both sides and the 50,000 or so missing Southern civilians. The analogy breaks down precisely because you must count that big war. As historian William Appleman Williams writes:

Americans remain haunted by the Civil War. . . . Underlying that persistent involvement is the realization that the war undercuts the popular mythology that America is unique. Only a nation that avoided such a conflict could make a serous claim to being fundamentally different. In accordance with the logic and psychology of myth, therefore, it has become necessary to turn the war itself into something so different, strange, and mystic that it could have happened only to the chosen people.

World government or World Empire, if we should ever enjoy such, would be the material cause of world civil war. "Leaguism" as we might name the ideology of collective security was meant, one supposes, to overcome what international political theorists call the "self-help" dilemma under international "anarchy." But so, too, were the big alliances at the beginning of the twentieth century, and they only succeeded in making World War I possible. Thus, the League of Nations and the later U.N. might reasonably be seen as the Entente Cordiale writ large. As Murray Rothbard liked to point out, the logical outcome of collective security was to ensure that no war could remain limited i.e., confined to two parties and fought over limited issues. Instead, the demand that the true "aggressor" be named and that all Good Powers rally to the defense of the injured party, stood guarantee that future wars would be as broad in scope as possible.

WINDS OF DOCTRINE II: KELLONG-BRIAND PACT, WORLD WAR II, UNITED NATIONS, AND NUREMBERG

War "Outlawed"

The rather innocent-looking Kellogg-Briand Pact of 1928 committed the nations signing it to the assertion that war was obsolete as a positive instrument of foreign policy.88 Since, at the same time, the contracting powers reserved the "right" to resort to self-defense when attacked, a deep contradiction arose, a contradiction that could not be papered over by rational means. Even so, the pact stands as a landmark in the rise of the New International Law of "collective security" because so much ideological hay was made from its supposed implications. In truth, a number of sovereignties, severally and under their own power, had ratified a vague agreement, enforcement of which was left to the imagination. Shortly thereafter, advanced thinkers began proclaiming that those states had unanimously committed themselves to an entirely new legal order from which they might not now recede. No less than Quincy Wright, a paladin of the new order, wrote:

> The law of the pact will not work unless the parties can agree at once on the position of the belligerents. Under the old law of war and neutrality, the obligations of neutrals flowed from the fact of war and not from the conditions of its origin. Under the new law, the obligations of nonparticipants depend, not upon the fact of war, but upon the position of the belligerents as is determined by its origin. . . . It is believed that the legal case against war and armed violence in international affairs is complete. War cannot occur without violation of the Pact, and armed violence cannot be justified except within the legal concept of self-defense. Neutrality posited upon isolation and impartiality has lost its legal foundation.

War, now "outlawed," was a crime, and the analogy with domestic jurisprudence came into full view. In the words of old-line international lawyer Edwin M. Borchard, the new gospel took sustenance from the extraordinary view that the system of international relations that prevailed before 1914 was "international anarchy," and that what we now have represents "law and order." Perhaps it is not unnatural, therefore, that the evangelism of the new "new order" is directed toward a disparagement of the international law which sustained the "old order" an attack which indiscriminately characterizes "war" as a common-law crime and would therefore deprive the laws of war of all legal standing, regards neutrality as "immoral," if not "illegal," and insists that collective intervention and force will, or should, alone assure "peace."

Given the supposed "outlawry" of war, the main task now became one of stipulating Good vs. Bad nations "aggressors" vs. defenders and deciding the best means of bringing aggressors to heel, whether by boycott, embargo, or stronger measures. Together with the League of Nations Charter, the Kellogg Pact was taken to have overturned the Old International Law in favor of a brave new order. The sect that believed this happy doctrine was especially strong in the United States. Acting on the newer conception of international law, U.S. Secretaries of State Henry Stimson and Cordell Hull "repeatedly talked as if the renunciation of war was one of the fundamentals one of the Ôpillars' of American foreign policy."

Outlawry of War Followed by World War II

For the new school, neutrality had become "obsolete" a reactionary vestige of the bad old days which, if practiced by any modern power, stood as an affront to the all-encompassing logic of the new order. Among the many spokesmen for the new outlook were such people as Quincy Wright, Denna Frank Fleming, various U.S. Secretaries of State, and Soviet foreign minister Maxim Litvinov. World War II became the proving ground of the new viewpoint via such pronouncements as the Atlantic Charter and other wartime agreements between the Allied Powers, culminating in the U.N. Charter. Thus, a not-very-subtle "antifascist" theme resonated within the new international law. Only "fascist" disrupters were to blame for World War II, or any other disasters of the first half of the twentieth century. To prevent future outbreaks of fascism and war, an international body with power of enforcement was needed, and it is no accident that Franklin Roosevelt and others began referring to their warmaking coalition as the "United Nations." As Charles G. Fenwick writes:

It was only with the adoption of the Atlantic Charter and the wider Declaration of the United Nations that it came to be realized that the hope of a new political order was dependent upon removing the economic causes of war and setting up an ideal of social reconstruction. The barriers to the trade and raw materials of the world must be removed; labor standards must be improved, and social security assured to the people of all countries.

These conceptions, it is worth remarking, looked forward to some undefined degree of socialism and social democracy, with the principle of the Open Door thrown in for the benefit of politically wellconnected American capitalists. The new order, imposed from the top down, would alleviate those "economic" conditions which had uniquely caused fascism, thus assuring peace and preventing war via an ever-leftward drift of policy.

A New World of Institutionalized Peace

The United Nations Charter reads like a weird combination of the U.S. Constitution, an old-fashioned treaty, a utopian manifesto, and a set of rules for a private club, as distinguished jurist Hans Kelsen, a legal positivist, implied in a critical essay on the Preamble.93 The new international law provided justification for the Nuremberg tribunal. According to the Allied prosecutors, planning, preparing, and carrying out the elements of an "illegal" war of "aggression" were separate counts, and something like an endless, upward plea-bargaining process entered the picture.94 The Korean War, too, was claimed as an instance of international police work in the interest of collective security, although the war's actual implementation showed, if anything, that the Charter did not work as planned. A fairly straightforward analogy, mooted earlier, construes world federalism as the cure for mankind's ills on the basis of a particular reading of U.S. history. Just as Messrs. Madison's and Hamilton's centralizing Constitution "saved" by Lincoln in its greatest crisis freed Americans from such perils as war (oddly enough, by having One Big War), so, too, would an increasingly sovereign world organization deliver humanity from the perils of major war between nation-states. One of the great partisans of internationalism, Quincy Wright, in 1956, made precisely this comparison:

It may be noted that in the theory of the United States Constitution, the military measures undertaken by the Federal Government in the South, usually designated as the Civil War, were not considered in Constitutional law action to coerce the Southern States as such, but action to stop the illegal conduct of the governments of those States in nullifying Federal legislation, preventing the functioning of Federal services, and attempting to secede from the Union. The Southern States, said the Supreme Court after the war, had never been out of the Union, and the unconstitutional acts of their governments were null and void. If this were otherwise, "the war must have become a war for conquest and subjugation."95

Certainly, on Lincoln's theory of the Union (and therefore of the war), all the above might follow, but I leave to one side whether his theory was a good one. Wright's argument by internal American historical analogy naturally turns toward the asserted need of the putatively "superior" to act directly upon individuals guilty of "crimes" as part of their cooperation with others in the larger "crime" of undertaking "aggressive war." As Wright expressed it:

Crime, as indicated in the trials after World War II, is thought to be committed only by individuals. Delinquency by a state creates liabilities of civil rather than of criminal character.

Referring to the U.N. Charter and the Universal Declaration of Human Rights, Charles G. Fenwick writes:

Here, for the first time in the history of international law, was an act of the whole community of states, looking behind the formal organization of their governments to the individual human beings who constitute the legal body of the state. It creates, in a sense, a bond of unity cutting across state lines and restricting the sovereignty of the state in a vital area of its domestic life. The individual has thus been accepted as a subject as well as an object of international law.

These views amount to a projection of the theoretical premises of municipal (state) law onto the world stage. The shadow of a global Social Contract theory hangs over what might otherwise be seen as mere cooperation of a number of states in pursuit of their power-political goals under cover of internationalist ideology. There is also an odd conflation of the notions of legislation, law, and jurisprudence at the level of mankind a body that cannot actually be shown to exist. Within certain limits, the federal-international analogy "works," as does the related federal-feudal one, but not necessarily in quite the way progressive thinkers would have us believe. Perhaps, indeed, the original political sin is that anyone ever delegated power upward at all. On second thought, the whole notion of voluntary "delegation" seems intended to obscure the actions of those at higher levels who successfully seized power from lower levels at some time in the past, or to obscure future actions of those who aspire to global "governance."

Persistence of an Older School

The intellectual victory of the new outlook on international law remained incomplete for some decades. An older school continued to set forth their ideas, albeit with a decreasing audience, into the 1950s. Thus, criticizing a peculiarly Wilsonian notion, John Bassett Moore could write in 1933:

The President of the United States has no power, either under the Constitution or under international law, legally to decide the question whether a foreign government is de jure, or, in other words, established in conformity with the constitution and laws of the country over which it actually rules.

Nor in Moore's view did the U.S. Congress or Courts have such a power under the Constitution or international law, although Congress could make specific rules about retaliation, property seizures, etc., once a state of war had come into being. Moore's critique of the collective security outlook was systematic and total, as in the following passage:

The tendency to confuse war and peace and to magnify the part which force may play in international affairs not unnaturally followed the so-called World War. During that great conflict there developed, in the ordinary course of things, a war-madness, manifested in the exaltation of force, and the belittling of the enduring legal and moral obligations which lie at the foundation of civilized life. Peaceful processes fell into disrepute.

We began to hear of the "war to end war"; and pacifists, enamored of this shibboleth, espoused the shallow creed that international peace could best be assured by the use of force or threats of force. We were told that preexisting international law had suddenly become obsolete, and that the world had entered upon a new era in which the general tranquility was to be maintained by "sanctions," by boycotts, and by war. But the final stage was reached in the spawning of the notion, now rampant, that peoples may with force and arms exterminate one another without breach of the peace, so long as they do not call it war. To this final stage belongs the supposition that the law of neutrality no longer exists, and that in future there will be no more neutrals.

Edwin M. Borchard also contested the notion that neutrality was obsolete:

The suggestion that it is not possible to remain neutral is negatived by the fact that countries much more closely affected by the late struggle than the United States, such as the Scandinavian countries and Holland, were perfectly able to maintain their neutrality. In all the wars fought since 1919, including that between Poland and Russia, Greece and Turkey, Japan and China, and those on this continent, the non-participating members of the League of Nations and the United States remained neutral. Neutrality has been stipulated in innumerable treaties since 1919, including treaties between European Powers and those concluded at Havana in 1928.

Later stages of this battle were fought out, among other places, in the pages of the American Journal of International Law, and certainly the broad outlines can be traced there. Suffice it to say that the new school had largely triumphed by sometime in the 1950s.

IDEOLOGICAL TRAJECTORY OF THE INTERNATIONALIST SCHOOL

Peace, Properly Understood, Through Armed Intervention

As indicated, the successful trajectory of the New International Law, as interpreted by (among others) friends of an activist U.S. foreign policy, can be followed in the American Journal of International Law. The writings of W. Michael Reisman, present editor of the journal, embody the transformations in question. An early piece (1968), written with then-editor Myres S. McDougal, justifying U.N. policy towards Rhodesia, is highly symptomatic of the evolving internationalist point of view. The writers argued for a kind of "loose construction" of the U.N. Charter in order to bring the Rhodesian case under the notion of "threats to the peace" warranting U.N. action including "sanctions" (blockade) and the "authorizing" of Britain to use force against the white minority government of the secessionist colony. It was good, they wrote, that the Charter's "framers, in rejecting all proposed definitions of the key terms Ôthreat to the peace,' Ôbreach of the peace,' and Ôact of aggression,'" had left to the Security Council "a large freedom to make ad hoc determinations of each specific situation of threat or coercion."

International "law" thus becomes legislation by a fleeting majority of delegates to the relevant U.N. bodies, a majority unconstrained by stable definitions of terms. The writers deployed injured British sovereignty alongside various notions of international (U.N.) jurisdiction centering on the admittedly under-defined rubric of "threat to the peace." Anticipating later post-modernist moves, they advanced a subjective standard of harm:

The promulgation and application of policies of racism in a context as volatile as that of Rhodesia and South Central Africa must give rise to expectations of violence and constitute, if not aggression of the classic type, at least the creation of circumstances under which states have been customarily regarded as justified in unilaterally resorting to the coercion strategies of humanitarian intervention.

Thus, it followed that the events in Rhodesia were neither internal matters, nor a dispute between Britain and its former colony, as in 1776, because, under present conditions, "peoples interact . . . through shared subjectivities" and, thus, "other peoples of Africa have regarded themselves as affected by the authoritarian and racist policies of the Rhodesian elites." Even worse, the bad example of Rhodesia could "easily spread to other communities and become international." We have here, on the one hand, a kind of psychic Interstate Commerce Clause modeled on the failure of the U.S. Constitution to limit central power and, on the other, a continuation of the founding antifascist theme of the United Nations.

Suppress Rhodesia, or Hitler will come back! There is more, but we must move along. Twenty years later, we find Reisman, writing with James Silk, on the legal character of the ongoing war in Afghanistan between Soviet forces and the Mujahidin. Unsurprisingly, the "law" was found to favor the positions then taken by the U.S. government with respect to that war. Some months before, Reisman had already issued a sort of Afghan Resistance Manifesto and recruiting poster, which claimed, on the basis of relevant law, that: (1) the Mujahidin are entitled to fight against the Soviet Union and the Soviet-supported Government in Kabul; (2) the Mujahidin are entitled to call upon third states for support in their struggle; (3) third states are under an obligation to provide such help to the Mujahidin in their resistance; and (4) neither the Soviet Union nor the Soviet-supported Government in Kabul is entitled to characterize the support that third states are obliged to and do, in fact, render to the Mujahidin as a violation of international law or in any way a violation of its own rights.

Support Islamic fundamentalists, or totalitarianism will come back! Since then, Reisman has addressed war powers under the U.S. Constitution and the sovereignty of states in relation to asserted human rights. The former essay calls for better division of labor among the branches of U.S. government to facilitate more effective overseas interventions while the second discovers that all recent U.S. interventions have been on the up-and-up and fully consistent with international law. Now, in some of these cases, I suppose, it is possible that Reisman has an argument, but the extreme "fit" between positions taken and the short-term needs of U.S. foreign policy does raise a question or two. Clearly on a roll, Reisman is next seen calling for establishment of a U.N. war college to train staff officers and organize command structures.108 Naturally, the task will be to "wage peace" since, by ideological definition, the U.N. never makes war, just as the U.S. never does wrong. Reisman's post-9/11 statement calls on the U.S. to defend "world public order."

Panamanian Interlude

While Professor Reisman was perfecting his unique style of proU.S. apologetics, another dispute rocked the pages of the American Journal of International Law. Three writers contended for the truth about George H.W. Bush's invasion of Panama. Anthony D'Amato argued that, by invading Grenada and Panama, the United States had modified international law. On the basis of two interventions, a new "rule" of customary law could be spotted just on the horizon. No longer could Third World despots hide behind "formalist" readings of the law, nor could they hide behind "texts" of existing treaties. There was far too much good to be done by ignoring rules and texts that sheltered the Bad from the wrath of the Good.

Unfazed by these conceptual shortcuts, two writers, Ved P. Nanda and Tom J. Faarer, dissented. Nanda asserted that redefinition of key terms could not save D'Amato's argument. In any case, nonintervention in the internal affairs of other states was the customary rule, not lightly set aside. Farer invoked the U.N. Charter, among other considerations, as a barrier to D'Amato's new doctrine.

The "Right" to Obey the Hegemonic Power

Thomas M. Franck shares some views with D'Amato and Reisman. In an essay published in 1992, he announced "the emerging right to democratic governance." On the strength of a piece of revolutionary propaganda issued in 1776, he derives in Straussian fashion a "democratic entitlement" of universal reach. Repackaging the Wilsonian claim that democracy is the only legitimate form of government, he somehow connects that form to the rule of law. The sleight of hand is dazzling. Since its feeble beginnings at Versailles, the democratic entitlement has risen above mere self-determination to become a fundamental right a right duly severed, however, from "any entitlement to secede." It has so risen on the basis of the usual international agreements, held by Franck to apply as "customary law" even to those who have not ratified them. As he puts it:

The Covenant thus foresees a continuing, growing body of law made by means of the interpretation and applications of its provisions by an expert, independent, quasijudicial body.

Coupled with this universal Fourteenth Amendment comes "the right of free political expression" which "originated conceptually in the antitotalitarianism born of World War II."114 A cynic might say that Franck's problematic is situated in the (brief) transition from War Liberalism to Cold War Liberalism, which entailed a redefinition of Soviet communism as "Red fascism" so as to preserve the continuity of "antifascism" so dear to American corporate liberals and their European social democratic allies.

After some discussion of visionary schemes mooted in 1990 in Paris and Copenhagen, Franck informs us that local sovereignty is dead and buried. There can be no legitimate objection against intervention by the powerful armed with slogans about human rights. Having blithely noted "three generations of democratic entitlement" (which calls to mind a famous judge's remark about "three generations of imbeciles"), Franck announces that the Genocide and Racism Conventions "qualify as rules of deportment imposed on all states by the community of nations."

This genial conceit presupposes a world constituency voting by states or as individuals? that imposes rules on existing states, neatly recapitulating the American experience. The global Constitution awaits its John Marshall and Earl Warren. Franck reasons that, in light of "the natural right of all people to liberty and democracy" note the assumption that these are compatible the older international law "principle of noninterference" has fallen by the wayside. At the same time, "established rights and duties implicitly validate a penumbra of unenunciated, yet legitimate, means necessary to give them effect." The evolved new order is praiseworthy because "it opens the stagnant political economies of states to economic, social and cultural, as well as political, development." Finally, an implication of these newfound rights is "that legitimate governments should be assured of protection from overthrow by totalitarian forces": a letter-perfect "antifascist" prohibition on "right-wing" political activity, including, one suspects, all strivings for local autonomy and freedom that are not of the Left.

There is, indeed, something for everyone here: the inevitable Open Door for U.S. business, and endless social work for the reformist, bureaucratic wing of the bourgeoisie. It is a hard thing to pronounce Hans Kelsen nave, but the readings of the Charter which I have just canvassed clearly refute his assertion that no one would ever seriously make such claims.

PRESENT TRENDS (THEIR MASTER'S VOICE)

All the high-toned internationalist doctrine surveyed above tacitly depends for its fulfilment on military violence directed against designated threats to the peace. Absent any genuine world political community, the U.S. has stepped into the breach to provide an imperial substitute or equivalent. The idea that the U.N. is, today, the source of such international law as exists is a delusion that has much appeal. For many people, if the U.N. "approved" a war, that would make the war "just" ipso facto without further discussion. This is about as true as the related idea that a state is the source of law in a given territory. If the one isn't true, neither is the other. It may be that neither is true, but that discussion must wait for another time.

The rhetoric of collective security has done well, but the wielders of the notion are operationally split between those who really believe in it as an ideology and those who know that it operates as a good ideological cover for the U.S. Griff nach der Weltmacht the present U.S. leaders' grasp at total power. For the latter, the "law" can always be reckoned on to legitimate U.S. military intervention anywhere. In practice, the two groups are hard to tell apart. Present Court Intellectuals are more than happy to proclaim the relativization of "sovereignty" except for the sovereignty of the U.S. and its few faithful allies. The obvious danger for everyone else is that of great power hegemony in the name of international "law." And it is precisely the would-be hegemon Britain in previous centuries, and the United States at the beginning of the twenty-first that breaks the "rules" and drives the law in its preferred direction. In 1805, James Madison protested just such encroachments on neutral rights in a state paper entitled "An Examination of the British Doctrine, Which Subjects to Capture a Neutral Trade, Not Open in Time of Peace." As Veale observes:

So long as the British Navy commanded the sea, the British people had no reason to fear a reversion of warfare to the methods of primitive times. If defeated in a war, a continental people faced the prospect of being dealt with in accordance with the standards then prevailing. To a continental people, therefore, it was a matter of vital concern whether these standards were civilized or barbarous. The people of Britain, on the other hand, enjoyed the comforting knowledge that, so long as their Navy ruled the waves, defeat at the worst would only mean a withdrawal for the time being from the Continent. In fact, until the conquest of the air, Great Britain could hardly be regarded politically as a part of Europe.

As for the United States, that power has been especially keen to find, invent, and proclaim new rules of warfare that favor air power the field in which it is predominant. Where other powers have adopted rules to limit that military arm, as in the 1977 protocol to the Geneva Convention, the U.S. leaders stand aloof and proclaim their own peculiar doctrines. They then carry those out, and who is to say them nay? In our time, the hegemonic power partly justifies its activities under a "living" U.N. Charter. This is held to be necessary lest the Bad should shelter themselves under narrow readings of settled law. At other times, the same power asserts its separate sovereignty and superpowerhood, with little apparent sense of incongruity. FrŽdŽric MŽgret observes, in the manner of Carl Schmitt, that an interesting spin-off from the argument that the U.N. Charter is a global constitution, is whether the U.S. might not also portray itself as accomplishing for the rest of the world and the U.N. Charter a decentralized version of what the executive may see itself as doing for the U.S. and the American Constitution, namely, breaching the "constitution" (or at least going against its spirit) in order to better defend its ordinary function.

Perhaps the central fallacy has been to assume that "law" international or otherwise is only law when it can be equated with force or the "will of a superior." From this comes the notion that international law consists, or should consist, of current legislation promulgated by a world body. This approach thrives on the failure to specify levels of analysis, the nature of law, and other matters, and with that, the failure to see that an understanding of international conflict necessarily entails considerable casuistry, in the proper sense of that word.123 Nor should it be forgotten that the seeming rationality, whereby a club of good states formed to bash the bad states can masquerade as the parliament of all humanity, has owed much to the guile and cunning of the major English-speaking powers, who have even managed at times almost to believe their own rhetoric. Woodrow Wilson shines forth as the most self-deluded of these rhetoricians. Recent wrangles over Iraq suggest that the U.N. is best seen not as the source of law or as the genuine organ of an incipient world society, but as a military alliance whose operational membership may vary depending on circumstances, such as bribery and genuine underlying interests. With its verbal claims to represent all of humanity, it is an unusual military alliance, to be sure. In 2003, the U.N.-as-military-alliance refused to yield to the wishes of its most powerful member, and that Super Power undertook a war of aggression "unilaterally" with a few other states in tow in a "coalition of the willing."

ARMED AND DANGEROUS NEO-KANTIANS

John Hall divides power into three types ideological, economics, and political-military. It is reasonable to say that, in our time, the first of the trinity has risen in importance, although those who are concerned with the second and third forms of power have not gone missing. Neo-mercantilist elites are as busy as ever rigging markets in favor of themselves and their friends via political-military power. This trend is widely equated with "free trade" and "free markets" under sundry neoclassical and Chicago School smokescreens. Having won most of their gambles, however, the political, military, and corporatist actors feel more need than ever for believable ideological cover.

Thus, the arrival of ideological power at center-stage reflects the quickened pace of U.S. (informal) empire building. Murray N. Rothbard gave much thought to the role of ideology and intellectuals in state-level political systems. He concluded that the state's distribution of economic benefits "only secures a minority of eager supporters" and "still does not gain the consent of the majority." Hence, the majority must be persuaded by ideology that their government is good, wise and, at least, inevitable. . . . Promoting this ideology among the people is the vital social task of the "intellectuals." For the masses of men do not create their own ideas, or indeed think through these ideas independently; they follow passively the ideas adopted and disseminated by the body of intellectuals. The intellectuals are, therefore, the "opinion-molders" in society. And since it is precisely a molding of opinion that the State most desperately needs, the basis for age-old alliance between the State and the intellectuals becomes clear.

The Philosophers Intervene in Favor of Intervention

For twenty-odd years, social scientists, international lawyers, and philosophers allied to U.S. power, by employment and sentiment, have been banging together new justifications for great-power intervention. Here we may name Fernando Tes—n, Michael Reisman, Thomas Franck, John Rawls, and Anne-Marie Slaughter. According to Gerry Simpson, these developments are, in the case of Rawls, linked to "liberal anti-pluralism or the liberal intolerance of intolerant governments."

Regardless of whether these persons are influential individually, their works play an important role in helping along the overall imperial project by giving high-toned reasons why we must support, acquiesce in, or put up with the project and its costs in money, blood, moral decay, and institutional change. Immanuel Kant (1724-1804) reasoned that, in the fullness of liberal time, more and more republics would come into being. Republics would be unlikely to wage war the sport of kings and therefore the proliferation of republican forms of government would spark a trend toward world peace. He wrote:

> If the consent of the citizens is required in order to decide that war should be declared . . . nothing is more natural than that they would be very cautious in commencing such a poor game, decreeing for themselves all the calamities of war.

Even letting republicanism stand in for liberalism here there is no need to quibble some problems arise. First, the assumption that under republicanism/liberalism, the "people" somehow control the state seems nave at best. It ignores the incentives presented to politicians and the ability of small cliques effectively to control policy from the top.128 The imperialist successes of "democratic" (especially Anglophone) states are the centerpiece of twentieth-century history and folklore, and we shall consider, shortly, possible reasons for this outcome. I cannot treat here the part played by shared Anglo-American Protestantism, but the title of a book by Samuel D. Baldwin, published in 1854, summarizes some persistent U.S. themes.129 Some "Kantian" imperialists long to invade under the U.N. flag; others are happy to reckon on U.S. firepower. But the paradox of blessing a long series of "elective," aggressive wars to install democracies everywhere, as the precondition of later eternal peace, has not gone unnoticed.

This doctrine of wars fought in the name of future peace, redeemable once the Good have sufficiently bombed the Bad, craftily substitutes the question of who is good and who is bad for the oldfashioned question of war and peace. The sheer genius of the new liberal imperialism lies in its decoupling of the asserted peacefulness of "democratic" states from any worldly pursuit of actual peace.

The key is now said to be that such nice states never attack each other. That they have attacked and do attack non-democratic states stands forth as further proof of their moral bona fides. This tendentious doctrine, raised up at just this historical moment, owes less to Immanuel Kant than to the felt need of U.S. policymakers for catchy rationalizations. Just as the twentieth- century collective security theorists undid the older international law, which focused on neutral rights and the rights of noncombatants, so, too, do the democracy gangsters outbid the security collectivists. One critic refers to the new position as "liberal millenarianism," nicely capturing the sheer scope of its claims.130 James Hathaway notes that the new liberal imperialism rides on the rather questionable heritage of American exceptionalism:

> The sense that the United States has a special moral status and mission has resulted in an intensive engagement by the United States in foreign affairs, predicated on a belief that America has a unique mission to lead the world. But even as it is a basis for the attribution to the United States of a special right to propose rules of international conduct, American exceptional status is also invoked to "plead the authority of its internal law to mitigate its international legal

obligations." The United States thus simultaneously asserts the right to lead, but also to be exempted from the rules it promotes. This looks like nothing more or less than an imperial claim to world rule, whatever the trimmings.

Pay No Attention to That State Behind the "Democracy"

Another advantage, to those in power, of the newest doctrinal wrinkle is that we never need look into the content of democracy; we never need undertake a critique of the internal realities of any conformist welfare-warfare state. Liberal corporatism and suffocating bureaucratization of the life-world get a free pass. Simpson almost sees this, when he refers, in passing, to systems having "free periodic elections in which the government is elected by the citizens of [the] state." Exactly! In the sainted democracies, the government is always reelected. There can be no question of reducing the scope and activities of any democratic state in the brave new world. As JosŽ E. Alvarez writes of one of the new liberals:

Slaughter's liberal theory is millenist, triumphalist, upbeat. The examples being set by liberal nations' treaties and their transgovernmental networks in the wake of the victory over communism mark the beginnings of a global "new deal" or a "new liberal democratic order." Liberal international law promises to replicate the liberal welfare state. In any case, states are states and have a lot in common on that basis alone. As G. Kitson Clark has observed, that conditions of survival "are in many ways the same for all states, totalitarian or liberal, and therefore all existing civilized states, totalitarian or liberal, share in part the same characteristics, use some of the same principles and to some extent pursue the same ends." Above all, "all modern states are Sovereign States or aspire to be Sovereign States." This last fact is decisive:

A Sovereign State is autonomous, it is the sole judge of its own actions, no appeal lies to anyone against it. The sovereignty of Sovereign States is most often considered in the international sphere, in connection with a State's autonomy in its relations with other Sovereign States; but it is important to remember that it exists in the domestic sphere as well. In a Sovereign State the subject has no legal right against the State at all, the power of the State is absolute. This is palpably true of the total State, but it is true of the liberal State also. It is true of Great Britain. In Great Britain the subject has important rights against the executive, he can sue the policeman, the soldier, the borough official, Her Majesty's Government itself, if he believes they have infringed his rights.

But he has no rights against the law. In England, a rule which is an acknowledged part of the English Common Law or the result of a statute duly passed by King, Lords and Commons, may seem to an Englishman to be absurd, unjust and generally intolerable, but he must obey it or take the consequences. There is a moral restriction on the actions which a liberal State may take against its subjects and it is very valuable, but there can be no legal restriction on those actions.

What looms on the horizon is the international Gleichschaltung ("co-ordination") by the Great World Hegemon aided by tractable NGOs ("nongovernmental organizations") of those "tolerant, liberal" forms of bureaucratic rule and interest-group plunder which came to characterize certain advanced states in the twentieth century.

The radiant future comes down to periodic but pointless elections, under cover of which the boot of armed bureaucratic "protectors" and wellconnected, state-sponsored corporations will stamp on the face of humanity for quite a long while, helped when necessary by the "precision" weaponry made possible by subsidized Big Science. Clearly, the idea of "liberal-democratic" world peace has already slipped its gears, and the clutch of history is about to burn itself out in conceptual futility. Blaming the aggressive potential of powerful states on forms of rule, e.g., democracy vs. autocracy, skirts the need to think about states as such. But, as Bolshevik theorist Nikolai Bukharin, a bit crudely, put it in 1916 as World War I dragged on, "the power of arms and murder has thus become a brazen law . . . of every form of state without exception." All Bolshevism aside, Murray Rothbard's analysis of states is more likely to be of help if we wish to think our way out of these corners, than is an analysis that credits "democracies" with inbuilt moral qualities readily cashable as foreign policy.

AMERICAN EMPIRE AND THE TRIUMPH OF ANGLOPHONE CUNNING

As already hinted, it was the commercially oriented Englishspeaking elites of Britain and the United States who successfully engrossed much of the world's political economy and bent the rules of the international system. Britain combined formal and informal empire, while the U.S. preferred an informal pattern of alliances and subsidies to local strongmen, which is not less an empire for all that. Since World War II, the U.S. leadership has sought to redefine (further) the state system. As Ian Hunter puts it:

In recent Anglophone political theory, Westphalia or the states-system it inaugurated has continued to undergo various kinds of assimilation, marginalisation, and repudiation.

At this late date, the whole thing takes on a kind of dreary inevitability. George Liska writes that the transition from British to U.S. hegemony has gone smoothly, as if the preordained end, America's imperial succession to Great Britain, was immanent in the beginnings of America's secession from the British empire; and as if the end shaped accordingly the intervening process of American expansion, while sanctioning its irregularities.

In the years between 1776 and 1971, U.S. leaders took on an "ideologically exaggerated sense of right to expand" along with "the equation of security with total immunity and of sustenance with unlimited growth."138 Similarly, New Left historian William Appleman Williams remarked U.S. policymakers' tendency to make the rest of the world answerable for American prosperity.

Hans-Hermann Hoppe notes that it is precisely the "liberal" states nineteenth-century Great Britain and twentieth-century United States that rose to global dominance. Their internal policies gave rise to unparalleled productivity from which state functionaries could extract, at modest rates of taxation, revenues far beyond the capacity of their less-enlightened rivals. This allowed creation of superior military forces with which to build empires, even as their domestic institutions ossified and their tax rates gradually climbed. Both powers' imperial projects rested, in the end, on military power and monetary preeminence. The lingering connection of the pound sterling to gold limited what Britain could spend on overseas adventures. The U.S. leadership, blessed with a system of paper money, has more freedom of action. As a state, the U.S. is in Hoppe's words "an autonomous counterfeiter of last resort to the entire international banking system."

[Further,] the typical Third World cycle of ruthless government oppression, revolutionary movements, civil war, renewed suppression, and prolonged economic dependency and mass poverty is to a significant extent caused and maintained by the United States-dominated international monetary system. Thus, the pool of economic resources available to U.S. leaders and the resulting military hardware seem the key to the so-called "Democratic Peace," as against any hypothetical magic qualities flowing from democracy, free elections, etc. The American policymakers' utterly self-centered conception of security blossomed in the context of Total War, an art form in which they were the main path-breakers. As a result, the U.S. now takes on the appearance of a heavily armed but mentally unstable colossus, rather than the "pitiful, helpless giant" about which Richard Nixon worried. Lessons that the U.S. rulers believe they have learned, together with certain objective realities of modern warfare, push the whole thing toward a breaking point. Already in the mid-1960s, John H. Herz observed that air power, foretold in World War I and perfected in World War II, allowed "direct action against the Ôsoft' interior" of an enemy state, by-passing outer defenses and thus foreshadowing the end of the frontier that is, the demise of the traditional impermeability of even the militarily most powerful states. Warfare now changed "from a fight to a process of devastation."

The Anglo-American Allies' blockbusters, firebombs, and, finally, atomic bombs underlined this change in unmistakable fashion. The age of Sovereignty, national independence, and fixed boundaries seemed to be over for all all but superpowers, that is. The logic of the classical Westphalian system came under siege. Herz comments:

One radical conclusion to be drawn from the new condition of permeability would seem to be that nothing short of global rule can ultimately satisfy the security interest of any one power, and particularly any superpower.

Thus, "security" and survival seemed to imply World Empire. This is certainly the conclusion drawn by U.S. policymakers. Their pre-existing aspirations and mental formation made this answer inevitable. Of course, this makes the United States a revisionist and not a status quo power, but that, too, is not exactly new. In developing a theory of cooperative "ultra-imperialism" just before World War I, Karl Kautsky overlooked the possibility that one power might emerge from unprecedented carnage with the capacity to impose its will on the major powers. After recovering from their defeat in Southeast Asia, U.S. rulers reasserted their domestic ideological (and physical) dominance, and embarked on a program to insure long-run global †berdominanz, exploiting the applied technological lethality for which they are rightly famous a lethality that turns enemies, soldiers and civilians alike, into "pink mist," calling to mind the crazed apocalyptic demons lodged right below the rich, if not very thoughtful, topsoil of the American official mind. Judged by their rhetoric and even more by their behavior, the U.S. resembles another empire, as described by Anthony Giddens: "The Romans . . . recognized no type of international rights or law, treating their own institutions as in principle generalizable across the rest of the known world."

U.S. apparatchiks define their imperial progress as the "expansion of the area of freedom," much as the Soviets defined their own, less successful efforts although the phrase itself may come from Andrew Jackson. Resistance to the Super Power becomes opposition to Freedom itself, since the empire presides over the only possible form of freedom. Peter Gowan's thoughts on the twists and turns of U.S. policy may be useful here. He sees the United Nations Organization as an American project designed "as a framework for the politics of the hegemon." Coming out of World War II, the U.N.'s architects based it on "an updated variant of Wilsonian internationalism" the only marketable collective security rubric then available. As sketched out by Franklin Roosevelt and his advisors, the U.N.'s electoral machinery was rigged in favor of the U.S., working in the Security Council with three, later four, great powers as official "world policemen." The inclusion of France and Britain among the Big Five nations was a temporary necessity that delayed U.S. liquidation of those powers' overseas imperial assets. Within a few years, the confrontation between the United States and the Soviet Union led the Americans to treat the U.N. as merely an "auxiliary instrument of American diplomacy." U.S. leaders repackaged the world order "through a series of friend-enemy alliances centered on anti-Communism." At the same time, they began "militarizing the American state on a permanent basis" to make possible the U.S. "role of guardian and manager of the entire core." Only the Old Right put up any real opposition, and its efforts failed. By giving theoretical hostage to the sovereignty of the U.N.'s members, the Charter froze in time the collective security notions of the late nineteenth and early twentieth centuries, which had sought "to bring great-power wars amongst (capitalist) states to an end, by laying down rules for collective action to stop them." Such thinking presupposed that no single power could rule all. However, the classic collective security model became irrelevant under U.S. hegemony for the simple reason that America, unlike Britain, possessed the resources to impose a unipolar control over all the other capitalist powers, both in Western Europe and in East Asia.

As U.S. policy took its postwar form, it became clear that the old security model was lumbered with "a juridical principle which was, at best, unhelpful: absolute national sovereignty." This was,

Gowan writes, a principle more attuned to the era of British than of American imperialism. The British never had the capacity to reshape coercively the internal arrangements of other capitalist societies. Their specialty was taking over and reshaping pre-capitalist societies.

The United States, Gowan continues, wanted first, to penetrate existing capitalist states and reorganize their internal arrangements to suit U.S. purposes; and second, to defeat any social forces there that rejected the American path to modernity in the name, not of traditionalism, but of an alternative modernity.

In 1991, the Gulf War allowed the U.S. "to exploit the U.N. to the full for a demonstration of the new reach of American hegemony." But the U.N. and its underlying legal notions remained an obstacle to U.S. aspirations. Equal state sovereignty, he argued, suggests that states are free to organize their domestic political economies as they wish, whereas the profit streams of U.S. (and much of the European, especially British) business depend crucially on internal arrangements in other states that provide unfettered freedom to external financial operators, unfettered rights for foreign companies to buy out domestic concerns, and unfettered protection of monopoly rents on intellectual property.

Owing to this ideological dead end, he wrote, during the 1990s, the U.S. and its European associates sought to rework the traditional discourse of the U.N., arguing that sovereignty was not unconditional, but should be viewed as a revocable license granted to states by the "international community," to be issued or withdrawn according to the palatability or otherwise of their internal regime. . . . The eclectic repertoire of the Charter itself . . . offered a ready antidote to any too narrow insistence on national sovereignty.

We have already reviewed these ideological innovations in the American Journal of International Law and need say no more about them now. As noted, "human rights" and armed intervention in their name, while looking like little more than a good excuse to attack weak states, have emerged as a leitmotiv of the new opera.147 Such ventures under U.S. auspices can make use of N.A.T.O., the U.N., or new coalitions thrown together on demand. Reviewing a recent book by post-Marxist war theorist Martin Shaw, Leo Panitch says:

As set out in Part II of the book, he [Shaw] argues that "the hey-day of the nation state (roughly 1870Ð1945) was also that of modern European empire" in which the "dominant form of state was not, therefore, simply a nation-state, but the nation-state-empire within an interimperial state system." For him, the crucial turning point that laid the foundation for what is today called globalization was the replacement of the classic (imperial) nation-state after World War II by a new "revolutionary" international state form that represented the "unprecedented integration of many autonomous major centres of state power in the world, under U.S. leadership." The new "bloc order" of the West, whereby the American superpower reconstructed the former nation-states of Europe and oversaw the creation of "legitimate international institutions" (NATO, the

U.N., the Bretton Woods financial institutions, etc.), was primarily constituted in terms of American military predominance. The nation-state lived on in the Western bloc-state, but did so in only "neutered form, in most cases a shadow of its former existence." The national form of the state was reinforced in the context of a cooperative international form through which "national state entities were penetrated by the international organizations of the Western state and adapted accordingly, finding new roles in pressing redefined, chiefly economic interests within their frameworks."

The path along which we have come is addressed by historian Norman Etherington:

Another possibility I would like to consider is that the great inter-systemic European wars of the period 1600-1945 were generated by the system itself. . . . At some point, however, new states stopped following the model.

Etherington tends to blame the warrior nobility, which survived into this period, for the debacle, and plays down the decivilizing role of middle class nationalism and democratic ideology, unlike Hoppe, but despite this, his point (about the system) seems well taken. His point about new states could be extended to Latin America, where states exist but seldom fight interstate wars as against internal conflicts. Thus, while the European state system qua system operated for several centuries as a loose imperial cartel vis-a-vis the rest of the world, it was prone to periodic bouts of struggle in its heartland. When the European states emerged, somewhat scathed, from the Napoleonic wars, they tacitly sought to displace their aggressions into regions suitable for colonization, but their ensuing rivalries in the extra-European world helped set the stage for World War I, which revealed the downside of the whole system. And by then, as noted previously, the rise of the middle classes, along with republican and democratic forms of government, had raised the stakes materially and especially ideologically. Present-day "globalization" via U.S. imperialism (with its alliances and coalitions) competing at the margins with U.N. bureaucracies and N.G.O.s does not appear so far to leave many interstices in which liberty could flourish. R.B.J. Walker notes an "increasing intensification of the problem of sovereignty as sources and sites of authority become increasingly inconsistent with any claim to a single authority in a specific territory." What we see now

is both a proliferation of sovereignties and a decline in the plausibility of claims about state sovereignty. Moreover, whereas state sovereignty was conceived as a more or less unchanging spatial, territorial affair, fixed on land, modern sovereignties seem to be highly mobile.

The possibility of "sovereign mobility" not hard to link with U.S. leaders' insistence of total world surveillance, air power, and now, control of outer space itself gives pause, and also seems to provide the only meaningful thread in the rather unreadable Hardt and Negri book. It also brings to mind the "Asiatic" pattern of empire in which formerly nomadic rulers never quite give up their roaming ways, as discussed by Hugh Nibley.

WHITHER SOVEREIGNTY AND THE STATE SYSTEM?

We seem to have come full circle, from the birth of sovereign territorial states to their absorption in a phase of renewed world empire. We begin to feel the mental anguish of a Late Hellenistic age. Where does this leave "sovereignty" as a "set of practices" (to use a currently trendy phrase) or as ideology? After all is said and done, what was sovereignty, what has it been, and what is it now, as a feature of international life? Constantin Fasolt notes that, from early modern times forward, important thinkers such as Machiavelli and Rousseau have denied that "natural justice" has any perceptible effect in the world. This view, he says, "is an article of faith," something "better called a revelation than an assumption." From this, it is concluded that no form of order at all is natural, and justice is impossible, and therefore both must be imposed. As Fasolt puts it:

It is only on the assumption that the laws of nature have no effect on human society that it becomes intelligible why we might need sovereigns who make purely positive laws in order to preserve human society. Sovereignty thus rests on foundations different from but no less religious than those of the medieval church.

Hence, the idea and theory of sovereignty have been important legitimizing devices for state apparatuses both at home and outwardly in the state system.155 As an accumulation of ideological power, it is simultaneously hard as iron and, under the right conditions, subject to overnight evaporation.156 As Walker writes:

Sovereignty works by giving authority to definitions. . . . The whole point of modern sovereignty is that it does not exist, and yet it has tremendous effects, it does not exist and yet it is constantly enacted, it has no foundations yet it is always foundational. Whatever it is, it is perhaps the strangest beast in the modern political world.

Worse luck, the apparent fragmentation of sovereignty, these days, does not necessarily imply a rebirth in the short run of freedom and laissez faire liberalism:

Theses about the decline of state sovereignty understood as a monopoly of authority in a specific territory are quite compatible with theses about the continuing or even increasing scale, size, influence, and so on of statist institutions.

He does not notice, exactly, that the process takes place under the aegis of the Super Power and its allies, but one can easily imagine multiple levels of oppressive bureaucracy loosely or tightly gleichgeschaltet by the distracted imperial center, itself beset by interest groups with sundry economic and sentimental agendas. After all, what does internal American "federalism" amount to now, if not such a system? The state system was problematic from the outset, precisely because it consisted of states a fact that many commentators contrive to ignore. In the century-and-a-half during which rules of warfare were generally followed, in Europe if not overseas, there was little moralizing about the internal arrangements of states. This had the advantage of reducing the ideological stakes of wars. It was far from perfect, but did make wars more manageable. What arose from such practical concerns was the pragmatic "right" of each state to its internal forms, whatever they might be.

This at least limited the goals of warring powers and, thereby, the scope of their wars. Already the French Revolution and the American "Civil War" foretold an end to equal sovereignty, which was, in any case, something of a fiction. In the real world, states in the system recognized and legitimated one another, but some states were "more equal" than others, and states generally declined to deal with peoples not having a proper state.158 Nonetheless, the somewhat fictive sovereign equality of states did work, a good deal of the time, as a barrier to intervention in the internal affairs of states. The point, after all, of a rule-bound cartel of sovereign states was precisely to limit their mutual competition in the production of public "bads" usually termed, for no obvious reason, "goods." Since their mode of competition was organized violence, this arrangement was perhaps the only upside in the theory and practice of Westphalian order an upside now undergoing deconstruction in favor of empire and armed doctrines. If nothing else, this circumstance gives us greater reason to complete the theoretical deconstruction of sovereignty from a standpoint quite opposed to the imperial one.

4

THE NATION-STATE AND GLOBAL ORDER

INTRODUCTION: THE STATE AND THE STUDY OF POLITICS

With the dissolution of the Soviet Union, the belief that a new democratic age has dawned is widespread. Paradoxically, however, many people are skeptical and cynical about the ability of government, even a democratic one, to provide peace and prosperity. This paradox is reflected in two common, but divergent, responses. While some people are embracing a world of multicultural connections by throwing off national identities in favor of global ones, others are retreating into more and more privatized worlds in which they cut themselves off as much as possible from people different from themselves. Despite these simultaneous celebrations of globalism and retreats from public life, states still persist in capturing the political imaginations and allegiances of vast numbers of people around the world. States continue to collect taxes, manage economies, organize collective identities, and make war. War, in fact, undoubtedly accounts for much of the state's endurance. Despite humankind's best efforts over the past three hundred or so years to eliminate it, war is still a global scourge, as devastating, if not more devastating, than ever! Moreover, it is still primarily states, or groups aspiring to form states, that make war, although in important ways this is no longer exclusively the case.

States, in significant and troubling ways, are also expanding their powers of surveillance and coercion. Some categories of people are being imprisoned by the states in which they live at ever-increasing rates. In many, censorship is on the rise, private communications are being monitored more frequently, and deviance from the "mainstream" is becoming more and more suspect and subject to interrogation. In spite of the end of the Cold War, the military budgets of the major protagonists have not fallen dramatically. The "peace dividend" many expected has not been realized. States continue to represent the world to their citizens as a dangerous place requiring a strong national defense and "the next generation" of advanced weaponry. States continue to exaggerate and fabricate external threats in order to present others as "enemies." Nationalism and patriotism show few signs of abatement. What is a state?

This is a difficult question to answer because the idea of the state conjures multiple meanings and associations. Sometimes the state refers primarily to an institutional apparatus: bureaucracies, armies, ministries, police, legislatures, political parties, and the like. At other times it signifies something broader, more in keeping with its reference to a territorial entity, such as the state of France. At still other times it refers to its legal and symbolic character as sovereign power. Defining the state in terms of any one of these alone—institutionality, sovereignty, territoriality—would be a mistake. Moreover, the history of the state is not a simple or linear process. Its development has been rather messy and unpredictable, complex and open to a multiplicity of possible trajectories. This book presents a historical approach that interprets how these different meanings of the state are constructed and interpenetrate to constitute the abstraction referred to as the state.

HISTORY, SOVEREIGNTY, AND THE STATE

Why take a historical approach to understanding the state? History is important because only by examining the state in historical perspective can it be shown that the state is not universal and given, not an immanent part of human nature. A history of the state reveals how it was created by people acting within the boundaries of the understandings and structures of their time and place, as well as through contingent conditions and circumstances. The state is an effect of the way peoples live. A historical approach reveals, for example, that sovereignty, although a crucial component of states, is not identical to the state. Sovereignty is instituted, as Hobbes said, not by states as if states preexisted sovereignty and took possession of it, but as part of the state's development.

Therefore, the historical specificity of sovereignty— the way it is formed, instituted, and reproduced at particular times and places—is important to an account of the state. Other important benefits of a historical approach are, first, that social constructions that appear to be universal, fixed, or given, such as the distinction between state and society, the relationship between domestic (inside) and international (outside) politics, the connection between institutions and ideology, and the separation of public and private, can be shown to be creations of particular historical state-sovereignty formations. Second, a historical approach also permits the inclusion of insights drawn from areas usually understood as outside the theory of the state, such as international relations and feminist theory. Third, a historical approach also allows the examination of the mutual embeddedness of the state in economies, religions, and everyday traditions, without collapsing the state into any one of these. As one scholar has put it:

> A construct like the state occurs not merely as a subjective belief, incorporated in the thinking and action of individuals. It is represented and reproduced in visible, everyday forms, such as

the language of legal practice, the architecture of public buildings, the wearing of military uniforms, or the marking out and policing of frontiers. The cultural forms of the state are an empirical phenomenon, as solid and discernible as a legal structure or a party system.

The historical treatment of the state presented in this book pays attention both to continuities and discontinuities over time. It will show that the sovereign, territorial nation-state is a fundamentally different ensemble of governing practices from city-states and traditional imperial states. The city-state is a territorially small, independent urban conurbation that constitutes an autonomous political entity. It represented itself within an ensemble of governing practices that involved an intensive logic of place. That is, its representations of power and authority invoked a history and mythology of its distinctive place.

The best historical examples of such entities are the city-states of ancient Greece (Athens, Sparta, etc.), the cities of the Hanseatic League along the coast of what is today northern Germany (Bremen, Hamburg, Danzig, etc.), and the republican cities in what is now northern Italy (Venice, Genoa, Pisa, etc.) during the early Renaissance. A contemporary city-state is Singapore, which occupies only 641 square kilometers, an area smaller than New York City. The modern nation-state is also different from the traditional imperial state. The central government of traditional empires, such as the Roman, Chinese, Inca, Syrian, and Zulu, had only limited, sustained authority over the extensive territory of the empire, which was internally fragmented and ethnically heterogeneous, being composed of numerous culturally distinct tribal societies. Empires governed through a representation of space as extending out from the center, not necessarily the same in all areas of the empire. Because the central government did not have a monopoly of coercive force, it required its army to take the field regularly against local warlords, armed tribesmen, and bandits.

Ordinary people within such empires had very little contact with imperial officials, except at taxpaying time. By and large, these empires did not interfere in economic life, although there were important exceptions. They did not exhibit a sense of what today would be called "nationalism." The frontiers of traditional empires were not internationally recognized as boundaries are today. Boundaries were simply the limits of military expansion that could be moved outward at will through additional conquests. Thus, there was no recognition of "interimperial" rights or law, that is, no globalized system of empires. The modern nation-state is a unique creation of specific historical, political, social, and economic circumstances. It is different from city-states and traditional empires in that the nation-state claims sovereignty over a fixed territory, both attributes being recognized, in principle, by other nation-states that are members of a globalized system of nation-states. Nation-states represent territory as an empty space to be filled in by the representations of the state's power and authority. Through their governing practices and artifacts, nation-states diffuse a singular identity within the bounded space their borders arbitrarily but legally enclose. The sovereign territoriality of a state is represented by a capital city, a flag, an anthem, a passport, a currency, armed forces, national museums and libraries, embassies in other sovereign states, and usually a seat in the United Nations. Today's global order comprises about 203 recognized nation-states.

As the sovereign territorial state is a historical creation, theories to explain its existence as well as the way it functions are themselves part of the history of the state. The connection between the history of the state and theories of the state will be explored in detail in the body of the text. What follows is a brief outline designed to distinguish our approach from others.

Politics and The Theory of The State

Throughout the nineteenth and into the early twentieth century the state received much scholarly attention. It was something that needed to be explained by political science, and the disciplines of history, law, and philosophy in which political science was then contained. After World War II, however, the state came to be taken for granted. Although the state's existence continued to be felt through the actions of its military apparatus, its bureaucracy, its ministries, and its police, its presence seemed unproblematic, routine, clear, and, above all, necessary and laudable, in no need of questioning. It was as if, at least in the United States, everyone knew what the state was supposed to do—reconstruct Europe, stop communist "expansionism," manage the liberal capitalist economy to prevent another depression, and provide welfare. Two approaches came to dominate political science during the post–World War II years: functionalism and pluralism.

Functionalism emphasized how social roles, norms, and individual psychology functioned to create social and political order. Pluralism sought out the ways in which the diversity of social interests, organized into pressure groups, could produce an ordered and fair distribution of collective goods and services. Both viewed the "state" as too ambiguous a concept for political science because it could not be defined in a way that eliminated all value judgments and, hence, could not be studied empirically. Moreover, both approaches assumed that society was separate from the state and established society as the primary focus. States did what societies wanted or pressured them to do. In short, politics was to be explained by what happened in "society," not the state. The focus on "society" and individual psychology was connected to the extension of American power after World War II. Political scientists in the United States sought to generalize the Western liberal democratic model of state and society, especially the U.S. version, to newly independent states.

In this way, new states could be more easily incorporated into a world order in which U.S. interests and values would prevail, and communism would be unable to gain a foothold in the non-European world. In order to project the Western, liberal democratic model of state and society, U.S. political scientists sought a "general" theory to explain how societies, no matter where they were, could function smoothly, if their economies, politics, and social structure were integrated and balanced. "Disequilibri-um" among these balanced parts, it was feared, would create an instability that could be exploited by leftist groups in their bids for power and, thus, increase the influence of the Soviet Union. Ironically, the disinterest of the discipline of political science in the state was, in part, a product of the state's success. In the advanced capitalist states, such as the United States, Japan, and the states of Western Europe, the state more or less successfully managed increasing economic prosperity and steady advances in the welfare of their subject populations. Public policies considered "socialistic" when initially proposed, such as social security, health care for the poor and aged, unemployment insurance, and the minimum wage, became staples of these states.

The "welfare state" did not need serious analytic attention from political scientists because it seemed to provide a common good that few questioned. This positive view was reinforced by the fact that Western European states and the Japanese state had successfully transformed war-ravaged economies into prosperous, dynamic capitalist powerhouses. By the early 1970s, however, all was not well and the state came under intellectual scrutiny and political challenge. Among mainstream political scientists a new subfield of the discipline called policy analysis arose out of new bureaucratic politics models of government and a new interest in decisionmaking. Policy analysis had two concerns in the United States. One was to explain how the United States became embroiled in the Vietnam War in spite of widespread domestic dissent and expert advice that the war could not be won. The hope was that models of bureaucratic politics would shed light on how foreign policy decisions could be better made to prevent future Vietnams. The second concern was the search for answers to the vexing question of how state programs could be more efficiently managed in the face of challenges by those who deemed them wasteful. While not reviving an interest in the state per se, and while accepting the prevailing individualism and rationalism of pluralist and functionalist political science, the policy analysis approach did refocus on the activities of government bureaucracies. Eschewing a concept of the state, policy analysis drew on theories of organizational behavior and decisionmaking that, in turn, were drawn from mathematics (game theory), social psychology, and cybernetic engineering.

As with functionalism and pluralism, the implicit normative emphasis of policy analysis was on promoting order, routine, and efficiency against the messy indeterminacy and contingency of politics. The first political and social scientists to renew an interest in the state were crisis theorists, many drawing on various Marxist traditions. Crisis theories sought to explain why the welfare state seemed no longer able to sustain the prosperity and security of the postwar era. Many of these theories were inspired by Marx and traced the failures of the state to its inability to extract sufficient resources or to maintain its legitimacy in the context of a capitalist economy. Some argued, on the one hand, that the state could not take in enough money to pay for all its programs, along with Cold War military budgets (which were seen as necessary to ensure foreign outlets for capital and sources of raw materials); and some, on the other hand, argued that the legitimacy of the state, which rested on its promotion of equality, could not overcome the class inequality produced by capitalism.

Increasingly, in reaction to both functionalism, pluralism, policy analysis, and crisis theory, some political scientists began to focus explicitly and look more favorably upon the state. These scholars examined how the state had functioned historically both as an organization of domination and as a promoter of reforms that might make good on the promises of the welfare state. This effort to "bring the state back in" was critical of the way the state had been subordinated to society and the economy by the functionalists and neo-Marxist crisis theorists. Instead, these scholars began to look at how state institutions made decisions, under what influences, and with what effects. These statist theories viewed the state as an agent in itself, as an autonomous entity in the sense of being institutionally separate from society, which could take independent action, even against society's wishes. Statist theories have led to fruitful studies of particular states by integrating historical sociology and political science. However, while statists have been attuned to the historical nature of particular states, they have assumed an ahistorical and reified concept of the state; states are historical but the state is not. For the most part, these theorists have largely ignored international politics, although some crisis theorists did locate the state in the world capitalist economy.

Also, functionalism had international parallels in functionalist theories of integration, which sought to identify those behavioral principles of social integration among states and international organizations capable of producing international peace. The statist theories that did introduce the international dimension into a theory of the state were not very successful because of their a historical concept of the state. Eventually, these theories accepted the point of view of realist international relations, that is, all states were, conceptually, the same; each sought to maintain sovereign territoriality against others in a systematic balance of power.

Just as the state was seen domestically as autonomous because it was institutionally separate from the economy and society, the same was assumed to follow for the states-system. That is, states somehow existed autonomously from their societies, on the one hand, and from the global system of states on the other. In the 1980s and 1990s several critical theories developed, which have contributed to a more thoroughly historical account of the state.18 These theories have explored how aspects of the state that pluralist, functionalist, and statist theories largely take for granted and do not explain historically are themselves historical constructs, especially the two primary aspects of the modern state: territoriality and sovereignty. These critical theories have also shown how war and violence constitute the state, and cannot be analyzed simply as resources or tools used by states, as well as how the distinction between the domestic "inside" of the state (a presumed sphere of order and law) and the international "outside" (a sphere of presumed anarchy and war) are not given ontological categories but are historically constituted of and by states.

Formation and Emergence of the Territorial State

The modern territorial state exhibits continuities and discontinuities with its past. In Part we examine the legacies of the Roman Empire, feudalism, and medieval monarchies in the genesis of the modern state. We focus on the emergence of institutions, such as standing armies, centralized administrations, and economies framed by territory-wide legal structures, as well as the transformations of political language and knowledge that made the modern territorial state possible. In addition, we establish an interpretive framework in which the specific histories of modern states, within and beyond Europe, can be understood.

The Ancient Roman State: Imperial Rule

The unique circumstances associated with the collapse of the Roman imperial state gave rise to the conditions that spawned the European medieval monarchies, which themselves eventually became the first territorial states. This development should not be understood in linear terms. It must be remembered that any image of continuities and discontinuities in the past is not part of that past itself but derives from the questions and understandings of contemporary analysts. We discuss the Roman state and the situation it spawned for Europe in order, first, to show how the situation created by the collapse of the Roman Empire conditioned the development of several key structures and institutions of the modern state. Second, we discuss the Roman state to show how it could be treated by the Renaissance and early legal apologists of modern sovereignty as the origin of the modern Western state.

That is, we show how the Roman state became a crucial nodal point in the past onto which was grafted an imaginary (or way of imagining) of the modern state as heir to a singular "Western civilization" that underlay not only the legitimation of those states but the globalizing of the state as a representation of a universal modernity. The political history of Roman rule can be divided into two broad periods: the first is the period of the Republic, which stretches from the founding of the city of Rome in 508 B.C. to the rule and assassination of Julius Caesar (r. 49–44 B.C.). The second is the period of the Empire, which extends from the rule of the Emperor Caesar Augustus (r. 27 B.C.–14 A.D.) until the sacking of Rome by a Visigothic chieftain in 410 A.D.

The Roman Republic

During the republican period the Roman state was governed by the Senate, which represented the patricians, or persons of high birth, wealth, and cultivation who could trace their ancestry to one of the original clan heads appointed to govern the city of Rome by its mythical founder Romulus. The patricians held most formal positions within the state administration, and articulated the ideology that justified or legitimated the institutions and structure of the Roman state. In short, the Senate represented the ruling aristocratic class of Rome. During the early Republic, class warfare between the patricians and the plebeians, or the ordinary people, was common. In order to still this internal strife, the Senate allowed wealthier plebeians to gain access to the consul, the highest office of magistrates in the Republic, as early as 356 B.C. It also created the tribunate, which was composed of tribal representatives and functioned as a parallel executive office to the consul. The tribunate was designed to give the poor a voice in governing Rome but was ineffective because, as one scholar puts it, "[t]he tribunes, normally men of considerable fortunes,... [were] for long periods docile instruments of the Senate itself."

In effect, the political institutions of the Roman Republic were "a complex mechanism that provided both an outlet for, and a restraint upon, the dynamics of class conflict, group rivalries, and personal ambitions." In addition to the institutional flexibility of the republic, a flexibility always kept from bending too far by the Senate, the Roman state managed political conflict and allegiance through the oratory of its politicians and their skill at playing the "seamier side of politics... patronage, bribery, vote-buying, tampering with electoral bodies, and the sale of public contracts." So long as politics remained centered in the city of Rome itself, this political practice managed to maintain order and secure for Rome significant wealth and power. It generated a remarkable military machine composed of all male citizens of Rome. By 275 B.C., the Roman army had conquered the Italian peninsula, defeated the Carthaginians in a century-long campaign known as the Punic Wars (264–202 B.C.), which gave the Republic control of the Western Mediterranean, and conquered Greece and Macedonia between 201 and 146 B.C.

The Roman Political Imaginary

Given the persistence of a political structure dominated by the patrician aristocracy, it is important to understand the ideas and cultural practices through which the state was imagined and represented under the republic. These ideas and representational practices portrayed certain ideals and values as normal for all Romans, and presented them as universally valid, as if inscribed in the natural ways of the world. The Roman political imagination imbued the city of Rome with a special significance as a place possessing its own spiritual gravity. The Roman sense of the space of politics was intensive, consisting of a dense mythology and history that marked Rome as a special and privileged place.

This gave its institutions and governing practices an assurance of their ethical rightness and superiority over vanquished enemies. It also constituted the Roman way: its traditions and especially its time-worn status and class distinctions, as rooted not in the contingency of political struggles and power but in the cosmological order, made Rome a special place. Even after absorbing a universalism drawn from Greek Stoic philosophy, which we will discuss shortly, Roman ideology assured Rome of its distinctive superiority and privilege as an ethical and political order. The political ideas of Rome focused on two attributes of the patrician class: virtus, and "nobility of birth and ancestry."

Virtus, or "manliness," as demonstrated by the great deeds and accomplishments of patricians, especially in the Roman army, provided the ruling class with a politically effective identity. To be a member of the Senate carried with it the honor of being the descendant of a family that had contributed greatly to the city in the past. The civic virtue of the ruling class carried both honor and responsibility to look after the affairs of the city, inclining that class to define the essence of politics in terms that transcended private "interests," such as responsibility and honor. Even as the lineage of senators came to be diluted by social reforms and the introduction of plebeians into the Senate in the later republic, civic virtue remained part of the identity of the senator. It is useful to talk about the conception of power embedded in the Roman republican state. To have power meant to act for the common good. Power prescribed a hierarchical decisionmaking structure, legitimating those "in power" to make and enforce decisions through a mixture of coercion, consensus, and organized violence.

This idea of power and politics replaced the less hierarchical practices of earlier tribal, clan, and kinship systems in which politics involved ritualized reciprocity, such as gift-giving, as well as noncoercive allocations of collective roles, privileges, honors, responsibilities, and resources. 6 In Rome, political authorities were to be obeyed because they exercised certain offices, which were conceived of as having been created for the public good, not for the person who exercised the office.

The idea that the public good was to be associated with political office rather than the particular office holder would make possible the reference to Rome as an original source of the bureaucratic and legal authority of the modern state, and help to establish a historical lineage constituting the modern territorial state as the culmination of a Western civilization. In the Roman political imagination, masculinity was privileged. The deference given to ancestry associated power and authority with patriarchy ; that is, the supremacy of the father of the family and the legal subordination of wife and children. Women were to be silent and invisible in the "public" world of Rome, considered by Roman law as under the patria potestas, or power of the father, which "committed women to male guardianship as perpetual minors."

In law, the power of the father was nearly absolute, although in practice women exercised some political power. Only fathers had rights before the law, could own property, and make contracts. Moreover, the ideology of Roman civic virtue, indeed of "armed civic virtue," relegated women to the private world of the household dominated by their fathers or husbands, and constructed their public role as "civic cheerleaders, urging men to behave like men, praising the heroes and condemning the cowardly." 8 The subordination of women in the political imagination as well as in the legal practices of Roman citizenship, which represented it, was an essential part of the Roman state. The durability of the Roman Empire was bolstered by Roman law, which, when it was finally codified by the Byzantine Emperor Justinian (r. 527–565 A.D.), largely followed the patterns set centuries before.

Because the revival of Roman law will be central to the formation of the modern territorial states of Europe, it is important to discuss briefly some of its details. Civil law was the most important element of Roman law. It dealt primarily with "the regulation of informal relationships of contract and exchange between private citizens." Public law, which set forth the rights and duties of the citizen toward the state, and criminal law, which was the law regarding crimes and punishments, were of considerably less interest and importance. The latter was especially concerned with keeping the lower classes in check, and was often arbitrary and harsh. Roman civil law was concerned to a great extent with the protection of private property.

With respect to indebtedness, for example, it protected the creditor far more than the debtor. Roman civil law did not give legal and political protection to the entire population, or even to all citizens, because it was based on the idea of "absolute private property," which separated property from political and moral restrictions. As the preeminent principle of civil law, the institution of property itself never required justification. Parallel to Roman civil law was another system of law based on the practical principles used by the governors of towns and justices when they tried specific cases in the law tribunals. This law was more sensitive to regional differences and the specific needs and customs of the people living in specific areas. Eventually, this customary law became known as the ius gentium or "law of the nations." It governed those economic and political relations which could not be adjudicated by the more traditional and inflexible civil law. With the introduction of the Greek philosophy of Stoicism into Rome, especially in the second century B.C., the ius gentium gained a philosophical basis. Stoicism emphasized order, and taught people to live their lives in conformity to the natural order of the cosmos, which governed all physical and moral being. As practiced by Romans, Stoicism meant peacefully accepting one's duties and responsibilities even if such acceptance involved great personal pain and sacrifice.

Roman Expansion and Imperial Policy

The political structure and ideology of the Roman Republic were most appropriate to a city-state, a geographical and cultural space in which political life focused on the city of Rome itself. However, the expansion of the Roman republican state into an imperial state was driven in good part because, to increase wealth, its economy needed additional land. The state's revenues were drawn largely from agriculture, and its more ambitious public works were funded from tribute paid by conquered peoples. Also, important social reforms, such as the grain subsidies and distribution of provincial lands to the poor during the tribunates of Tiberius and Caius Gracchus (r. 133–121 B.C.), were paid for largely by wealth drawn from Roman colonies in Asia Minor.

Moreover, the Roman economy was dependent on a continuous supply of slaves, whose primary source was conquered territory because slaves practiced various forms of birth control, which limited their numbers. Expansion from a republic into an empire was also implicit in the idea of virtus, which militarized Rome. War provided an important social and cultural arena where Roman citizens distinguished themselves in the eyes of their fellow citizens. In the words of one historian, "Loyal soldiers were rewarded with generous grants of land." The "result was a growing territory that needed ever more troops to defend it, and a growing army that needed ever more land to support it." The Roman Empire, which expanded greatly under Caesar Augustus (r. 27–14 B.C.), reached its greatest territorial extent during the reign of Trajan (r. 98–117 A.D.). Rome's army was stationed along the empire's limes (frontiers), which were demarcated with walls and fortifications. Rome's legions constituted the world's first standing army ; that is, a permanent military force paid, fed, uniformed, and armed by the state. It was the finest military organization of its time, highly trained, superbly disciplined, and extremely mobile. It was virtually invincible from the Punic Wars to the third century A.D. At the time of its greatest strength, the Roman army numbered about 30 legions of 6,000 men each.

Administratively, the Roman Empire was divided into Italy proper and the provinces. The city of Rome and the Italian peninsula were governed by the Senate, the supreme council of the empire. The eastern and western provinces outside of the peninsula were governed by the emperor, the supreme ruler of the empire and commander of the army. The purpose of Roman imperial administration was to collect the taxes that supported the army and paid for public works such as roads, temples, baths, and aqueducts. Administration and control were facilitated by the Roman road network (originally built to allow for the rapid movement of troops), which created a communications system within each province and connected each province to the capital city; hence the expression "all roads lead to Rome." The practice of Roman imperial policy was not the same in all of its provinces, however. In Italy and the eastern provinces, especially Greece and Asia Minor as well as Egypt, Rome established its domination indirectly by spreading Roman ideology and manipulating local rulers.

The Romans generally left local power struggles to work themselves out so long as they did not threaten Roman control and Pax Romana (Roman peace). When the Romans believed their hegemony was threatened, Roman provincial governors, called prefects, intervened militarily. In the western provinces, military campaigns were constantly necessary to subjugate the largely seminomadic tribes of Celtic peoples, whom the Romans called "barbarians," meaning foreigners, who inhabited these provinces. Roman policy in the West required more direct forms of rule, which often amounted to brutal and violent repression of local populations and extensive exploitation by Roman businessmen, money lenders, and tax collectors. Although the eastern provinces had provided Rome with much of its culture and wealth, the western provinces remained a perpetual battleground, where generals of the Roman army gained power and prestige. Julius Caesar, the general in charge of military operations in the western province of Gaul, and other generals like him would play an important role in eroding the power of the Senate and, eventually, replacing the oligarchic Republic with an imperial state centered on the emperor.

Roman imperial expansion caused tremendous social upheaval, which strained and eventually transformed the state.

Expansion impoverished the small independent farmers, who had been the backbone of the Roman economy, and enhanced the wealth and power of the patrician aristocracy. As these farmers were drafted into the army to increase its size so that the empire could be expanded and maintained, their farms were taken over by the patrician aristocracy. Such takeovers created latifundia, or large estates, and intensified the use of slave labor. 19 The republican state created conditions that transformed the state from a republic into an empire dominated by emperors and military strongmen, who came to rule more and more autocratically. As one historian has put it: "The Republic had won Rome its Empire: it was rendered anachronistic by its own victories." 20 The Senate gradually declined in power. The position and role of the army changed. Its ranks were filled increasingly by dispossessed farmers and the poor, as well as by "barbarians" who agitated for land and, most important, Roman citizenship. When the traditional aristocracy refused and resisted demands for land and citizenship, legionaries became increasingly loyal to their local military commanders, who promised such rewards. As the citizenry expanded to include the poor and non-Romans, the centralized political power and authority of Rome and the ideology that justified rule by the senatorial aristocracy were undermined and eventually collapsed.

Political Economy and Imperial Decline

The collapse of the Roman Empire was gradual, extending over several centuries. The fall of the empire was caused by four interrelated factors involving the inextricably interconnected state and economy. Note that the conception of economic and political life as separate and distinct spheres of activity is not characteristic of Rome but is a modern invention of liberal states, as we will see in a later chapter. First, the empire ceased to expand during the reign of Hadrian (r. 117–138 A.D.). Lacking the booty and tribute from newly conquered peoples, the empire could no longer pay for its vast army, large bureaucracy, and extensive public works. The only resources available to the state were drawn from the agricultural sector within the empire. Rome did not have a rich and extensive industrial and commercial base from which to draw revenues.

As the expenses of the state increased, taxes had to be increased. In addition to money taxes, a tax in kind was levied on land and labor. A percentage of what was produced by farmers had to be turned over directly to state warehouses and granaries. Manual labor of a certain number of days per week had to be rendered on public roads, buildings, bridges, and aqueducts. To pay these taxes, farmers had to keep land under cultivation. Therefore, laws were passed that compelled farmers to stay on their land and urban dwellers to stay in their occupations for life. Gradually, the extraction of resources necessary to maintain the army and the civil service as well as build public works became confiscatory and the Roman state became despotic. Second, Rome's reliance on slave labor as the major source of economic productivity also contributed to imperial decline.

Although the Roman economy was in certain respects quite innovative, having invented new agricultural techniques and machines, such as bread-kneading devices and the screw press to extract olive oil, which increased productivity and wealth, throughout its history the economy remained predominantly agrarian. However, the aristocracy limited the use of laborsaving devices because it wanted to moderate unemployment and prevent idleness among slaves. With the concentration of land ownership in the latifundia system of the later republic and empire, reliance on slave labor expanded. This system of agricultural production depended on the state's continuing to expand militarily because military campaigns on the frontiers of the empire were the most significant source of new slave labor. Third, the empire's economic problems, especially the inflation of prices caused by falling productivity (a result of the dwindling supply of slave labor), were compounded by urbanization. Rome was an urban culture because Romans imagined political order and the political good as being possible only within cities. Its distinctive architectural and engineering innovations were the arch, dome, and vault, which made possible the construction of large public buildings and aqueducts necessary to city life. Therefore, Romans constructed cities wherever they conquered. Each of these cities was a small replica of Rome itself, with a central square, colonnaded streets, public buildings, forums, triumphal arches, baths, amphitheaters, and aqueducts.

This urbanization, which accelerated as power shifted from Rome itself to the provinces, became increasingly difficult to pay for with the financial resources provided by a largely agrarian economy. Fourth, Rome's policy of recruiting barbarians into the army to maintain its strength eventually led to the de-Romanization of the army. Gradually, the ranks of the army were filled with legionaries whose commitment to Rome was slight. The influx of barbarians into the army was speeded up after the third century A.D. because the Roman state was facing a serious manpower shortage brought on by a declining birth rate and a high mortality rate among Romans, both the result of civil war, epidemic diseases such as the plague, and increasing economic hardship produced by confiscatory taxation. The civilian reign gradually gave way to military dictatorship. From 193 to 285 A.D., Rome was ruled by a succession of soldieremperors from the provinces who were elevated to and removed from office by their troops. Military dictatorship exacerbated the empire's economic problems because more of its wealth was given to soldiers to buy their loyalty.

In an attempt to stave off further disintegration, the empire was divided, for administrative purposes, into eastern and western portions by the emperor Diocletian (r. 284–305 A.D.). Diocletian ruled the eastern portion and appointed a co-emperor in the west. Each portion was subdivided into dioceses, or regional governments under the control of civil and military rulers appointed by the co-emperors. When Diocletian abdicated in 305 A.D., he was followed on the imperial throne by Constantine (r. 312–337 A.D.), who established a new capital city on the Bosporus, called New Rome, on the site of Byzantium in 330. Eventually, the division into Eastern and Western Empires became permanent and Byzantium, the capital of the Eastern Empire, was renamed Constantinople in honor of its founder.

Roman Religion and the Rise of Christianity

Something must be said about Roman religion because developments in this sphere eroded the ideology that allowed the Romans to imagine and maintain an imperial state centered at Rome. The official state religion of Rome was paganism (i.e., the belief in many gods). Romans worshipped the gods of the Greco-Roman pantheon, such as Jupiter, Juno, Minerva, and Mars, as well as dead emperors who had been deified. These gods were tied to the life-world of the Romans and were seen as protecting Rome itself. As the disintegration of the empire and the harsh methods taken to counteract it created extreme economic hardship, Romans began to turn away from official paganism. They turned either to foreign gods, such as Mithras, the militant god of the sun from the Persian Zoroastrian religion, especially popular with Roman legionaries; Isis, the Egyptian goddess of motherhood; or to ancient natural and fertility gods from pre-Roman times.

They also turned to a variety of mystery cults from the eastern provinces of the empire. Initially, the state allowed people to follow these new religions, provided that they continued formally to recognize the gods of Rome and the cult of the deified emperors. The devotees of these new religions were largely, but not exclusively, from the lower and most economically distressed classes of Roman society, especially slaves and the very poor, who were desperately seeking relief from economic misery. Roman aristocrats continued to be loyal to the gods they believed had made Rome great. One of these oriental religions was a Jewish sect that originated in the eastern province of Judea. At first the disciples of Jesus of Nazareth, an early nonconformist, itinerant teacher, and the sect's founder, proselytized among Jewish communities elsewhere in the eastern portion of the empire. After Jesus's crucifixion by the Romans, his disciples began to proselytize in the empire's western portion. Christianity (from the Greek Christos or Messiah, meaning annointed one) was a revolutionary social movement that spread rapidly, especially among the lower social classes as well as aristocratic women, because its theology (1) was clear cut (good versus evil), (2) was universalistic (all are equal in the sight of God), (3) satisfied emotional and psychological needs (belief in life after death), and (4) emphasized concern for the poor (charity). Christianity's rapid spread was facilitated by the Pax Romana and the existence of good Roman roads, which made movement about the empire relatively easy for its missionaries. 24 At first the Roman state tolerated Christianity.

However, because Christians refused to acknowledge the pagan gods of Rome and the cult of the deified emperors, they came to be seen as enemies of the state. Its monotheism (i.e., the belief in the universality of the one God) and its idea that all people everywhere were equal in the eyes of God threatened the way Rome had understood its distinctiveness. The Christian emphasis on humility, charity, and love for one's neighbor proffered an alternative understanding of virtue, which in turn undermined the Roman association of virtue with manliness and war. Christian virtue was manifested in private acts of piety and charity rather than in civic acts of courage and honor. Consequently, the most pious and energetic adherents to Christianity were women. In spite of persecution, the greatest of which came during the third century when many thousands were tortured and put to death, the number of Christians within the empire increased during the fourth century. Converts began to come from the upper classes of Roman society. The early church, which was composed of small, independent congregations that elected their own deacons and bishops, was replaced by an ecclesiastical hierarchy modeled on the Roman system of provincial administration.

In 313, Constantine lifted the ban on Christianity and a few years later became a Christian himself; probably from religious conviction, not political expediency, he fostered Christianity throughout the empire. When he died in 337, the Roman Empire was thoroughly Christianized. The Emperor Theodosius (r. 379–395 A.D.) declared Christianity to be the official religion of the Roman Empire and outlawed paganism. As the empire disintegrated, the Christian Church replaced the politico-military institutions of Rome with its own law (canon law), ecclesiastical courts, and administrative hierarchy of priests, bishops, and cardinals. The capital of the empire became the capital of the Catholic (meaning universal) Church. In the fifth century the bishops of the diocese of Rome were able to achieve ascendency over the Church's religio-administrative hierarchy by reference to St. Peter, the first bishop of Rome and the Apostle to whom Christ reputedly gave the "keys of Heaven" and established the papacy. Christianity's message of kindness, humility, patience, mercy, purity, and chastity was fused with the governing practices of the Roman imperial state: hierarchy, order, virtus, patriarchy, and law. In effect, the Church had become the Roman Empire. In the words of one scholar, the Church "took over the vestments of pagan priests, use of incense and holy water in purification, burning of candles before the alter, worship of saints, the architecture of the basilica, Roman law as the basis for Canon law, the title Pontifex Maximus for the pope, the Latin language, and the vast framework of the government of the Empire." 26 At this point the Catholic Church had grafted itself onto the framework of Roman administration and became a form of organized rule that did not recognize territorial boundaries to its authority over its community of believers.

Germanic Invasions

At the time the Roman Republic was expanding northwestward, Germanic tribes of Franks, Lombards, Frisians, Burgundians, Alemmani, Jutes, Angles, and Saxons were moving westward from the Baltic region and overran the indigenous Celtic inhabitants of Europe. By 200 B.C. they had reached the Rhine River and by 100 B.C., the Danube. Other Germanic tribal peoples such as the Suevi, Visigoths, Ostrogoths, and Vandals moved to the south and east. The Rhine and the Danube became the frontier between the seminomadic Germanic peoples and the Roman

Empire. Only in Scotland, Wales, Cornwall, the Isle of Man, Ireland, and Brittany did the Celts survive. In about 378 A.D. the Huns, a nomadic warrior people from central Asia, swept westward and pushed some of these Germanic peoples across the Rhine and Danube into Roman territory. The Romans settled them on uninhabited land within the empire as self-governing allies of Rome and under obligation to furnish troops for the Roman army in exchange for land and money.

The Germanic tribes accepted Christianity after being settled within the empire. The Germanic tribes were by and large communal groups. Their economies were based on primitive agriculture and animal husbandry, which required them to move perpetually, probably annually, to seek virgin land to cultivate and new pastures for their herds. Land was considered the property of everyone. Because tribes lacked formal institutions of government, decisions affecting the tribe, such as which clans and families would work which areas of land, were made by assemblies of leading warriors according to custom. Many of the clans that made up these tribes were matrilineal (i.e., they traced descent and inheritance through the female line), which gave women important social roles as clan leaders and involved them in decisionmaking. Finally, because the tribe was considered to be the family writ large, no distinction existed within the Germanic tribes between the public and the private. In places where tribes had settled within the empire, there grew a hybrid society, which blended Roman and Germanic institutions and practices. In many places Germanic peoples abandoned communal ownership and accepted the Roman idea of private ownership. Leading warriors carved out latifundia for themselves, creating differences in social standing and status that had not existed before the encounter with Rome. Increasingly, women were subordinated to men as the Germanic tribes accepted Rome's patriarchal inheritance laws and Christianity's definition of the identity "woman" in relation to God and "man."

Barbarian Invasions of the Fifth Century

For their part, the Romans gradually accepted the Germanic institution of the comitatus (from the Latin comes, or one who dines with the king), which was a band of young men who attached themselves to a famous warrior to whom they pledged unswerving loyalty. Such a warrior's followers were companions who were treated with distinction and given gifts, such as weapons and horses, rather than wages for their support. As more and more Germanic peoples were brought into the Roman army, most generals during the last centuries of the empire were of Germanic origin. Gradually, loyalty to Rome was replaced by personal loyalty to a particular commander.

Thus, the chain of command from the emperor downward was broken and the Roman imperial state was left without a reliable means of defense. 28 Eventually, the slow infiltration of Germanic peoples became a full-scale invasion. From 407 to 429 the provinces of Italia, Galicia, and Hispania were invaded. In 410 Visigoths invaded the Italian peninsula and sacked Rome. Rome was sacked for a second time in 455 by Vandals who invaded from Africa after having overrun the Iberian peninsula. The frontier provinces were also overrun: Jutes, Angles, and Saxons invaded Britannia between 441 and 443; Galicia fell to the Franks, Burgundians, Alemmani, and Visigoths. Hispania was overrun by the Suevi, Vandals, and Visigoths. In 476 the last Western Roman emperor was deposed and replaced by the German chieftain Odoacer (433–493), who ruled the Italian peninsula as a king. The Roman Empire in the west had come to its end. Visigoths attacked Constantinople in 378 but were defeated by the Byzantine emperor. After this victory, the Eastern Roman Empire was able to maintain itself until defeated by Ottoman Turks in 1453.

Summary

Rome grew from a primitive tribe of herdsmen living on an estuary of the Tiber River in the Italian peninsula of Europe into the most powerful and extensive empire of the ancient world. The situation it left was one of political disintegration amidst the growing unity of a Christian community. The fragmentation of the Western Roman Empire by the successor Germanic kingdoms, combined with the spiritual universalism of the Catholic Church, produced a particular political space called "Europe" and had significant consequences for the emergence and globalization of the modern state.

THE FEUDAL "STATE": INDIRECT RULE

The Western Roman Empire was succeeded by a collection of Germanic kingdoms. Over time, these kingdoms were subdivided into semiautonomous politico-military units and eventually came to be treated as the private domains of those whom the king had appointed to administer them. Gradually, centralized, public politico-military power and authority all but disappeared and became a private possession that could be bought and sold, divided among heirs, mortgaged, and given in marriage. In other words, public power had been essentially privatized. The development of the modern territorial state during the late medieval period, as will be shown in the next chapter, involved the gradual deprivatization of public politico-military power and authority. To help understand this modern public space, we first review elements of the Germanic kingdoms; they continued to influence later political structures even if the kingdoms themselves did not survive intact. We then describe "feudalism" to set the stage for the emergence of the modern state, that is, to describe the institutionalizations of power through which the modern territorial state could be imagined and constructed.

Germanic Kingdoms: Privatized Rule

Kingship as a form of rule originated in Germanic tribal custom. As was mentioned in the previous chapter, the Germanic peoples were ruled by chieftains selected from certain clans. Chieftains were military, political, and religious figures who were expected to lead the tribe into combat, settle disputes among the tribe's members, and act as intercessors with the gods through the performance of religious rituals, such as making sacrifices for successful hunting and good crops, or victory in battle. Successors were chosen from among a chieftain's direct, male descendants. The choice was made by the still-living chieftain but had to be confirmed through an act of acclamation by an assembly of the leading warriors of the tribe. Thus, loyalty among Germanic peoples was based on persons, which meant that followers were loyal only to a certain chieftain from a certain clan.

Politics and power did not operate according to the same logic in Germanic tribes as it did in the Roman Empire. The chieftain was the leader of the tribe, not the ruler over the tribe's people. Chieftains did not have the power to command the obedience and actions of persons in the tribe. Rule was a matter of performing religious rituals, maintaining peace among the tribe's clans, and leading the tribe into battle. These activities accorded the chieftain honor and respect and, hence, authority, but did not give him "power over" fellow tribespeople. After the conversion of Germanic peoples to Christianity, an incomplete and uneven process that took place from around the second through the ninth centuries, the Catholic Church was called upon to consecrate, and thereby authenticate, a new chieftain. According to the Church, a king was appointed by God to maintain order, protect the weak, support the Church, and defend the faith.

Thus, Germanic kings in the area of the collapsed Western Roman Empire held secular authority under the sacred authority of the Church—in contrast to the Eastern Roman Empire where the emperor, seen as representing Christ on earth, held both secular and sacred authority. Consequently, in the West, kings wielded secular power, which they acquired through heredity, and the Church wielded sacred power, which it had acquired, in its view, from God. 4 Thus, in the West, a political imaginary emerged that defined politics both in terms of the clanbased, personalized, lateral connections of Germanic tribal rule and in terms of the translocal, depersonalized, and hierarchical politics of the Roman Catholic Church.

The Germanic kingdoms had no formal political organization, no specialized administrative departments, no civil service, and no standing army, as did the Roman Empire. Governance was handled by the king's household, which was not a problem when the kingdoms were small. As they grew larger, new governance structures were invented. When a kingdom reached a certain size it was subdivided into counties, and a representative of the king, called a count, was selected to govern each one. Counts ruled their counties as the king ruled the kingdom: they had full military, judicial, and financial power, which they exercised with the aid of their household companions. Thus, the problem of governing the Germanic kingdoms was solved by breaking them into subunits small enough to be ruled by a few individuals. This way of governing had a significant drawback: counts could become independent of the king and challenge his power in their counties. Kings attempted to prevent such challenges in several ways. First, they tried to prevent counts from becoming too strong by directly supervising them, but such supervision was intermittent.

Second, they sought to counterbalance the power of strong counts by establishing rival authorities in each county. Thus, at an early date the Church was taken under the protection of kings. Abbots of the monasteries and bishops of the dioceses were placed on the same level as counts, who were forbidden to enter Church property or territory. Third, kings would establish a few close and unswervingly loyal companions on estates scattered throughout various counties of the kingdom. 6 Gradually, the large Germanic kingdoms, already fragmented into counties, were themselves fragmented into a bewildering array of smaller kingdoms and independent principalities and duchies, each possessing its own military, financial, and judicial powers. Although this fragmentation resulted in part from the practice of delegating rule downward to counts, it was also in part the result of dynastic struggles provoked by the dissatisfaction of the king's heirs with the subdivision of the kingdom at his death.

The breakup of Charlemagne's Holy Roman Empire in 840 is the most famous example. Toward the end of his life Charlemagne's son Louis, who had received the Holy Roman Empire intact, willed the empire to his oldest son, Lothar, and subkingdoms to his younger sons. When Louis died in 840 a war broke out among Lothar and his brothers for the throne of the empire. After a bloody internecine struggle, the combatants agreed according to the Treaty of Verdun (843) to partition the empire into three new kingdoms: West Francia (France), East Francia (Germany), and the Middle Kingdom (Lotharingia), which included the northern half of the Italian peninsula. Fragmentation was also the result of a series of invasions: by the Saracens (a derogatory term derived from the Arabic sharakyoun, meaning easterner), a nomadic, Muslim people from North Africa, in 711; by the Vikings or Norsemen, a seafaring people from Scandinavia, whose descendants, the Normans, spread throughout western Europe, including England (1066) and Sicily (1091); and by the Magyars, a nomadic people from the steppes of central Asia, who eventually settled in the tenth century in what is now Hungary. The brunt of these invasions was borne by local counts and their retainers and encouraged their independence. Few kings were able to raise an army quickly enough to be effective against bands of swiftmoving raiders. Therefore, local counts had to defend themselves. This led them to believe that the land they defended was their own personal property, not the king's. The people whom they defended also came to believe that the local count was their ruler, not the distant king. Great families began to take root in specific counties. In this way the principle of strong monarchy, which had been synonymous with the early Germanic kingdoms, was undermined, and rule became fragmented and indirect.

EUROPE: POLITICAL DIVISIONS AND INVASIONS, 800-900

Feudalism

The politico-military practices in the fragmented successor Germanic kingdoms have been known since the seventeenth century as feudalism. "Feudalism," then, is a representation, not a mirror, of this period. The concept organizes a complex, heterogeneous reality by reducing it to forces and dynamics important to later times and places. The term was never used during the Middle Ages, that period of European history beginning with the collapse of the Western Roman Empire in the fifth century and ending with the overthrow of the Eastern Roman Empire in the fifteenth. It was invented by lawyers and antiquarians of the 1600s to describe customs and institutions, such as the possession of public power by private persons and rules governing the transfer of land, that did not meld well with the new laws and institutions of the emergent territorial state.

These customs and institutions appeared to be connected to the medieval institution of the fief ; therefore, they were lumped together under the term feudalism, which comes from the medieval Latin feodum, itself from the old German fee, meaning cattle or property. 8 As such, the construction of the idea of "feudalism" as a unified, coherent system of social relations was used to help legitimize the modern state by contrasting modern conditions (those of the seventeenth century and later) with a "premodern" condition (the previous feudal epoch) whose "primitive" organization, it was argued, had been overcome and surpassed by a "better," more "modern" one. We therefore look at feudalism with two of our own aims in mind: first, to introduce some of the elements of this historical period that established political, economic, and social conditions within which the modern state emerged; and, second, to see how the representation of this period as "feudalism" could be used, as was Rome, as a system of signs pointing to the emergence of the modern state.

Feudal rule consisted of five interrelated activities and practices. First, vast castles were built with high, stone walls for defense, which generated loyalty by providing security to those living nearby. Second was the carrying out of military campaigns against rival lords, which made reputations and established particular lords as leaders to be respected, obeyed, and feared. Third was providing religious leadership and patronage, which furthered the reputations of certain lords as defenders of the Faith and ensured support from the Church. Fourth was pursuing dynastic alliances, primarily through strategic marriages, which expanded the wealth and politico-military power of rulers. Fifth was providing justice throughout the territory being governed, be it kingdom, principality, duchy, or county. Such practices did not constitute a "state" in any formal sense, however.

Feudal governance lacked key features of a state, such as permanent structures for decisionmaking, a standing army, or an extensive administration that operated according to codified law. Most important, though people were personally loyal to counts and kings, their identity as human beings was not bound up with a secular political order to which all belonged. To the extent people recognized an intersubjective social unity that linked them to people outside their immediate local surroundings, it was a vast Christian community of believers under the authority of the Catholic Church that came to be called Christendom.

By the tenth century, feudalism had spread more or less to all former territories of the Roman Empire. Although more highly developed in some areas than others and exhibiting local variations, each feudal "state" was a pyramidal structure of individuals bound together by oaths of loyalty. The king was at the top of this pyramid and was the suzerain, or overlord, of the entire kingdom. Several dukes, who held huge tracts of land within the kingdom, were his direct vassals. Dukes, in turn, retained a number of direct vassals, and so on. At the bottom of this pyramid were the simple knights, who held sufficient land to maintain themselves and their families. All land was someone's property and all landholders, except the king, were someone's vassals. 10 In some cases, kings were considered vassals of the pope, who, of course, was considered God's vassal on earth! The glue that held the feudal "state" together was vassalage, which can be defined as "a system in which a free man binds himself personally to a lord, offering him loyalty and military service in return for protection and the use of property (usually land)." It was entered into by doing homage, which was a ceremony in which the lesser man, kneeling before the greater man with hands joined as if in prayer, pledged himself and his loyalty to the greater man. In some areas, the pledge was "sealed with a kiss." Ties of vassalage lasted during the entire lives of both lord and vassal.

Vassalage was thus a complex politico-military system based on ties of personal dependence within which all men were the "men of other men," to whom they owed obedience and loyalty and from whom they expected unwavering assistance and beneficence. Thus, dukes, counts, marquis, and even bishops and abbots pledged themselves to their kings. Lesser knights pledged themselves to counts and marquis, and so on. As will be seen in the next chapter, the rise of the territorial state involved replacing an idea of politico-military power and authority rooted in the personal ties of loyalty and obedience to individuals with a conception of politics rooted in identity with and loyalty to the institutions of the sovereign territorial state. Although some vassals resided in the households of their lords, more significant were those who were granted an estate called a fief, from which the vassal could derive sufficient income to feed, clothe, and arm himself and, if the fief was large enough, keep an armed retinue. Political power in the form of immunities, that is, the right to collect taxes and tolls, dispense justice, and coin money, were often delegated by the king to local lords. The granting of land from which the vassal could derive personal income became the most common way of rewarding service, because land was the primary source of wealth. From the king's point of view, granting fiefs to vassals was a way of shifting the cost of maintaining an army of heavy cavalry to the warriors themselves.

Vassals provided the king with three forms of service. The first was military, which involved appearing fully armed when summoned by the king. The second was counsel, or advice on important decisions, a legacy of the German practice of involving all warriors in decisions affecting the tribe. The third was financial, which involved payments of money to the king to help him meet unusual expenses such as ransoming himself from his enemies, paying for the great feast given when his eldest son was knighted and given horses and armor, or when his eldest daughter was married. As will be shown below, such aid evolved into modern systems of general taxation. The feudal contract was binding on both lord and vassal for life, although it could be broken by mutual agreement or individual public renunciation. Nonetheless, at the beginning of the medieval period, the status of the lesser vassals was precarious. Their fiefs could be seized by the king for no reason at all or exchanged for others. Vassals had no assurance that their lands would be inherited by their heirs, because after a vassal's death, the fief legally reverted back to the king. In other words, the vassal had no hereditary right to the fief. As a consequence, vassals became obsessed with strengthening rights of inheritance any way they could.

The transference of a fief exclusively from father to son did eventually become hereditary under laws of primogeniture, although it was never automatic and had to be reaffirmed by the king. Kings gladly acquiesced to these efforts because they did not want fiefs to become too small by inheritance to provide protection. Laws of primogeniture replaced the earlier Germanic custom that favored equal inheritance among sons and daughters. Therefore, although there were occasionally exceptions, as a rule, women were unable to inherit fiefs. When a woman was permitted to inherit, it was always with the proviso that her husband perform vassalic duties in her stead. If the firstborn son was too young to meet the obligations of a vassal, an adult relative, usually a maternal uncle, was chosen to exercise vassalage until the minor came of age. Fiefs were subdivided into manors, the basis of the feudal agricultural economy. The lord of each manor was a free man who owed feudal obligations to the lord of the fief. Thus, political and economic life were thoroughly intertwined within the feudal "state." The peasants who lived on the manor were free, half-free, or tenants called serfs. They tilled a plot of land owned by the lord of the manor, who gave the serf life tenure and military protection for as long as he paid an annual rent in produce, labor, and money.

The Estates

In the feudal "state," rights and privileges were attached to corporate groups called estates, not to individuals. Political power was inseparable from social status, just as it was intertwined with economic wealth. There were three main estates. The first estate was the clergy, which was composed of the official hierarchy of the Church (bishops, priests, archbishops, and cardinals) as well as the monks and abbots of its religious orders. The second estate was the nobility, which comprised a privileged politico-military ruling class. The third estate was the bourgeoisie, which was composed of the merchants and artisans who lived in towns (bourgs). In addition, there were various other groups—serfs, free peasants, servants, beggars, prostitutes, and thieves—most of whom were poor and, except for the serfs, without legal status in the estates system. Although not part of the formal estates system, women were often treated as a separate and distinct corporate group, a "fourth estate." In the feudal "state," women were dealt with under the sign "woman," which was not a description of a particular person but a social category. 16 In order to represent women as the social category "woman," medieval society primarily drew upon two Christian teachings. The first was the biblical narrative of the Creation, in which woman was seen as being created from Adam's rib and serving as his "helpmate."

In this narrative women were the incarnation of Eve's sins in the Garden of Eden, and hence were seen as inclined by their nature to sin and as responsible for sin in men, who could not resist women's tempting. The second was the story of the virgin birth of Christ, in which woman, of whom Mary became a dominant representation, was seen as innocent and chaste. The former teaching was openly misogynistic (i.e., hating and distrusting women), and the latter valorized "woman" as representing absolute purity, innocence, and goodness. When women failed to live up to the ideal of purity, they were subjected, and subjugated, as sin incarnate. Hence, these two seemingly opposite characterizations formed part of a singular representation of women that effectively subordinated them within medieval life. In general, women could not exercise politico-military power and, as one contemporary source put it: "They must devote themselves to their feminine and domestic occupations." Women had no rights at all against ennobled males and were both legally and in custom subordinate to men in nearly all spheres. Once married, a woman could do little without the consent of her husband.

Describing the condition of women in marriage, one historian says: "In marriage, the husband predominated by force of law and with the guidance of homiletic [i.e., religious] literature. Many women feared their husbands, and some were even beaten by them. Law and custom permitted a man, whatever his class, to bring his superior physical strength to bear against the woman who was supposed to be his helpmate." Although they had no rights, women were in charge of the household, whether it be castle, manor house, or hut, and shared the status of their husbands. This occasionally gave some women significant power and importance, especially because the life expectancy of their knighted husbands was quite low.

For example, in some places in medieval Europe, such as France and Catalonia (although not in England), noble wives not only took responsibility for educating children but also protected their inheritances and otherwise safeguarded their futures. In several cases, noble wives took on the role of local governance and administration in the absence of their husbands.

The First Estate: Clergy

The clergy included the priests, bishops, archbishops, and cardinals of the regular Catholic Church hierarchy; the monks and abbots of its religious orders, such as the Cistercians, Benedictines, and Franciscans; and the knights, masters, and grand masters of its military orders, such as the Templars and the Hospitallers. Bishops, archbishops, abbots, masters, and grand masters were equal in status and power to the greatest dukes and counts of the secular nobility. Many dioceses and religious orders became extremely wealthy and controlled huge tracts of land. The military orders were especially powerful because they were composed of armed monks. The great power and wealth of certain dioceses and religious orders created tension between the Church and feudal rulers. Feudal kings frequently sought to control the appointment of bishops and abbots and were always watching for any attempt by the Church to rob them of their rightful revenues and patrimony, that is, their property. The threat of excommunication was usually sufficient to persuade a recalcitrant king to bend to the Church's wishes. However, as feudal monarchs began to centralize their political power during the late medieval period, they were able to gain control over the appointment of important bishops and abbots within their realms. Eventually, the military orders were suppressed and disbanded and their lands and properties were confiscated by the crown.

The most famous of the disbandments was the brutal suppression of the Knights Templar in France in 1310. The French king Philippe IV (r. 1285–1314) arrested all Templar knights within his kingdom on charges of heresy, tried and tortured many, and executed about sixty who refused to recant, including the order's grand master, Jacques de Molay. The clergy served an important politico-cultural function in medieval Europe. They comprised its intellectuals, and as such they interpreted the meaning of Scripture, elaborated Church doctrines, and carried on the traditions of classical philosophy and science inherited from Rome. Through its networks of monasteries and its cathedral schools, as well as its dominance of emerging universities, the clergy came to be respected for its learning as well as feared for its enforcement of canon law, under which, among other things, it could accuse people of heresy (i.e., adherence to a religious teaching contrary to Church dogma) and execute them, usually by burning at the stake. Few people outside the clergy and the nobility were literate, and within the nobility, men were more likely to be literate in Latin, the language of religion and government, and women in the vernacular, or the language of the common people. This gave the literate clergy enormous power because the Church communicated legal and moral ideas. As one historian put it, the Church was "the main, frail aqueduct across which the cultural reservoirs of the Classical World now passed to the new universe of feudal Europe, where literacy had become clerical."

What unity there was beyond the local village or town came not through identification with a political association (e.g., a state), but through the system of religious signs institutionalized by the Catholic Church throughout Europe. This semiotic system was visual and aural. Therefore, the cathedrals and liturgy (i.e., rituals and ceremonies) of the Church served not only the religious function of reinforcing and strengthening faith, but the sociopolitical function of anchoring identity in Christendom, that universal community to which all Christians belonged. Note that many areas within Europe were not thoroughly Christianized until well into the high Middle Ages, that is, the twelfth and thirteenth centuries. The clergy did not simply pronounce and propagate Catholic dogma on an already believing and, hence, accepting people. The establishment of Catholic dogma was a struggle, a political act that often involved persuasion, the use of terror, and military force. For example, Charlemagne ordered 4,500 defeated Saxons to convert on the battlefield or die. They chose to remain loyal to their pagan gods and were put to the sword. Moreover, the Church's official liturgy was continually contested by local religious practices drawn from pagan religions. People of all ranks prayed to local saints, practiced magic, and believed in miracles, practices that the Church combated. With respect to witchcraft, the Church targeted women especially, believing, according to one historian, that "legions of the Devil were led by evil women who anointed themselves with grease from the flesh of unbaptized children, who rode stark naked on flying broomsticks or on the backs of rams and goats, and who attended their nocturnal 'sabbaths' to work their spells and copulate with deamons." Thus, medieval political theory conceived of the world, God's creation, as a unity, a whole governed by Him for the good of His subjects. Humanity was potentially a single unity under God's rule. To define and interpret the meaning of community and collective life, the clergy relied on the idea of the corpus mysticum, the mystical body of Christ, which had roots in the early days of Christianity. Christ's body, the human element of which was believed to have died on the cross at Calvary, and the spiritual element, which is supposed to live forever at God's side, symbolized the unity of the spiritual and the secular, of faith and reason in human life.

In St. Augustine's famous phrasing, human life is divided between the City of Man and the City of God. The City of Man referred to man's physical and secular needs, a world of necessities in which the potential for sin and evil was great, but in which men also needed to develop reason. The City of God referred to the spiritual in human life, the orienting of men and women toward eternal happiness in God. Reason, especially as expressed in classical philosophy, was the human means toward knowing God; hence the continuing importance of Roman and Greek legacies in feudal Christianity. The universal idea of Christendom, then, both retarded the emergence of an understanding of a territorialized political community and made available a powerful alternative communal identity across the otherwise politically fragmented lives of medieval peoples.

Within this alternative imagined Christian community, the political was subordinated to the religious, as was reason to faith. Christianity rested on what one historian, trying to make sense of the motivations behind the Crusades, has called a "spiritual restlessness," the emotional, passionate, and all-consuming longing for God that was inscribed in the Christian idea of faith. Rather than considering social conflicts as mediated and resolved by the institutions of secular rule, people in the Middle Ages relied on local religious practices informed by the Church's teachings. In order to use Christianity in constructing the modern territorial state, its principles and signs would have to be reinterpreted; and they were, as we will see.

The Second Estate: Nobility

During the early centuries of the medieval period, no social or legal distinctions existed among vassals. By the twelfth century all members of the feudal hierarchy, from the greatest lord to the pettiest knight, believed they belonged to the same social group, a belief based on their ownership of politico-military power. Thus, a nobility (or aristocracy) was created whose social purpose was governing and fighting; it dominated European political and military affairs until the nineteenth century. Initially, the nobility was a military caste whose members often came from humble backgrounds. When they were not making war, vassal-knights passed their time practicing with arms, carousing, and intriguing in the lord's court. Hunting and hawking were popular sports. They engaged in tournaments, or mock combat, designed to maintain and improve their martial skills, in search of which some knights traveled far and wide across Europe. These knights-errant, as they were called, spread medieval culture and feudal institutions from northwestern Europe, where they had developed, to the Iberian Peninsula, southern Italy, eastern Europe, the British Isles, and the Holy Land during the Crusades.

The Crusades, which were military expeditions instigated by popes and undertaken by the Christian kings from 1096 until 1270 to take the Holy Land from the Seljuq Turks who had themselves taken Jerusalem from the Fatimids, gave rise to the idea that the vassal-knight was a soldier of God, a defender of the church, a protector of widows, orphans, and the poor, an avenger of evil, and a savior of "damsels in distress." This ideal was codified into a system of personal conduct called chivalry (from the French chevel, meaning horse), which prescribed that knights live according to strict rules called courtesy (from the word court). The gentleman (from the French gentilhomme), or man of good lineage, in addition to being a great warrior, was expected to have polished manners, a high moral sense, and knowledge and skill in the social arts of courtly life.

This cult of chivalry enhanced the misogyny that was common among the nobility. The development of the notion that vassal-knights were socially superior to others because of their bravery and devotion to duty, honor, and good manners eventually gave rise to the idea that such status could be acquired only by birth, although lords could acquire more vassals, some even low born. Thus, the right to be made a vassal-knight became hereditary. Gradually, the nobility became privileged, that is, subject to its own legally recognized rights and obligations. Certain occupations, deemed incompatible with noble status, such as trade or commerce, were legally forbidden to the nobility. Nobles were also forbidden from working with their hands in agriculture or at manual occupations. Such activities were considered to be contrary to the honor and breeding of the nobility.

The nobility itself came to be subdivided into various legally recognized ranks based on wealth and power, to which specific legal privileges and obligations were attached. The most powerful and prestigious were, of course, kings, followed by dukes, counts, viscounts, and knights. The development of recognized ranks and hereditary privilege gave rise to the art and science of heraldry, which arose from the need to identify armored knights, whose faces were hidden by their helmets during combat, and involved the painting of individual signs of recognition, such as a chevron, lion, or cross, on shields. Such signs came to be legally associated with a particular knight and were passed from father to son through the generations. Thus, the heraldic device became a legal symbol of family continuity and noble standing.

The Third Estate: Bourgeoisie

In some kingdoms, especially England, the third estate referred to all commoners, whereas in others it referred primarily or exclusively to town dwellers. In all kingdoms, the third estate was dominated by the bourgeoisie, or burghers (town dwellers), who were for the most part merchants and artisans. Towns came into existence when commercial activity in Europe revived after the collapse of the Western Roman Empire. Initially, trade was of little importance for the Germanic kingdoms. Manors were self-sufficient and produced almost no surplus. Roman roads over which trade could flow had fallen into disrepair. By the eleventh century, however, commercial activity began to grow and urban life revived. Trade began between certain areas of western Europe where a surplus of a locally produced good, such as woven woolen cloth in Flanders, was traded to another area that had a surplus of other locally produced goods, such as the honey, furs, and hunting hawks of Scandinavia. Surpluses of French wines were traded for the tin, lead, and silver of England, especially after the conquest by the Normans, who preferred wine to ale. The Crusades also were made possible by increased trade: the Crusader kingdom in the Holy Land needed supplies, and pilgrims needed transportation. Thus the northern Italian towns of Genoa, Pisa, and Venice became important shipbuilding and trading centers.

As commercial activity grew, a class of merchants who traveled from place to place developed. The fragmented structure of feudal governance created special problems for these merchants, especially the localized customary law that limited the validity and uniformity of contracts over time and across space. Laws governing commerce were "under the rule of a patchwork system of local customs, influenced in varying degrees by Roman law."

Moreover, "procedure in the secular feudal courts was uniformly slow, arbitrary, and unfair to the lower orders of society . . . characterized by reliance upon an oral tradition of custom maintained by the lord and his officers and judges." 33 Eventually, these itinerant merchants looked for places where the local lord would allow them to settle and extend them the privileges necessary to carry out their commercial activities. This included stabilizing and extending the law that applied to commerce, often by combining elements of canon law and the law that traveling merchants had themselves devised to facilitate and normalize trading practices across multiple feudal legal jurisdictions, called " merchant law. "

Usually, merchants settled near ports, river crossings, castles, monasteries, or cathedrals. It was not long before major castles and monasteries had bourgs (from the Latin burgus, a district removed from a castle) or merchant settlements, nearby, which had been granted a charter, or franchise of privileges and rights in exchange for the payment of a sum of money or an annual income to the local lord. Thus, those who lived in such settlements, which eventually grew into towns and cities, enjoyed a distinctive legal status that distinguished them from the nobility, clergy, and serfs. Town charters applied to the collective whole, not to individuals. Towns, because they were centers of commercial activity, became economically and militarily self-sufficient. Town dwellers surrounded themselves with defensive walls and raised their own militias. People who lived in towns were free because they were immune from laws that regulated the feudal system beyond their walls. Serfs who escaped to a town and lived within its walls for a "year and a day," without being claimed or identified, became free persons and received the town's protection. The merchants who settled the first towns organized themselves into a guild (from the Anglo-Saxon geld, meaning self-governing) for protection, mutual aid, and governance. As the towns grew and attracted artisans, such as cobblers, weavers, dryers, fullers, butchers, bakers, tanners, wheelers, coopers, pullers, and smiths of various kinds, new guilds were formed in each trade or craft. Guilds regulated these occupations and their levels of activity by controlling the training and licensing of those who practiced them and by preventing competition.

Each guild set forth detailed regulations concerning the method of manufacture, price, and quality of its goods. Before being admitted to a guild, one had to learn its trade or craft by becoming an apprentice to a master practitioner, the number of which in a particular area was controlled by the guilds. After a certain amount of time the apprentice had to produce a masterpiece to be inspected by the officers of the guild to prove his ability to practice the trade or craft. At the bottom of the lord-vassal system were the serfs, the lowest of whom were attached wholly to the land of the lord on whose manor they resided. Above these serfs were serfs who had land of their own. Serfs were not slaves because, unlike slaves, they had certain rights and privileges.

The lord could not harm his serfs and was obligated to protect them from enemies. A serf had a right to his land and to his wife and family. As with the nobility, the male was considered the head of the serf's family, although women often performed considerable work. In addition, serfs enjoyed the right to rest on holidays (holy days), which could number as many as fifty a year in addition to Sundays. In exchange for these rights and protections, the serf gave the lord a portion of his produce or rent or labor for special tasks, as well as a tithe, that is, 10 percent, to the Church. He was also obliged to work several days each week on the lord's land as well as perform extra work for him during ploughing, sowing, and harvesting. The serf also had to pay to use the lord's mill, bake-oven, brewery, winepress, and stud animals.

Feudal Constitutionalism

Recall that rendering the king counsel was one of the major feudal obligations of every vassal. A king received advice from two sources: his curia, or court, composed of his closest companions and household retinue, and a great council, usually convened on major holidays such as Christmas and Easter, composed of the upper members of the nobility and higher clergy of the realm as well as important members of the bourgeoisie. When the upper nobility and clergy became too numerous for the council to perform useful work, delegates were chosen from the three main estates of the realm—nobility, clergy, and bourgeoisie—to attend. These delegates did not represent individuals but were delegates from the estates from which they were chosen—that is, the group of people having the same legal status or position to which bundles of rights, privileges, and obligations were attached. Thus, representation in the feudal state meant the representation of corporate groups such as the nobility and clergy, and eventually included other corporate groups such as lawyers, professors, and physicians.

Thus the feudal "state" was "constitutional" in that the great council of the three estates represented the realm to the king, voiced protest, restated rights, gave advice, and agreed to financial requests. Together, the crown and the estates governed the feudal "state." However, because the king needed the consent of the estates to obtain access to their financial resources, especially to raise taxes to fight wars, a struggle ensued between the crown, on the one hand, which needed the money, and the council of estates, on the other, which had it to give but expected justification. This struggle intensified in the late feudal period when a military revolution increased the cost of war well beyond that which any individual monarch could afford from his private coffer.

Summary

Reflecting on the feudal period of fragmented political communities presses us to recognize that the modern territorial state is a historically contingent creation. The feudal constitutional struggles between crown and estates, out of which the political space of the modern state would emerge, developed from a complex juxtapositioning of Germanic and Roman institutions and understandings of the political world. The distinctive political architecture of the feudal "state" was one in which economics, social status and custom, and political power were tightly intertwined. In the modern state these will become separate fields related hierarchically. In the next chapter we turn to the long historical process in which this new political space was invented.

THE MEDIEVAL STATE: DIRECT RULE

Changes in warfare, together with centralizing administration and the invention of a new language of politics, marked the transformation of feudalism into rule by the centralized, medieval states. 1 By the end of the late Middle Ages, roughly from 1100 through the 1500s, a number of important elements of territorial states would be in place: large standing armies, hierarchies of government functionaries loyal to territorially based rulers, and new ideas about human beings and their bodies as objects, about which secular knowledge was possible. In this chapter we will see how these developments made human beings, the state's subjects, available to be used as objects by the state apparatus in the name of order and as expressions of the power of the state.

Military Revolution

With the advent of the feudal "state," the large standing infantry-based army of imperial Rome was replaced with a multitude of small private armies composed primarily of retinues of mounted aristocratic warriors. From 1000 to about 1400, a band of heavily armored knights mounted on specially bred and trained warhorses became the principal military formation of the medieval age and the massed cavalry charge its chief tactic. Heavy cavalry was made possible by the arrival of large horses from Persia by way of Byzantium in the fifth century, the invention of the horseshoe, and the introduction of the stirrup into Europe from Asia. A feudal army, known as a host, was a temporary coalescence of many private retinues called into military service by the prince or king. Knights were obliged to render this service in exchange for their fiefs. The non-noble groups of the feudal "state"—clergy, bourgeoisie, and serfs—had no military obligations and were, for the most part, excluded from military service. Knights were responsible for procuring their own military equipment, which included a chain mail coat, helmet, sword, shield, lance, and mace.

Because of the expense of this equipment, especially the chain mail coat, the number of men-at-arms in medieval armies was low. Knights were assisted by one or two squires, who were apprentice knights responsible for the packhorses and the maintenance of equipment. During this period, thousands of castles and fortified manor houses, first built of earth and wood and later of stone, were constructed throughout Europe. Castles and fortified manor houses were physical sites of the fragmented and delegated politico-military authority of the feudal age. In medieval warfare the advantage was with the defense. Sieges of castles and towns, usually long, drawn-out affairs lasting many months, frequently ended in failure. Between 1300 and 1600, three technological innovations were introduced onto the European battlefield; these revolutionized medieval warfare and shifted the advantage to the offense. The first was the longbow, the traditional weapon of the Welsh, which was capable of shooting arrows per minute at targets 300 yards away with great accuracy and penetrating power.

The second was the pike, which, in the hands of well-drilled foot soldiers, could dislodge armored knights from their horses. During the century and a half after 1300 a number of battles—such as the Battle of Agincourt in France in 1415, where English longbowmen and pikemen were able to defeat a larger army of heavily armored French cavalry— demonstrated the effectiveness of these two weapons. To defend against longbows and pikes, armorers replaced the chain mail coat with plate armor, which was worn by horses as well. Thus, heavy cavalry became even heavier, capable only of the direct charge. Infantry, or foot soldiers, when formed into phalanxes (i.e., closed into deep ranks and files), could easily break such charges and dislodge knights from their horses. On the ground, knights weighted down by their armor could be easily overwhelmed by infantrymen. As a consequence, armies increasingly became composed of infantry units armed with longbows and pikes.

The third technological innovation that revolutionized medieval warfare was the introduction of gunpowder from China during the fourteenth century. The dominance of the heavily armored knight and the high, stone castle ended with the development of two weapons that used gunpowder: the arquebus and the cannon. The arquebus was a primitive, handheld firearm that fired a lead ball capable of penetrating the thickest plate armor. Gradually, longbows and pikes were replaced by arquebuses and, eventually, by muskets and, finally, rifles. The second weapon that used gunpowder was the cannon. At first, cannons were small, poorly made, inaccurate, and unable to do more damage to medieval fortifications than the traditional, mechanical siege engines, catapults, which fired stones by means of counterweighted levers. Gradually, metallurgical techniques were developed that permitted the manufacture of larger, more powerful, and more accurate cannons. Stone shot was replaced by round cannon balls of lead and iron. Improvements in the composition and manufacture of gunpowder increased the penetrating power, range, and accuracy of cannons.

The development of effective artillery had a dramatic impact on the balance between offense and defense in medieval warfare. The offense gained the advantage because more powerful cannons were able to puncture the stone walls of medieval castles with ease. Castles that had held out for many months against traditional siege engines were reduced to piles of rubble within a matter of hours when cannons were fired at them. Consequently, the high stone-walled castle was gradually abandoned and replaced by a low-profile fortification, first designed by Italian engineers and called the trace italienne, whose low, angled earthen bastions could absorb the shock of concentrated artillery fire. As a result of the emergence of infantry, artillery, and the trace italienne, armies increased in size and complexity.

As armies became bigger, they were divided into infantry, artillery, and light cavalry units. Training and discipline were introduced. Logistics (i.e., procurement, maintenance, and transportation of military matériel) systems developed. Privateers (i.e., armed private ships) were organized into navies and sailors were trained. To withstand the shock of rounds fired from ever more powerful artillery pieces, the trace italienne fort became larger and its earthen walls thicker. Highly trained and disciplined infantry units, which were organized independently of their members and commanded by a hierarchy of officers, including noncommissioned officers, became the backbone of these massive armies. Troops began to wear distinctive, standardized clothes, called uniforms, and were issued standardized arms. Individualistic displays of fighting prowess and heroism, which had been so important in medieval warfare, were discouraged. The warrior aristocratic caste and the feudal host were gradually replaced by a professional standing army.

Initially, the ranks of most early infantry-based armies were filled by mercenaries, that is, individuals who were paid to fight. Eventually, mercenaries began to be replaced by soldiers recruited exclusively from the monarch's own population because mercenary armies were notoriously unreliable: they frequently rebelled for higher pay, deserted the battlefield, changed sides, and even threatened the monarch's own throne. Troops recruited from one's own subjects and officered by individuals from one's own ruling class fought better and were more reliable, less dangerous, and cheaper. The summary effect of these technological innovations, then, was to change fundamentally the social and political reality of warfare. In the words of one scholar, "standing armed forces began to conform to bureaucratic regularity."

War itself became an object for the state, not just a series of battles fought by the king, but a complex of practices that required the regular disciplining of subjects and the organizing of logistics that could be used not only for defeating the enemy but also in the general production of social order. More and more, armies became objects, a uni fied (as in uni form) "body" of soldiers onto which the state could be inscribed, through the design and color of uniforms and of various accoutrements such as insignia of rank, belt buckles, and buttons. Armies no longer just fought battles; they increasingly came to represent the state they fought for—which tended to render mercenaries an anachronism—and to symbolize its power, thereby helping create its right to govern. Thus, the military revolution encouraged a new general view of the person and the body as an object to be molded and upon which could be inscribed signs of the state's power and legitimacy. As we will see in the next chapter, this imaginary of the body as an object to be inscribed by the state fundamentally altered the relation of sovereign and subject.

Emergence of A State Apparatus

A king who was able to recruit, train, equip, and maintain a large standing army as well as build low-profile fortifications could prevail over others. Hence, the advent of standing armies, regular navies, and trace italienne fortifications transformed the indirect, fragmented, decentralized rule of feudalism into the direct, concentrated, centralized rule of the medieval state, an early form of the territorial state. In the words of one historian, "The modern state without the military revolution is unthinkable. The road from the arquebus to absolutism, or from the maritime mortar to mercantilism, was a direct one." 9 Recall that feudal kings were not all-powerful rulers.

They faced the three estates of the realm—nobility, clergy, and bourgeoisie—who had their own rights and privileges as corporate groups. Kings were primus inter pares (first among equals) with respect to the nobility and had special responsibilities to the realm: providing justice, minting coins, designating bishops and abbots, granting town charters, and defending the realm. During the feudal period, wars were largely private affairs, paid for by revenues collected from the king's own demense as well as by tolls charged for the use of his roads and bridges, fees for fairs, fines levied by his courts, customs placed on imports, and money from vassals. As armies and fortifications became larger and more expensive to maintain, kings increasingly found themselves in debt. Medieval kings were unable to tax or confiscate property except that of Jews because their power was circumscribed by the rights and privileges of the estates. In order to raise funds, kings borrowed money, debased the coinage of the realm, sold crown lands, and pawned the royal jewels.

Eventually, medieval monarchs began to levy taxes on the estates. At first, the concessions granted to the king to levy such taxes were valid only for the estate that had granted them and only for the purpose for which they had been requested. The idea of a general tax on all subjects came about slowly. Gradually, the financial institutions set up by kings to collect revenues from their private lands became public institutions that collected taxes conceded by the estates. Medieval monarchs were helped in their centralizing efforts by the support they received for such efforts by the bourgeoisie and the lower nobility. The burden of direct taxation fell most heavily on the bourgeoisie because movable property (i.e., commodities bought and sold) could be more easily taxed than such fixed property as land. Nevertheless, the bourgeoisie did not much resist because it benefited from the territorywide legal systems that were also being developed by medieval kings at the time. Towns began to renounce their privileges and autonomy and integrated themselves into these emerging territory-wide legal frameworks, which came to link capitalism and state power in a single political formation. For its part, the lower nobility was also in favor of the centralizing efforts of medieval kings. Many lesser vassals were barely able to live as gentlemen because their lands were too small and unproductive. It was from their ranks that kings recruited tax collectors and judges. They were paid good salaries and given gifts of additional land. From the ranks of the lesser nobility, then, medieval monarchs began to build a corps of professional administrators; in this way monarchs could bypass the upper nobility.

Emergence of Professional State Administration

Although certain practices of feudal governance remained within the medieval state, such as dispensing justice through personal rule, and dynastic politics based on family ties and feudal obligations, increasingly a new apparatus of power—a new set of institutions, offices, and techniques of exercising power—emerged; it was envisioned and created as separate and distinct from the persons of the rulers themselves. As was mentioned in the previous chapter, all feudal lords, including kings, kept retinues of knights and household servants who helped them defend and run their castles and lands. The most important members of the king's household staff were the chancellor, who was in charge of the chancel (the altar area of the lord's chapel), and the steward, who was in charge of the great hall of the castle or manor house. The chancellor, in addition to saying Mass for the king, kept the king's seal, wrote his business letters (in Latin) to other kings or the pope, and directed the work of the king's scribes, clerks, and messengers. The steward, who was in charge of the household and the management of the king's demense, required knowledge of accounting and document preparation. The steward was assisted by a number of bailiffs, who were put in charge of the sections of the king's demense called bailiwicks.

The king's properties were not contiguous, that is, they were scattered throughout the realm. Revenues from them were also shared with members of the nobility. Therefore, collecting what was due the king was difficult even when the exact amounts were known. The first permanent officials of the emergent state apparatus were the estate managers sent out by the king to collect revenue from crown lands and properties. In medieval England these estate managers were called reeves and in France prévôts (provosts). After the Norman conquest, England was divided into shires (counties), within each of which a reeve was appointed. These shire-reeves, or sheriffs, were responsible for collecting the king's revenue. As fines from local courts were part of the king's revenue, sheriffs and provosts were also responsible for ensuring the king's justice. Sheriffs and provosts frequently held court for petty offenses. Thus, the collection of the king's revenue and the provision of his justice were intertwined activities in the early medieval state. Gradually, feudal kings began to consider the administration of justice as more than a source of money. It was a way of asserting monarchical power and authority. Therefore, they began to increase the jurisdictions of courts. Serious criminal cases, such as murder, were reserved for the king's court; this allowed him to intervene in districts where he had no estates or local rights of justice. In civil cases special procedures were developed that allowed litigants to bypass the local court and present their cases directly to a royal court.

This allowed the lower nobility to protect themselves against their immediate lords. Because it was the duty of feudal kings to see that justice prevailed throughout the realm, appeals were allowed from lower courts to royal courts as a way of remedying injustice. Eventually, throughout medieval Europe the tasks of collecting revenue and providing justice were disentangled and two parallel sets of institutions and offices—legal and financial—began to evolve. While the same individual might be both judge and tax collector, when hearing a case he followed certain procedures and formalities that were different from those he followed when collecting revenue. As the law became more complicated, individuals who had been trained in the law, called judges and lawyers, began to appear and take charge of the provision of the king's justice. At the same time individuals trained in accounting began to take over the collection of the king's revenue.

As legal and financial institutions and offices evolved separately, their work had to be coordinated. This was accomplished by the king's chancellor, who was always a high-ranking clergyman, either a bishop or a cardinal. The king's scribes and clerks, under the direction of the chancellor, developed and preserved regular administrative routines. They drafted orders and instructions, using language that could not be misunderstood. The chancery, or the office of the chancellor, became the nerve center of the medieval monarchy.

A group of individuals thus appeared who spent their entire working lives as professional, full-time administrators. They were assisted by part-time agents who were willing to work for a portion of the year as estate managers, tax collectors, or judges. Although few existed at first, these individuals significantly increased in number during the thirteenth century. This growing band of administrators was recruited from the lesser nobility, who needed the money, and the bourgeoisie, who wanted the prestige and potential influence that came from being in the service of the king or prince. The development of financial and judicial institutions staffed by a small but growing number of professional judges, tax collectors, law-trained clerks, and scribes meant that monarchs were able to control and administer wide territories without the help of the feudal aristocracy. Because the king's administrators were dependent upon the king for their livelihoods, they were loyal to him. Thus, the vassal-lord relationship ceased to be the glue that held the feudal politico-military system together. The development of territory-wide law courts and direct systems of revenue collection, as well as the growth of the general right to tax, led to the commercialization of economic life and the decline of the nobility as an effective political force.

The nobility began to lose ground to the bourgeoisie and the king. It should be recognized that this was a gradual trend; it did not happen all at once. Medieval kings continued to support the nobility, although increasingly on the king's terms. The nobility was more and more subordinated to the king; those who were not recruited into the administrative apparatus were converted into the officer corps of the new infantry-based armies. Thus, medieval kings gathered to themselves the instruments of rule that had been hitherto dispersed among the estates. They began to construct an administrative apparatus for the formulation and execution of centralized, territory-wide rule. This structure became more and more public, official, distinctive, and visible. Society came increasingly to be envisioned as peopled by a multitude of private individuals, not corporate groups. 20 Larger, territorial political units emerged, and politico-military power and authority became concentrated in the hands of the king and his court. Public officials eventually replaced individuals who held political power as a private possession. In this way, the centralized medieval monarchy, the precursor of the modern territorial state, came into being.

Emergence of the Modern Sovereign

As power and authority became more centralized and more abstract, in the sense of being lodged in the institutions and offices of monarchical power rather than in the person of the king, they were increasingly depersonalized. This involved, first, the development of impersonal systems of law and taxation and, second, the emergence of a new language of politics and rule. With respect to the first, the emergence of the king's legal and financial institutions encouraged the evolution of uniform, impersonal systems of law. Two legal systems developed in medieval Europe. One was English common law (i.e., law common to all), which was an amalgamation of local customary law created by the king's judges, who were sent out to hear cases in local courts. The decisions they made in a multitude of local cases gradually became the law of the realm. Common law was based on cases, and as each case was different, judges were able to make constant changes in it until the nineteenth century, when the principle of stare decisis (i.e., to stand by the decision), or precedent, emerged and was consistently applied. Thus, English common law was judge-made law that became uniform across the realm when individual judges followed precedent. The legal systems that emerged on the continent were heavily influenced by the "rediscovery" of Roman law.

The Romans developed a homogeneous body of codified law, which provided a framework that regulated political, economic, and social life throughout the empire. Medieval courts on the continent, influenced by canon law, looked to the Roman legal system as a model. Quite early, medieval monarchs on the continent began to write legal codes—which were published in the vernacular, not Latin—that regulated the management of the realm's forests, rivers, shipping, trade, fairs, and the like. Such codes fostered the development of official state languages such as French, Russian, English, Spanish, and Portuguese. Thus, whether the judge-made law of England or the Roman-inspired code law of continental monarchies, uniform systems of public law came into existence that eventually replaced the various rights and privileges (literally, private law) claimed by each estate. Law came to be applied territorially, meaning that the same rules were applicable to all groups and in all regions within the realm. The law became an instrument for governing entire populations dispersed throughout the realm. At this point, the king's power to make law transcended his ability to do so based on discrete rights and privileges adhering to his person.

The second element of the emerging depersonalized mode of governance was the development of a new language of political power and authority revolving around the idea of state sovereignty. In feudal "states," the king was sovereign only in the sense of being "first among equals," and therefore his authority was limited by clearly recognized rights and privileges accruing to the estates. As centralization increased, medieval kings claimed a different kind of authority as the "head of state." Authority, that is, the legitimate right to exercise power, came to be lodged in the state itself, and in the person of the king only insofar as the king represented the imagined unity of the state. More important, as sovereign head of state, the king claimed to be not simply first among equals but a separate, overarching sovereign —that is, one whose power was free from control by all others. In doing so, the king exploited a legal fiction that had emerged, especially in England, according to which the king's body had a dual nature: it was simultaneously the physical body of the king and the symbolic, collective body that mediated between his realm and God.

The object of governing and government changed during this period. In the classical Greek city-states and the Roman Republic, the object of governance was "the city," which was understood as the highest and most noble form of human association. The institutions and techniques of governing the city aimed at realizing a just and harmonious human community that embodied the best, most virtuous qualities of human beings. In feudal "states," the object of governance was the soul. To the extent that the king (and his vassals) governed, beyond protecting his private holdings, he understood himself to be acting for the moral and spiritual well-being of those he ruled, his subjects. In the late medieval period, from about the thirteenth century, there began to emerge a new idea about what governing meant that contested these earlier conceptions of political rule. The object of governing was neither to realize human virtue nor to serve religious redemption. Although politics and rule were not in this period completely severed from these ends—they continued to be discussed using the language of virtue and salvation—both came to be described as good in their own right. As the aim of the art of painting was to produce a perfectly formed picture, so the art of governing increasingly aimed at producing a perfectly formed government.

In this new language, the king became more and more the symbolic representation of the apparatus that managed public affairs, his symbolic body gaining precedence over his physical body. The state became identified less with the authoritative decisions of private persons who governed, and more as an ongoing apparatus of processes, offices, and institutions under the direction and supervision of the king. Its logic became less one of personal loyalty to rulers and overlords and more one of representation; that is, political power became hierarchical and mediated by a language and culture that represented to the people their own collective being. Once the state was understood in this way, and a language formed that made such an idea intelligible, the state could take itself as its own object of rule. That is, the art of governance could become the act of managing the governing apparatus so as to ensure its own power and security, and to secure the health and well-being of the state. It is important to recognize that the development of the modern language of sovereignty was gradual, and, hence, we will look at its development further in the next chapter. The authority and the growing power claimed by centralizing monarchs were contested throughout this period, in some cases successfully, by the Catholic Church and the nobility.

Moreover, kings did not yet clearly see themselves as representatives of the sovereign power of the state. Most kings, well into the early modern period, that is, into the seventeenth century, continued to frame their claims to authority and power in terms of their being the representatives of a universal Christendom in Europe. This allowed them to claim rightful authority in areas outside their territorial area and to extend their authority to inherited but noncontiguous areas. Nonetheless, from the twelfth and thirteenth centuries on, a new mode of governing based on the sovereignty of the state rather than personal rule developed. The principle of state sovereignty first and foremost unified political rule within a specific territory. The stage was being set for the imagining of political space in a fundamentally novel way, as a unified, contiguous territory. The king came to look on his subjects, the population of the territory he ruled, as an object, bounded by the limits of the physical space he ruled, as parts of the whole to be ordered and administered.

Secularism and the Emergence of Modernity

The formation of centralized politico-military power together with the idea of sovereignty affected the traditional Christian way of understanding the relationship between human actions and God; this, in turn, provoked a crisis in Christian beliefs. As the politico-military power of the medieval state grew and strengthened, the natural and human worlds began to appear more contingent; that is, more of what happened to human beings appeared to be the result of mere chance or the result of their own actions rather than being directly determined by God. The power of the emerging, centralized medieval state to order human affairs made the world increasingly subject to human will; this presented a challenge to the Christian idea that all human actions and laws fit neatly together as part of God's plan over which humans themselves have no control. In the early fourteenth century, this crisis in Christian belief found expression in a philosophical movement called nominalism, which began to sever the link between reason and faith. Nominalists, like William of Ockham (c. 1280–1349), defended the new power of the medieval monarchy by arguing that considering the world as a preexistent order prior to human action and determination was inconsistent with the Christian idea that God was omnipotent, an all-powerful being who created the world according to his own will. The way the world is at any particular moment is finite and contingent.

One contemporary political theorist describes the importance of nominalism this way: "Nominalism saves God's omnipotence by pushing him higher into the heavens, disconnecting him from the reason, experience, texts and signs that make up the mundane world. It thereby sets the table for later secularization." This theological and spiritual crisis would continue to affect the rise of the state for several hundred years, and we will have occasion to return to it later. Here we introduce three developments of the late medieval period that would be important to the development of the secularized, territorial state:

(1) The idea of a civil society;

(2) The revival of Roman republicanism, including the idea of "reason of state";

(3) And the idea that knowledge can and should improve human life.

Civil Society As early as the writings of the Dominican friar Thomas Aquinas (1225– 1274), the idea of a body of law that governed human social and moral life independently of direct religious supervision developed. Aquinas revived Aristotelian ideas concerning the ability of human reason to discover for itself the moral laws that governed human beings. To do this without denying God and defying the Church, he defined natural law as developing from the "participation in the eternal law by rational creatures." In Aquinas's view, however, mankind still required direction from God. To express this need, he set natural law within a hierarchy of law. At the pinnacle of this hierarchy was the eternal law by which God regulated the universe. Divine law —the law as expressed in the Bible—governed mankind's higher spiritual life. Natural law reflected humankind's nature as a rational being possessed of both a natural inclination to do good and the innate reason to discover moral laws. Below natural law was positive or human law, the body of law made by the state. For Aquinas, human institutions and actions, such as politics, were to be directed according to principles of natural law and were distinct from the canon law of the Church, which expressed divine law. Aquinas used the idea of natural law derived by reason to justify the growing autonomy of medieval kingship from the church, and even went so far as to argue that the king was bound by natural law to do what was good for his subjects.

The implications of the idea that politics is bound by a realm of universal rational rules that sought the good of the "society" as a whole would develop over the next several centuries. It led to the concept of the "social" as a distinct realm of human actions and institutions. Natural law would become especially important in the seventeenth and eighteenth centuries when it would be used to describe a system of social relations that were based in human nature itself, and only indirectly linked, if at all, to God's law. Of particular importance to the construction of the idea of a society was the way in which women were related to natural law. This would lead to the subordination of women in the modern state by enabling them to be assigned to a private sphere cordoned off from the public world. Although natural law referred to both men and women, it did not do so in the same way or to the same degree. In both Aristotle's thought and in Christianity, the two sources of Aquinas's theory of natural law, women were secondary to men in a natural hierarchy. Aristotle believed that women were biologically inferior to men. Their natural function in the hierarchy of nature was to reproduce and care for children. Their natural place was the household and home.

Christianity considered women to be the "helpmates" of men, created by God to assist him in the Garden of Eden. Thus, Aquinas's theory freed the natural world from direct religious control, but continued to place women in a subordinate position within a presumed "natural" gender hierarchy. The result was that the modern state and society became domains of male activities. Although individual women might occasionally participate in them, this was not the norm, and such women were most often viewed with suspicion and open disdain. The modern idea of society was constructed according to a presumed "natural" gender hierarchy and a sharp division of public and private spheres, the latter proper to women and the former proper to men. Perhaps the most important consequence of natural law's conception of an independent social realm was that it freed commercial and economic activity from medieval constraints. The medieval church taught that commerce was an immoral activity because it encouraged people's passions and desires and put material life above spiritual life. However, Aquinas's writings provided a justification for commercial activity and the accumulation of wealth and private property based on the idea of natural law. Aquinas argued that although God had given the world to human beings as a whole for the purpose of sustaining and reproducing life (the traditional Christian belief), this inheritance would be best taken care of, and peace would be more likely, if individuals owned property for themselves. Aquinas reasoned from his observations of his fellow human beings that they took better care of property they personally owned. Here is how Aquinas put it:

Community of goods is said to be part of the natural law not because the natural law decrees that all things are to be possessed in common and nothing held privately, but because the distribution of property is not a matter of natural law but of human agreement which pertains to the positive law, as we have said. Therefore private property is not against natural law but it has been added to natural law by the inventiveness of human reason.

By justifying commerce and private ownership in this way, Aquinas marginalized women within economic activity, because it was men who legally owned property and therefore were the privileged caretakers of it. Aquinas did not go so far as to describe an independent society, that is, the self-regulating, individual action that would later underlie the free market economy. Nor is the theory of natural law in Aquinas's meaning a part of the concept of civil society that emerges in the eighteenth century.

However, Aquinas's idea helped generate a linguistic space, which made the idea of civil society possible by leading people to think of their social world as a creation of individual reason and their social interactions as governed by moral law, which they could know and justify to themselves. The Revival of Republicanism Another effect of the general trend toward centralized politico-military power in later medieval monarchies was the increasing construction of the political realm as independent of religious authority. This trend was bound up with the development of state sovereignty, which imbued the political realm with a spirit of self-confidence. Just as the idea of natural law allowed a freeing of the commercial spirit, the revival of Roman republican ideas of a distinct political realm operating according to its own principles freed the political will from the constraints of a divinely ordered world.

The new spirit of politics emerged most forcefully in the city-states of Renaissance Italy. From the thirteenth through the sixteenth centuries powerful Italian city-states such as Florence, Venice, Pisa, Milan, and Siena struggled to establish their independence from both the Catholic Church, which claimed the right to control them directly, and the Holy Roman Emperor. Political theorists such as Marsiglio of Padua (c. 1275–1342) and Dante Alighieri (1265–1321), among others, established the idea that the pope had no jurisdiction at all over political matters. They described the pope as "a mere administrator of sacraments who could have no power and make no laws in temporal fields."

Although this claim was made for the specific purpose of establishing the supreme authority of the Holy Roman Emperor in Italy, the arguments about the autonomy of political matters would go on to have more general significance. The important legal thinker Bartolus de Saxoferrato (1314–1357) used the rediscovered Roman law to claim not only the autonomy of politics from religion, but the supremacy of particular secular rulers.

Roman practices of self-governance had never been fully eradicated from the northern Italian cities during the Middle Ages; the peoples in them developed a fierce spirit of independence, which by the twelfth and thirteenth centuries led to the establishment of self-governing republics against prevailing monarchies. Thus, the political realm—the realm of struggle for independence and the conflicting strategies and passions of the factions, which sought to rule these independent city-states—became a subject of interest in its own right. Literati (i.e., educated individuals) began to write pamphlets and books giving advice to rulers on how to maintain independence from outside forces as well as peace among different factions at home.

The most significant proponent of this new spirit in politics was Niccolò Machiavelli (1469–1527), a Florentine bureaucrat and diplomat who served in the republican government of Florence until it was overthrown in 1494. Machiavelli reinterpreted the Roman republican ideas of citizenship and civic virtue as actions in the spirit of self-sacrifice for the good of the state. He most fully presented this concept in his commentary on Roman history, the Discourses on the First Ten Books of Titus Livy (1519).

Machiavelli's political theory has been called "the first great experiment in a 'pure' political theory." Machiavelli described politics as an arena of human action governed not by religion and high moral purpose but by necessity and contingency (i.e., chance and unforeseen causes). He saw it through a new imagery drawn not from religion but from the Roman idea of virtus and from his long experience of the political realm itself. Politics, he declared, demanded that the ruler know the people and that the people know the ruler, and involved the power and manipulations inherent in such knowledge. Knowing politics from the lofty heights of the heavens was replaced with an earthly imagery:

For in the same way that landscape painters station themselves in the valleys in order to draw mountains or high ground, and ascend an eminence in order to get a good view of the plains, so it is necessary to be a prince to know thoroughly the nature of the people, and one of the populace to know the nature of princes.

Thus, for Machiavelli, the political spirit is within politics itself, within its struggles for power, honor, privilege, and security. For him, the laws that govern political action are those of strategy, prudence, and daring. To learn politics one does not study theology or morals but the "deeds of great men" and their successes and failures in past political struggles. For Machiavelli, the spirit of the political realm was distinctly human, able to recognize and, when possible, master the contingencies of Fortune (i.e., chance). In this struggle great men could not afford either religion or its morals. They had to reduce the contingencies of Fortune through the prudent and instrumental use of violence for the "interest of the state," in order to maintain its glory, longevity, and greatness. One commentator on Machiavelli has called his focus on necessity and contingency an "economy of violence."

This emphasis on mastery, prudence and valor in war, and violence reinforced the masculine character of the emerging state and continued the trend of estranging women from politics and public life. Fortune, Machiavelli said in a famous passage in The Prince (1513), "is a woman, and it is necessary, if you wish to master her, to conquer her by force." 38 Machiavelli's revival of the Roman ideas of virtus and citizenship relied on the individual's (i.e., male's) own abilities to master the circumstances he finds in the world. Machiavelli's writing became associated over the next two centuries with a distinctly secular and "modern" attitude toward politics and government. By liberating the political will from its medieval religious and traditional restrictions, his writings allowed explorations of the way states could actually maintain and enhance their power. Reflections on the state in the Machiavellian mode could become reflections of the state itself, on how to efficiently order its affairs to maximize its power. This way of thinking about the political realm as embodying a distinctive, even ruthless spirit of political intrigue and action is called Machiavellism or, alternatively, "reason of state."

Science for the Benefit of Mankind A third aspect of late medieval life that led to the emergence of the modern territorial state was the development of a new attitude toward knowledge in general. Increasingly, knowledge and science came to be seen as having intrinsic value, which satisfied human curiosity about the basic makeup of the earth and the heavens, and as means that should be used to improve the material condition of humankind. The renewal of curiosity about the natural world and the practical applications of that knowledge challenged the traditional presumptions about the nature and purposes of knowledge. As we discussed in the previous chapter, the Catholic Church during the Middle Ages held a monopoly on advanced knowledge. This allowed the Church to define the standards of truth and the proper uses of science. To the medieval Church, knowledge was important because it led people to know God and therefore directly affected how people could live a good, moral life. Knowledge was to lead to a spiritual awakening and purification of the soul.

Thus, knowledge was closely linked to religion through its role in teaching people how to "know and love God." While knowledge remained connected to the moral life throughout the medieval period, links between scientific knowledge and the moral life became more indirect. "Modern" science did not tell people what the moral life was, but it could be an important tool for accomplishing specific tasks and solving specific problems, such as how to build bigger ships to meet the demand for more goods, or how to count populations accurately so that taxes could be more efficiently collected. Rather than being limited to the Church and a hierarchy of knowledges that defined God's will as supreme and the unity of the human world as part of God's plan, knowledge became technologized; that is, it became an instrument to be used by those who wielded power in order to accomplish specific tasks or solve certain problems. This new use of knowledge would have two important effects. One was to produce among human beings a sense of power and control over the natural and social world. The second was to produce a sense among human beings that knowledge of the natural and social worlds was of intrinsic value because it could lead to a better, more comfortable, and "civilized" way of life. By the early sixteenth century this new attitude would be reflected in the emergence of a new genre of literature, the utopia. These fictional narratives described a perfected social order that could be produced by applying scientific knowledge. Among the most popular of such works were Utopia (1516) by Thomas More (1478–1535) and The City of the Sun (1623) by Tommaso Campanella (1568–1639). The most influential in promoting the secular and political power of science was New Atlantis (1627) by Francis Bacon (1561–1626), which proposed a government based on a scientific technocracy.

Summary

This chapter has described both continuities and discontinuities between the elements of the medieval state, the precursor to the modern territorial state, and the feudal and Roman worlds out of which it grew. Central elements of the modern territorial state, such as large standing armies and professional administrations, emerged in the medieval period, roughly from the eleventh through the fifteenth centuries. By contrasting elements of the new language of politics that emerged in medieval monarchies, we have illuminated how the modern, territorial state was made possible by both its past and the contingent history in which it operated.

5

FORMS OF THE MODERN TERRITORIAL STATE

THE ABSOLUTIST STATE: SOVEREIGNTY INSTITUTED

The modern territorial state took several centuries to become established. In this chapter we discuss the first form the territorial state took in Europe, from roughly the sixteenth to the eighteenth centuries, and focus on how territorial sovereignty was imagined and instituted. Specifically, we look at the transformation of political structures, the rise of capitalism, and the transformation of the relation of state to capital. The emphasis is on the transformation of political space, in thought and practice, into an idea of territoriality that linked the local to the national and the rest of the world in ways that broke with the traditions of medieval Christendom. After painting each of these transformations in rather broad strokes, we turn to two specific case histories that show how sovereignty was instituted in two early modern states, England and France.

The Emergence of Sovereign Territoriality

An important catalyst for the transformation of medieval monarchies was the Reformation and the religious violence and wars it spawned. The Reformation was a revolt against the Catholic Church by those who considered it corrupt, more concerned with maintaining its power and privileges than with guiding the spiritual salvation of Christendom. At first, reformists were members of the clergy, such as the German monk Martin Luther (1482–1546). But soon the reform religions, such as Lutheranism, Presbyterianism, and Calvinism, spread throughout Europe, especially among the bourgeoisie, but also among some of the nobility. Reformers, known as Protestants, argued that salvation depended on faith alone. Protestant religious practice emphasized the private, personal relationship between the individual person and God; this relationship, they argued, obviated the need for the Catholic Church's liturgy, sacraments, and official hierarchy of priests, bishops, and pope. Indeed, Protestants argued that the Catholic Church's statues and images of its saints amounted to false gods; some even viewed the Catholic hierarchy, including the pope, as the Antichrist.

Religious conflict between Catholics and Protestants developed in every European monarchy, especially in northern Europe. States began to advance the religions of their rulers by attacking states whose rulers professed opposing faiths. These wars, known as the Thirty Years' War (1618–1648), began in Germanspeaking kingdoms, principalities, and dukedoms and pitted Catholic and Protestant rulers against each other. The fighting was bloody because the combatants thought they had God on their side and that the enemy was the instrument of Satan. It is estimated that about one-third of the population of Germanspeaking Europe died as a result of the fighting. Eventually, the desire to end the bloodshed and the resulting economic devastation led to a new concern with peace in Europe. Peace treaties, signed at Münster and Osnabrück in 1648, known collectively as the Peace of Westphalia (1648), sanctioned the division of Europe into states according to the religious principles of their rulers. The Peace of Westphalia recognized the principle of state sovereignty and enshrined the concept of secure and universally recognized state borders in law. It accepted the principle of nonintervention in the territorial space of other states and pioneered a rough standard for relating different currencies to limit the fluctuation of the value of money across different states; this encouraged trade by making financial transactions more predictable. Such a standard made it important for each state to control the value of its coin of the realm. The treaty also encouraged further development and use of diplomacy, that is, the art and practice of conducting relations among states through embassies and ambassadors, which had begun in the sixteenth century.

Modern diplomacy, with its concepts of extraterritoriality and diplomatic immunity, reflected a new sense of estrangement in Europe. Increasingly, the political other was conceived of as a state, with a specific geographic location, rather than heretical religious group, a rival noble family, or a person of inferior rank. Gaining knowledge about and communicating with other states required different norms, rules, and formal institutions than did overcoming the estrangement from heretics or rival nobility.

The new institutions of diplomacy, then, both presupposed the organization of territorial states and helped to further their entrenchment into a system of states. The Peace of Westphalia is perhaps the most important historical benchmark in the formation of the modern territorial state. Through it the principles of state sovereignty became normalized into a new political imaginary that, inside the state, sovereignty referred to legitimate, controlling authority, while outside, sovereignty referred to the reciprocal right to self-determination against dynastic or other claims, as well as to freedom from external religious interference. Territoriality arose, then, in good part as a historically contingent resolution of a spiritual crisis in Christendom. By sanctioning the division of the Christian commonwealth into territorially bounded states, the Peace of Westphalia also consolidated and gave a new political form to Europe.

Europe as a political identity began to take hold; that is, the term "Europe" increasingly was used to refer to an imagined political space defined by its own rules. Within Europe there obtained a system of states and an international society with an international law to regulate conflict and trade. The peoples outside Europe came to be understood not only as non-Christian others but as extralegal peoples who were not governed by the same rules of the international society of Europe; this had enormous consequences for colonial and imperial policies. Estrangement of European peoples from themselves becomes a double estrangement, simultaneously religious and political. A third estrangement, through colonialism, was also in the making.

Representing Territorial State Sovereignty

The Peace of Westphalia created a problem: how to imagine and represent a combined religious, moral, and political authority in a secular, earthly entity confined within territorial borders and boundaries. Finding a solution was imperative given that these territorial entities were created by conventions and agreements, which gave some measure of peace to the Europe of religious wars and which had to be grounded and secured. The first and predominant solution to this crisis of the representation of territorial authority was to imagine the state as a symbolic body, a body politic. Such a discursive practice had two notable sources. First, locating authority in a symbolic body had a long history and resonance in Christianity and was recognizable by both Protestants and Catholics. Christians located authority in the human world in the body of Christ, who, as the son of God, had a dual nature. He was both flesh and blood and ethereal at the same time; that is, "man and God." Second, legal discourses during the Middle Ages had similarly endowed the body of the king with a special significance and dual nature.

Political factions in the early modern state, in spite of their differences, could appeal to the fiction of the king's two bodies. One side emphasized the tradition of the divine right of kings in which the king's authority was traced through the patriarchal lineage of Adam, the first male given authority over other men and women by God. The other side appealed to the king's body as a collective body composed of his subjects. The latter, which was to have lasting influence, was developed in England, for example, by Thomas Hobbes (1588–1679) in Leviathan (1650). For Hobbes, the basis of the state, which he called a commonwealth, was the interest of individual subjects in securing their own peace and protection. He hypothesized that without a sovereign, people lived in a state of nature characterized by a war "where every man is Enemy to every man," which made "the life of man, solitary, poor, nasty, brutish, and short." According to Hobbes, individuals living in a state of nature created a sovereign power to defend themselves "from the invasion of Foreigners, and the injuries of one another, and thereby to secure them in such sort, as that by their own industries, and by the fruits of the Earth, they may nourish themselves and live contentedly." Hobbes saw the sovereign as a unity of the wills of the individual subjects who composed it: "The only way to erect such a Common Power . . . is, to confer all their power and strength upon one Man, or upon one Assembly of men, that may reduce all their Wills, by plurality of voices, unto one Will." Moreover, he argued that to create this sovereign, one consents to a " social compact, " a promise on the part of all individual subjects to "Authorise and give up my Right of Governing my self, to this Man, or to this Assembly of men, on this condition, that thou give up thy Right to him, and Authorise all his Actions in like manner."

Blending the religious and legal conceptions of the symbolic body, Hobbes describes the sovereign as an "Artificial Soul" residing in the "Artificial Man," which is the Commonwealth, or, alternatively, as a "Mortal God." This new way of imagining and representing the sovereignty of the state had two primary effects. First, it rendered the state more abstract and enacted the dualistic structure (inside/outside) of the Westphalian settlement. The sovereign treated his subjects inside the territory as a collective being, a population to be regulated and molded for the good the state. At the same time, it mediated their estrangement from those outside (who were increasingly presented as threats), which required the internal organization of the subjects by the sovereign. The head/soul (sovereign) needed to organize, coordinate, and regulate the physical body (subjects, territory) to protect it from the outside. The second effect of the new way of imagining sovereignty was to deepen the patriarchal domination of women. The state, or collective body, comprised a robust public life in which war, intrigue, and the pursuit of wealth were reserved largely for men. States now protected something increasingly referred to as "society."

"Society" came to refer to a private, interior world, first in the court life among the courtiers of the king, and then in the social world of art, high culture, and fashion, which was generated by the court, and through which capitalism was rapidly spreading throughout the population. Increasingly, the state depended on a private sphere in which male subjects were socialized to participate in public activities, such as owning property, serving in the state bureaucracy, or fighting in the army—activities reserved for men. In this private sphere men learned to be individuals, to cultivate their particular talents, which could then be appropriated and used by the sovereign. Rather than being viewed as individuals whose status resulted from personal abilities, achievements, and wealth, as was the case for men in public life, women continued to be understood as products of nature, better suited to the private than the public sphere. The functions of this private sphere, such as nurturing and caring for children, giving emotional support, and developing personal habits of hygiene, increasingly came to be associated with a new norm of "femininity," which was held in opposition to the public world's "masculine" characteristics, such as competing in business, gaining a rational education, and exercising governing power. Changes in the basic idea of the family, then, were crucial components of the new sovereign states. The family became bound up with a new idea of privacy. The family became the institutionalized form of the private sphere; here men developed their individuality and here, too, they cultivated their usefulness to and participation in the body politic. Spaces such as the bedroom, in which, during the medieval period, it had been the custom to entertain important guests, became private enclosures from which outsiders were excluded. Women came to be seen as belonging "naturally" in this private space. This prevented them from becoming individuals themselves and rendered them aides to the development of men's individuality.

Reimagining Political Space

The early modern state reimagines political life and sovereignty within territorial boundaries. We have seen various ways in which states at different times imagined the boundaries and key components of political space. Classical republican city-states, such as those of ancient Greece and Rome, considered the state as an association of human beings that provided for the common good. Politics properly took place in cities because this was where citizens met to discuss common needs and make common decisions. Because the republic meant the association of citizens, territorial boundaries were less important. Cities were separated from other cities by open areas rather than by fixed boundaries. Political space was associated with the specific place in which citizens met to debate and decide about laws and the common good. This classical republican idea of political space was manifested in the city-states of northern Italy during the Renaissance and still informs some elements of modern states. Nevertheless, the republican imaginary of political space is not the predominant one in modern states. Modern states are defined in terms of sovereignty and territorial boundaries. Political space is not the specific place in which citizens meet to debate and decide political matters, but refers to the area inside the territorial boundaries under the state's control. Politics comes to be associated less with the debating and deciding of the common good and more with securing borders and maintaining the territorial integrity and sovereignty of the state. The political space of the modern state becomes something to be pacified, administered, and defended.

Unlike republican theories of political space, which refer to the specific place where politics occurs, and includes all the specific attributes of that place (especially its people, with their distinctive culture and traditions), political space in modern states is more general. It refers to territory that states control. This idea of political space draws on the concepts of space that were invented in Euclidean geometry during the early modern period. Space was increasingly seen not as separated places having little to do with one another, but rather as a continuous field, a singular and empty space. Political space for the modern territorial state, then, in principle, included the entire planet, and was seen to enclose particular political spaces on the planet that particular states could pacify, administer, and defend effectively. The political ordering and governance of specific places was contingent, not natural or sacred. In this way of imagining political space the type of government a state has is less important than its being a state. Whereas the modern state can be designated in various ways, its designation simply as a state, that is, as an entity that exercises administrative control over a specific territory with fixed and secure boundaries, becomes predominant.

Not tied to place, state sovereignty could become an abstract and general model; it could be transplanted, and sometimes reconfigured, to suit different locales. Being based on such a generalized model allowed particular states to expand into the space outside, and permitted the state form to be exported via European colonialism and imperialism. By the end of the nineteenth century, the entire planet came to be divided into separate states. This was made possible by the new idea of the planet as space filled by the contingent organizations of territorial states, rather than the naturally differentiated spaces of ancient or medieval conceptions, or the non-Western conceptions of space, which either sacralized place, as did the Chinese and Mayan Empires, for example, or which considered human societies as embedded in their natural environment, as did the native peoples of North America, for example. Other forms of political life, such as nomadic tribes, traditional empires, and republican city-states, were no longer recognized as legitimate ways of organizing and practicing politics.

Economy and State/Public and Private

Territoriality and the new imaginary of political space that constituted it broke sharply with the past. They made possible both an intensification of internal consolidation by the state and the modular extension of the state to the rest of the world. In order to understand the different forms the state took in this period, we need to look at the reconstitution of economic life and its relation to the state. In medieval states economic accumulation was still largely considered the province of corporate groups, especially the nobility who owned the land, from which the greatest amount of wealth derived, and the bourgeoisie, whose guilds regulated manufacturing and commercial activity in the towns. During the sixteenth and seventeenth centuries fundamental changes occurred in economic activity and the way it was understood and envisioned. Two developments were crucial.

First, the type of wealth characteristic of the bourgeoisie—that involving manufacturing and trade—became more and more important. Mobile property such as money and the financial instruments necessary for trade, as well as those commodities produced for the local market, accounted for an increasing proportion of the state's wealth. These commercial practices were developed first and most fully in the city-states of northern Italy, as well as the Hanseatic cities on the north coast of Germany, but eventually spread throughout Europe. They spread especially to states such as the Netherlands and England, which depended on longdistance trade because local supplies of important goods, such as wheat, grain, wood, and wine, had been exhausted or had to be imported. The second development, closely connected to the first, was the general acceptance of the principle of individual ownership of property. Property came to be seen as a right of the individual, not the corporate group, and thus the individual was allowed to buy and sell it at will. Early modern states attempted to use these new economic conditions of mobile and individual property in policies called mercantilism by eighteenth century economists.

The specific ways they did so had much to do with the development of different forms of the state. It should be remembered, however, that an economy based on private property (i.e., capitalism) and the modern state developed together, each intertwined with and required by the other. Only later, at the end of the eighteenth century, would a science of political economy emerge that tries to disentangle them. Mercantilism assumed that a state's wealth was based on the amount of gold and silver it could accumulate and that the quantity of these precious metals that one monarchy accumulated was an equivalent loss by another. States therefore wanted to colonize lands rich in gold and silver, and export as many manufactured goods as possible. By exporting as much as possible and minimizing imports, states gained what economists call a favorable balance of trade. To make sure that exports exceeded imports, states levied tariffs (i.e., taxes) on imports in order to keep foreign goods out and subsidized the development of domestic industries by granting them monopolies, or by founding the industries themselves. Such policies created a mercantile sector of the economy that related differently to the rest of the state's economy, depending on the circumstances of the particular state. Two broad types of economic structure can be distinguished. In certain states the landed nobility continued as the dominant economic power. Most wealth within these states derived from land ownership, which largely remained in the hands of the nobility. The private sector consisted primarily of petit bourgeoisie, i.e., shopkeepers and small manufacturers engaged in local markets. The portion of the private sector that engaged in long-distance trade and large commercial ventures was small, in part because of the relatively undeveloped financial sector, especially banks.

The result was that the revenues generated by the mercantile sector —consisting largely of enterprises created and chartered by the king to control specific aspects of long-distance, colonial trade, especially joint-stock companies, or to engage in large manufacturing enterprises—did not filter through the general economy to generate further growth of the private sector. In other states, such as England and the Netherlands, a substantial private sector engaged in long-distance trade and large-scale manufacturing, which utilized newly invented machines and the factory system. Indeed, in these states, the private sector now predominated over the landed nobility. Such ventures were facilitated by highly developed financial industries (banking and credit). 18 Joint-stock companies chartered by the state controlled much of the colonial trade, but given the relatively large private commercial sector and the financial industries, its profits were circulated through this sector and fed further growth. This economy created a very different situation for the state than was the case in those states where the landed nobility remained predominant.

Absolutism

The world absolutism (from the Latin absoluta, meaning unbound) usually refers to rule by an all-powerful, all-embracing monarch who faces no checks or control on his power. The absolute monarch rules his realm directly through a staff of administrative officials whom he has rendered totally dependent upon him. The assembly of estates has been "put to sleep" by the crown; that is, it has been suppressed and is no longer consulted by the king. Moreover, local entities have been brought under the direct authority of the crown. Power is exercised without the concurrence of the estates, and the monarch has become absolute territorial sovereign. Monarchical absolutism was generally justified by the theory of "divine right of kings." Absolutist monarchies as a form of the early modern state are usually counterposed to parliamentary monarchies—that is, to a form of the early modern state in which the estates have won the struggle for power with the crown and the king's ability to rule his realm on his own has been reduced or eliminated completely. In place of the feudal constitutional order of joint or mixed rule, an assembly embodying the estates, called a parliament (from the French verb parler, meaning to speak), has defeated the king and become the territorial sovereign.

We believe that the dichotomy between absolutist monarchies and parliamentary monarchies is a false one. In our view both are varieties of absolutism. Recall that the military revolution that took place from the fourteenth to the sixteenth centuries, and transformed the feudal host into the standing army of infantry and artillery, led to the creation of an incipient centralized governing apparatus and practices realized primarily for the purpose of directly extracting from the realm the men, money, and matériel needed to fight wars. War and preparing for war generated a great struggle in all medieval realms between the crown, on the on hand, and the estates, on the other, over which would be the absolute sovereign of the emerging territorialized state. This great struggle evolved in two main directions: one was toward the crown, which became the absolute territorial sovereign to the total exclusion of the estates; the other was toward the estates, which became the absolute territorial sovereign at the total expense of the crown.

Varieties of the Absolutist State

Which of the two institutions, crown or estates, became the absolute territorial sovereign in a particular emerging early modern state depended on the outcome of the struggle between the two. The outcome of this struggle was conditioned by the contingent "situational factors" of the monarchy in question—factors such as the realm's geographical position with respect to rival monarchies, the "starting condition" of the realm, the personal strength of individual kings, and the ability of the estates to resist. The way these situational factors and the starting condition of the realm have influenced the instituting of absolute sovereignty can be seen in the following brief comparative histories of early state formation in England and France. In England, contingent situational factors, such as the insularity of the realm, its small size, its early centralization by conquest, and the importation of feudalism allowed the estates to win the struggle for absolute territorial sovereignty. In France, on the other hand, contingent situational factors, such as the realm's indigenous feudalism, strong regionalism, and its geographical location near emerging rival kingdoms (especially Spain), allowed the crown to win the struggle for absolute territorial sovereignty.

England: An Absolutist Parliamentary State

In 1066, William, Duke of Normandy (r. 1066–1087), invaded England and defeated the Anglo-Saxon king Harold, at the Battle of Hastings. William the Conqueror, as he is known, imported feudalism from France. He distributed among his Norman barons the choicest lands in the kingdom as fiefs. The barons had to supply a certain quota of knights, whom they supported by dividing their fiefs among their vassals. Thus, a feudal hierarchy was imposed, which gave rise to a struggle between the crown and the baronage as each attempted to increase its power against the other. William was a strong king who did not hesitate to jail great barons and assert his right to appoint bishops and abbots. To finance his court, he did not hesitate to extract heavy taxes. He warred against the king of France over the territorial boundaries of his realm. When William died in 1087, his eldest son inherited Normandy as a separate dukedom, and a younger son, William Rufus, inherited England. Rufus, who was unpopular with the Church because he was satirical and also homosexual, ruled until he was murdered in 1100. He was succeeded by Henry I (r. 1100–1135), who persuaded the barons to accept him as king provided he would stop the objectionable practices of his brother, which included charging unreasonable taxes and forcing widows to remarry.

Henry restored Normandy to his realm and developed a central administration and an efficient financial system. The kingdom was divided into shires, to each of which he assigned a reeve recruited from the lower ranks of the feudal hierarchy. His shire-reeves, or sheriffs, were made to appear before the barons of the exchequer to pay the revenues they had collected for the king. Henry's heavy-handed rule resulted in a series of revolts by the baronage, which he was able to put down. When Henry died in 1135 he left no heir but a daughter, Matilda; as a result, a dynastic war broke out among rival claimants to the throne. During the strife, the barons were able to build much local autonomy by promising support to the claimant who offered the most extensive privileges. Thus, when Matilda's son Henry II (r. 1154–1189) ascended the throne in 1154, the kingdom, which reached from Scotland to the Pyrenees and included half of today's France, had been pulverized into numerous powerful baronies. Henry fought these barons and took away many of the lands and privileges they had gained during the previous fourteen years of turmoil. Henry II's sons, Richard I (r. 1189–1199) and John (r. 1199–1216), continued to expand the power of the crown at the expense of the barons. Richard, the Lion-Heart, was a crusader who taxed his realm to the utmost to pay for his campaigns in the Holy Land. John, who faced high inflation, taxed the realm inordinately for his wars in Scotland, Wales, and Ireland, violated laws, and demanded frequent scutage (payments of money in lieu of military service). John's actions resulted in a baronial revolt. The barons demanded a return to the laws of Henry I, which recognized the rights of the nobility and limited the powers of the crown.

On June 15, 1215, John accepted the demands of the barons and drafted a document called the Magna Carta, sealed at Runnymede, in which he agreed not to levy taxes that had not been approved by an assembly of the barons. After the Magna Carta, the barons gained the upper hand in their struggles with the crown. They forbade the king's sheriffs from entering their lands, took possession of his courts, and usurped the powers of his local administrators. Rather than being a victory for the liberty of the common people as it is often claimed today, the Magna Carta was actually a victory for England's powerful barons. Henry III (r. 1216–1272), who needed money and troops, expanded the Great Council to include two knights from the shires, two leading citizens from the cities and towns, and the clergy. He consulted this "Model Parliament," which was divided into two chambers, the House of Lords and the House of Commons, when he levied taxes, especially for fighting wars. The financial exigencies of fighting wars strengthened Parliament rather than the king, however, because it was able to exchange approval of tax requests for extensions of parliamentary rights and privileges.

The power of Parliament was strengthened greatly during the Hundred Years' War (1337–1453) by granting the king's request for money to fight the French king over conflicting dynastic claims in exchange for the right to meet regularly, to control royal ministers, and to examine the crown's accounts. The wars against the Irish, Welsh, and Scots extended the territorial boundaries of the English monarchy and had an important influence on the military defense of the realm. As with medieval monarchies elsewhere, the feudal host of heavy cavalry was the core of the king's army. However, wars against the Welsh and Scots, who were able to defeat mounted cavalry thanks to rough terrain and guerrilla tactics, encouraged the English to incorporate more foot soldiers into their armies. These foot soldiers were recruited by the barons, under whose control they remained as local militias. This meant that the English crown was not able to build a strong army under its direct control. Moreover, the crown had come to depend upon Parliament for the money to fight wars. The lack of a centrally controlled, standing army was not a problem, however, for the survival of the realm because England was an island kingdom and was not directly threatened by the increasingly centralized and powerful monarchies on the continent. What efforts the crown made to strengthen its military capacity went into the navy, upon which it came to rely to defend the realm.

Dominions of Henry II, 1154-1189

During the reign of Henry VIII (r. 1509–1547), the crown sought to strengthen itself by forming an alliance with the landed gentry, a group of farmers below the nobility who were becoming rich thanks to the gradual commercialization of English agriculture. Henry regularly sought approval for his taxes and his policies, one of the most important being the reformation of the Catholic Church in England. Henry separated the English Church from Rome, made himself its head, and confiscated the property and lands of the great monasteries and convents. During this period, the House of Commons became the focus of the gentry's power. Despite increasing military involvement in wars with other centralizing monarchies, especially France and Spain, the English crown did not become absolute during the reigns of the two strongest rulers of the House of Tudor, Henry VIII and his daughter, Elizabeth I (r. 1558–1603). Parliament remained a force to be reckoned with. No large standing army was created. To a great extent the ranks of England's army were filled with mercenaries and freebooters, who were demobilized and sent home at the end of a war. Emphasis was placed on the navy, which was, in large part, composed of privateers —that is, ships belonging to private owners authorized by the crown to conduct hostilities in its name.

The crown's wars were paid for, in part, by selling crown lands, confiscating Church property, and borrowing money abroad. Additional money came from taxes granted by Parliament. Parliament became a steady source of revenue for the crown. Thus warmaking, even during the period of strong Tudor monarchs, was conducted within the limitations of England's feudal constitutionalism. Moreover, a small standing army and reliance on privateers for a navy meant that the English crown did not need a large, centralized bureaucratic apparatus of direct rule. Parliament was strengthened by granting the crown the money it requested in exchange for the recognition that certain forms of taxation were illegal. Eventually, Parliament became so strong as an independent institution that it was itself able to go to war against the crown. This war, known as the English Civil War (1642–1648), was precipitated by a breakdown of the agreement between king and Parliament concerning taxation. Charles I (r. 1625–1649) needed money to put down rebellions in Scotland and Ireland, which Parliament was unwilling to grant.

Charles imposed taxes to pay for his military campaigns without Parliament's consent. Parliament responded with the Petition of Right (1628), which restated its traditional right to be consulted. Charles answered by dissolving Parliament and attempting to rule alone; Parliament then took up arms against the crown. The king's army was small, poorly equipped, and irregularly paid. Moreover, Charles did not have an administrative structure through which he could extract the financial and human resources to support his army. He had to rely, instead, upon donations from wealthy supporters and proceeds from the sale of land seized from the supporters of Parliament. Parliament's army was also small, but it was well supported by funds raised from the sale of confiscated royal property as well as forcibly collected taxes. Owing to its superior ability to raise revenues necessary to support the army, Parliament won the war and abolished the monarchy. Charles was beheaded in 1649, and England became a republic. 30 After the war, the unity of the Parliamentarians collapsed into factionalism and backstabbing, which ushered in the rule of Oliver Cromwell (r. 1649–1660).

During the Protectorate, as Cromwell's rule is called, Parliament continued to sit and exercise its right to approve war subsidies, however. Despite disagreements with Parliament, Cromwell was committed to it as an institution and to the concept of the gentry's representation. The Protectorate was unstable, and in 1660 the monarchy was restored. When Charles II (r. 1660–1685) of Scotland became king, he attempted to circumvent Parliament. Cromwell's "New Model Army" was demobilized, leaving only a small force. Charles was succeeded by his brother James

II (r. 1685–1688), a dedicated absolutist, who also attempted to rule without Parliament by relying on loans, increased customs revenues, and the taxation of religious dissidents—in other words, by relying more and more heavily on the wealth generated by the private sector. This continued to increase the power of the bourgeoisie and to limit the power of the monarchy. The result was a strengthened Parliament. James was opposed by Parliament and driven into exile. A new dynasty was founded when Parliament installed William III (r. 1688–1702), of the Dutch House of Orange, on the throne. In the Act of Settlement (1689), William accepted the crown on terms set by Parliament. The ouster of James II and the installation of William, which is known as the Glorious Revolution (1688–1689), demonstrated the absolute power of Parliament and the utter futility of any monarch's challenging its authority.

Parliament had become without question the sovereign of the emergent modern English state. Over the next two centuries the power of the crown continued to decline and that of Parliament to increase, so that by the eighteenth century absolute sovereign power had been completely acquired by Parliament.

FRANCE: AN ABSOLUTIST MONARCHICAL STATE

When Hugues Capet (r. 987–996) was chosen to be the king of West Francia, that portion of Charlemagne's empire that had been ruled by his son Louis, the entire kingdom, except for a small royal demesne called the Île-de-France around Paris, was in the hands of six great barons: the count of Flanders, the duke of Normandy, the duke of France, the duke of Burgundy, the duke of Aquitaine, and the count of Toulouse. The new king's power was severely limited by these powerful barons, who believed that they, who had helped Hugues gain the crown, had established an elective monarchy. Although early Capetian kings, such as Philippe I (r. 1060–1108) and Louis VI (r. 1108–1137), increased the size of the royal patrimony, the kingdom remained for the next two centuries a loose aggregation of baronies protected by feudal limitations on the king's power. Philippe II (r. 1180–1223) was the first of four late Capetian kings who centralized and expanded royal power. He reconquered Normandy from the English crown in 1204 and later annexed Brittany, Anjou, Maine, Touraine, and Poitou to his directly ruled domain. Philippe supervised local courts and made alliances with the bourgeoisie against the nobility. Many towns were given charters, and trade was encouraged by granting privileges to merchants.

Philippe's son, Louis VIII (r. 1223–1226), gained portions of Aquitaine and Languedoc. His son, Louis IX (r. 1226–1285), also known as St. Louis, did not extend the crown's territory but centralized its power. Although he respected the rights and privileges of the nobility, Louis did not tolerate feudal infringements on royal authority. He suspended the baronial courts and replaced them with his own and gradually established a common law for the realm. The third powerful king, Philippe IV (r. 1285–1314), extended the boundaries of his kingdom to the Atlantic in the west, the Pyrenees and Mediterranean in the south, the Alps in the east, and the Rhine in the north; this established the present territorial dimensions of the contemporary French state. Initially, the administration of the kingdom was simple. Officials of the king's household managed the affairs of the realm. The steward had general supervision over the demesne. The king's constable and marshal, who cared for his horses, commanded his knights in battle. Since the time of Hugues Capet, royal lands were looked after by officials called prévôts who collected revenues, performed judicial functions, and maintained peace. As the kingdom expanded it was divided into bailiwicks and a bailli (bailiff) was assigned to each. The baillis, who represented the royal presence, controlled various prévôts, sat as judges, and carried out police functions. Prévôts and baillis were recruited from the lower nobility and bourgeoisie. The French monarchy continued to centralize under Philippe IV's descendants, and by the beginning of the fifteenth century it had an extensive administrative system in place supported by a regular tax called the taille.

France, 1035-1328

Like other medieval monarchs, Philippe convoked an expanded curia regis (royal court) called the Estates General (in medieval fashion, this was composed of clergy, nobility, and bourgeoisie) that gave advice on major decisions affecting the realm and approval for the taxes he levied. Unlike the English Parliament, however, the Estates General did not evolve into a strong institution capable of resisting the demands of the king. It was convoked only when the king wished for it to meet and usually only during an emergency. Because each estate met separately in Paris and Toulous, the Estates General was easily manipulated by the king's lawyers. Using his own administrators, the king was easily able to bypass the Estates General and forge direct links with the pays d'états, or local assemblies. Later, the crown was able to destroy these local centers of power and replace them with its own centralized, bureaucratic apparatus to extract resources in order to make war and maintain a large standing army.

French kings continued to rely on the feudal host for military defense long after the superiority of the infantry had been demonstrated. Disastrous defeats of French chivalry during major battles of the Hundred Years' War at Crécy (1346), Poitiers (1356), and Agincourt (1415), where 6,000 French knights were annihilated by a small English army armed with longbows and pikes, did not bring about military modernization. After watching English armies march across France and defeat French knights during the Hundred Years' War, the French crown decided to modernize its military. In 1439, the Ordonnance sur la Gendarmerie created a regular military force composed of cavalry, artillery, and infantry units armed with longbows. Although this initiative gave the crown a stronger and more reliable military force, discipline and training were lacking. In order to pay for these units, which were garrisoned and supplied locally, the crown levied a uniform tax without the approval of the pays d'états. The uproar that resulted forced the king to negotiate a series of complicated taxes with each pays d'états. Although some early French kings occasionally resorted to raising taxes without the consent of the pays d'état, at no point in the early history of the French state was the power of the pays d'états destroyed. 35

This situation began to change during the reign of Louis XIII (r. 1610– 1643). Louis's finance minister, Cardinal Richelieu (1585–1642), realized that the armed forces were the backbone of the king's power within the realm and beyond.

In 1626, he ordered the destruction of all private fortresses and forbade the construction of fortified private dwellings. In that same year, he created a standing army of 20,000 soldiers under a disciplined chain of command and with regularized pay, uniforms, arms, and quarters provided by the king. Richelieu also created a royal navy of 30 ships, fortified French harbors, and established arsenals. In order to support the army and navy, both of which rapidly grew in size, Richelieu reorganized the bureaucracy and imposed stringent taxes. These taxes were directly collected by thousands of administrative agents, called intendants, who were loyal solely to the crown. The intendants supervised local administration, finance, justice, law enforcement, and the conscription of troops. These measures, and even more stringent ones applied by Richelieu's successor as finance minister, Cardinal Mazarin (1602–1661), taken in order to fight a war against the Spanish Habsburgs, resulted in a rebellion of the nobility, known as the Fronde (1648–1653).

The Frondeurs sought to restore feudal rights and privileges against the crown, but were crushed. 36 The policies of Richelieu and Mazarin allowed Louis XIV (r. 1643– 1715) to establish monarchical absolutism in France. Louis, who believed that he had been ordained by God to rule France with absolute power, centralized all the functions of government at his palace at Versailles. He personally chaired the meetings of the councils that managed provincial affairs, taxation, expenditures, and major policies, and involved himself in every detail and decision. Louis XIV became known as the "Sun King," around whom the realm revolved. In 1661, the supreme practitioner of mercantilism, Jean Baptiste Colbert (1619–1683), became minister of finance and proceeded to organize the entire economy of France to serve the state, and especially its industrial sector. He issued detailed standards for manufacturing, established new industries protected by tariffs, and created state monopolies financed at public expense. He provided scientific and technical education, kept wages low, abolished all internal tariffs, improved France's network of roads and canals, and expanded the navy to protect French commercial interests abroad.

Under Louis's minister of war, the Marquis de Louvois (1641–1691), the army was expanded to well over 100,000 well-disciplined men equipped with the latest weapons. French monarchs ignored the Estates General after 1440 and eventually abandoned the policy of frequent convocations. From 1484 until 1560 the Estates General did not meet. In the words of one scholar, "After having battled over three centuries to achieve . . . sovereignty vis-à-vis foreign and domestic rivals, by the late 1400s the kings of France were not prepared to share that sovereignty with the Estates General." 38 The Estates General stopped being called in 1614. The crown had centralized itself sufficiently by that time and no longer needed the consent of the Estates General for the extraction of revenue. Thus, the monarchy excluded the estates of the realm from any role in governing the kingdom. The nobility had been rendered useless and the rising bourgeoisie of industrialists, merchants, and professionals were cut off from any significant involvement in the affairs of the realm. The crown had become beyond all question the embodiment of absolute sovereignty in the early modern French state.

Summary

The early modern state, developing roughly from the late sixteenth through the eighteenth centuries, pioneered a political organization based on a new understanding of sovereignty. Fundamental ideas of a unified, indivisible state ruling over people within a given territory emerged and took shape. Economies came to be envisioned as spaces within states in which wealth is produced, and wealth became the object of state control in order to build large armies and, in some cases, navies. Contingent situational factors encouraged the institution of sovereignty in either absolutist parliamentary monarchies or absolutist monarchical ones.

6

THE LIBERAL STATE: SOVEREIGNTY UNIVERSALIZED

From the sixteenth century, states in Europe came to take for granted that their survival depended on absolute control over a bounded, territorial space. Sovereignty was imagined as the unifying "soul" inscribed on the landscape and population within the state's territory, which was protected, and extended, by a centralized military and economy under the control of the absolute sovereign, whether crown or parliament.

In order to institute sovereignty, states such as France had to conquer and draw into their centralizing orbits local nobles and the independent centers of power such as the bourgeoisie of the towns. Absolutist monarchical states, then, inscribed sovereignty on the territories they ruled through the grid of bureaucratic and administrative units that linked local jurisdictions to the central monarchy. In states in which the parliament emerged as absolute sovereign, the struggle to institute territorial sovereignty focused more on the juridical, legalistic struggles over forms of property rights. Although these states also developed bureaucracies, including a military, in order to link the local to the central state, this institutional grid meant something different for state sovereignty.

Facing a different configuration of social power in which the state much earlier came to depend on the bourgeoisie for its revenue and was forced into compromises with it, parliamentary states eventually subordinated the state apparatus and crown to parliament. In the eighteenth and nineteenth centuries, developments in capitalism and reactions to absolutism (both in absolutist monarchies and absolutist parliamentary states) combined to produce a new imaginary of sovereignty and a new form of the state. We call this new formation the liberal state, at the center of which is a new imaginary of sovereignty as inhering in the people. The focus of this chapter is on the way liberal states arose out of the dilemmas faced by early modern states, especially the dilemma of procuring the resources needed to make war and managing the expanding capitalist economy while maintaining the legitimacy of state power.

THE PARADOX OF POPULAR SOVEREIGNTY

As the modern state came to be more highly developed, the problematic of instituting sovereignty shifted. Sovereignty came to be seen as inhering in the population of a territory, and not in the ruler (the king) or ruling assembly (parliament). This new imaginary of sovereignty, which came to be called popular sovereignty, had roots in the republican theories of the Renaissance, especially those of Machiavelli, which described the common good of the state as the necessary outcome of political power. In seventeenth century England, the republican idea of the common good was combined with, and transformed by, arguments that individual subjects had a prior right to private property. This led to the association of the interests of the state with the protection and furtherance of the property of its subjects. Sovereignty could be represented as "popular," that is, as inhering in the population of the state, in two primary ways. One was as a possession of the people, as a utility, a tool for the protection of their property and their private lives. This was the idea enacted by the Glorious Revolution (1689) in England. The other representation of popular sovereignty was as the expression of the collective, or general, will of the people. This was the idea formulated most clearly by the eighteenth-century French-speaking Swiss philosopher Jean-Jacques Rousseau (1712–1778), whose ideas would influence the French Revolution. The American Revolution would oscillate between both, and come to rest in the constitution of 1789 with the former, more conservative version. In both cases the meaning of the state's population shifted from being an object of administration by the state apparatus to being an almost organic entity endowed with a separate being and will of its own. Both versions of popular sovereignty positioned the sovereign as protector of a separate private sphere consisting of the market economy and the sphere of private conscience.

Therefore, both were inseparable from the gendered structure of individualist and capitalist societies. In the imaginary of popular sovereignty, the state was conceived as a creation of a preexistent people either as its useful property or as its expression. The "people" was constituted as prior to the state primarily via two processes and institutions: the economy, in which private property was produced, and the family, in which the rational individuals who authorized the sovereign were nurtured. Both were by law and custom the preserves of men, as we discussed in the previous chapter. Owning and managing private property were considered male pursuits. Innovation and competition were thought to require physical and mental toughness, attributes coded as masculine. The world of private property was opposed to a sphere of love, nurturing, and tenderness in the family, a sphere associated with the feminine. States based on an imaginary of popular sovereignty continued to perform those functions performed by the early modern territorial states. Armies continued to be raised. Such states continued to mediate class conflicts between the bourgeoisie and landed nobility, and increasingly between the bourgeoisie and the working class (i.e., the class of laborers dependent on wages). States based on popular sovereignty remained dependent on their ability to impose taxes, put tariffs on imports, and otherwise extract economic resources to make war.

States based on the idea of popular sovereigny developed an idea of politics as police power to regulate the population and maintain order. Police power was needed to regulate the working classes and those caught in the often painful and unsettling transition from rural peasant to wage laborer. Such states also kept the inequalities of the capitalist economy from erupting into open social conflict. The "science of the police," as political science was often called during the eighteenth century, encompassed the regulation of the social habits of the population to ensure that people conformed to the model of the rational individual, necessary to the functioning of the private property economy and the private family. Maintaining order meant not only doing what the bourgeoisie expressly considered to be in its economic interests, but also the state's intervening in the direction of everyday life to ensure those social habits of behavior that would lead to civil order. In short, the representation of sovereignty as popular sovereignty created a new realm of individual freedom that weakened the absolutist state in favor of the individual, while paradoxically subjecting the individual to new forms of power, exercised by the state and others and aimed at molding and regulating public behavior. Behavior came to be watched, catalogued, measured, anticipated, calculated, and managed. Rather than weakening the state to the point of near disappearance, the interpenetration of capitalism and the state and the new imaginary of popular sovereignty made possible the expansion of state power, although in new forms.

Liberalism

From the late seventeenth century, attempts to reform the absolutist state to make it protective of private property rights and responsive to the freedom of individuals to pursue profit in the market became popular, both among intellectuals and the bourgeoisie. By the nineteenth century this reformist movement would be called liberalism, and its defenders would be called liberals, a term first used to refer to the party of the bourgeoisie in early nineteenth-century Spain. By the middle of the century it had spread throughout Europe, becoming a name adopted by major bourgeois political parties. 5 Liberal ideas circulated not through religious channels or through official state-sanctioned media, but through the new commercial markets of civil society, primarily in the political pamphlets and books made possible by combining the technology of the printing press with the increasing wealth of the middle class.

Public opinion was created by the new newspapers and magazines, such as The Spectator and The Tattler, published by two English liberals, Joseph Addison (1672–1719) and Richard Steele (1672–1729). On the European continent, especially, liberal ideas circulated through the private clubs of intellectuals and the middle class (the most famous of which was the Freemasons) and in the scientific associations in which intellectuals published and otherwise circulated their writings. The most important of these was the initiative in France of the Encyclopedia, a massive publishing project under the direction of the French philosopher and intellectual Denis Diderot (1713–1784), which brought together in a unified set of volumes all the latest knowledge of natural and human sciences. In some places, the German states and Scotland, for example, universities played an important role in developing and spreading liberal ideas.

Liberalism developed in opposition to dogmatic religion, arguing that all forms of knowing, including religious knowledge, should be subjected to rational (i.e., reasoned) forms of discussion and debate. To be a "subject"—increasingly used to refer to individuals not only in a political but also in a moral sense—was to be an agent who acted rationally. Liberals set out self-consciously to reform the state so that it would support the private world of the individual in civil society, which they understood as the voluntary social interactions and organizations of rational individuals. They did so not only for economic reasons but for moral reasons as well. In Enlightenment liberalism, the economic and moral were intertwined. Liberalism developed a distinctive form of ideology that accepted the state only insofar as it could be justified by a rational discourse appealing to universal standards of human nature and justice. By positing a universal rational knowledge as the basis of truth, liberalism solved one of the most vexing problems of the early modern territorial state: that is, how to make war and effectively exercise power, yet, at the same time, maintain the willingness of the people to provide the state with the necessary human and economic resources to do so. In return for subordinating the subjectivity of the individual to the rules of a reason that would maximize productivity and social wealth, which the state could then appropriate for its military and other purposes, the state would subordinate itself to the universal laws of reason and thereby limit its own power.

In this way, liberalism, by promoting an ideology based on universal principles, made room within the sovereign state for capitalism and civil society, as well as for state sovereignty within capitalism and civil society. To see how liberalism and the liberal state emerged out of the absolutist state, it is necessary to look briefly at the relation between politics and morality. During the religious wars of the seventeenth century, absolutist monarchies sought to resolve moral conflicts politically—that is, by distinguishing morals from politics and subordinating the former, especially in the form of religious beliefs, to the latter by granting to the state the power to do what was necessary to maintain order. Although morality was considered a matter for the individual subject's conscience (i.e., his or her inward belief), the absolutist state compelled that inward belief in the name of public order. Public order was the supreme good, and private conscience and morality were to be subordinated to it. Against absolutism, the philosopher and political writer John Locke (1632–1704), in his Letter on Toleration (1689), articulated a position that would later come to define liberalism. In this pamphlet, Locke accepted the idea that morals are a matter of individual conscience and that they should be determined by reason and not by custom, nature, or political power. Counter to the logic of the absolutist state, Locke wrote that toleration is a universal good that states should accept and that should guide their acceptance of the rule of law. Locke's point was that the state, rather than reigning supreme over the individual conscience, as the absolutist would argue, should be subordinated to the universal principles of reason that govern the private conscience. Religion, Locke argued, should not dictate laws for the state, which exists in Locke's view "for the procuring, preserving, and advancing" of the individual's "life, liberty, health and indolence of body; and the possession of outward things, such as money, lands, houses, furniture, and the like." Neither should the magistrates of the state "forbid the preaching or professing of any speculative opinions in any church, because they have no manner of relation to the civil rights of the subjects."

THE LIBERAL STATE AS A RIGHTS-BASED STATE

By subordinating the territorial state to universal principles derived by reason, individual subjects and the civil society they circulated in came to be seen as existing independently of and prior to the state. This meant that subjects came to be seen in the liberal state as bearers of certain rights, which accrued to them as autonomous individuals. To justify this, many liberal thinkers drew initially on the tradition of natural rights, as when the drafters of the American constitution argued that all individuals were endowed by "their Creator" with "inalienable rights to life, liberty and the pursuit of happiness." Specifically, two rights, which Locke alluded to in his Letter on Toleration, were most important to liberals: the right to private property and the right to be protected from arbitrary and unfair treatment by the state. Each of these requires brief mention.

The general right to private property entailed, first, the right to secure possession of one's belongings, which was based on the belief that individuals had a natural right to choose how they wanted to live their lives by selecting their own occupation, religion, associates, leisure-time activities, and so forth. Second, it entailed the right to private property, which included the right to alienate one's possessions, that is, to be able to buy and sell property at will. Third, the general right to private property entailed the right to accumulate as much wealth as one wished, so long as one did so through buying and selling. In effect, natural rights supported a capitalist market society, that is, a society in which the economic market is paramount. Adam Smith (1723– 1790), the Scottish philosopher and political economist, developed the theory of the market and its implications in his book The Wealth of Nations (1776). In this work, Smith introduced the idea that the market was self-regulating. Smith's liberalism is based on the assumption that human beings are rational creatures who should be permitted to develop their inherent capacities to the fullest. Moreover, he assumed that all are born with "the propensity to truck, barter, and exchange one thing for another."

All barriers to the individual's inherent ability to achieve his or her capacities must be removed. Doing so would encourage people to act according to reason, and subordinate their passions by subjecting them to the rule of rational self-interest. In The Wealth of Nations, Smith argued that the economic restrictions of mercantilism retarded economic growth and with it the general welfare of the subjects because it restricted individual economic freedom. Smith argued that an economy free of state interference and monopoly would produce prosperity efficiently if the law of supply and demand were allowed to operate unfettered by state controls. Efficient producers would prosper and inefficient ones would fail. He believed that the unseen hand of the market, that is, the rational calculations of a myriad of individual consumers making their buying decisions based on economic self-interest, would automatically produce economic growth and prosperity for all. This presumed harmony of interests extended to the international economy, which Smith did not explicitly distinguish from the domestic economy, although nineteenth- and twentieth-century liberals would. If states were left free to trade without any tariff barriers, everyone subject to the world capitalist economy would benefit and a general peace would prevail among states.

Or so liberals argued. The liberal state, then, is in one respect a minimal state; that is, it is deliberately structured not to be itself a threat to the "natural right" of property ownership, which is the ultimate justification for the dominant position of the bourgeoisie within the state. Participation is restricted by property-owning requirements to eliminate a threat to the bourgeoisie's control of the state from economically less advantaged groups from below. 13 The second right that liberals considered inalienable was the right to protection from arbitrary and capricious treatment by the state. Being free of the arbitrary and capricious state power characteristic of the absolutist states meant first and foremost the application of the principle of the rule of law. The theory that a state was legitimate only when it was subordinated to the rule of law, and not the rule of men unrestrained by law, went back to the ancient Greek and Roman idea of a republic. For Greek political philosophers such as Aristotle and Plato, and for the Roman statesman and philosopher Cicero, states were to be ruled by the laws made by citizens. The rule of law for them was justified because citizens themselves made the law.

The aim of politics was to ensure that those citizens who were best able to make the laws actually ruled, although different republican philosophers differed on how this condition could best be met. This idea was revived by the civic republican tradition in the Renaissance, whose most famous theorist was Machiavelli. In the civic republican tradition, the rule of law was grounded in the idea of the public good. That is, the rule of law was justified because it served the public benefit, and any state that did not respect the rule of law would, in the long run, work against the public good and lead itself to a general decline. States governed according to the rule of law, this tradition believed, would be secure, prosperous, and less inclined to factionalism, civil war, and general violence than states in which rulers could impose a personal and arbitrary authority. This republican tradition provided considerable ammunition for the critical struggle against the absolutist state. Liberalism defended the rule of law, but did so on different grounds. It supported the rule of law because it would protect citizens best from arbitrary and capricious personal rule and leave individuals the most freedom to pursue their own private lives and, especially, to trade and accumulate wealth and property.

That is, liberalism grounded the rule of law negatively: the law should rule not because it promotes the public good but because it allows individuals the greatest freedom by protecting their private interests. Liberals recognized that the law might itself treat individuals unequally or might contradict some of their rights; to prevent this, liberalism committed to the equal treatment of individual subjects. Liberals reduced all subjects to a common denominator, an abstract concept of the person that eliminated his or her particular differences, the so-called abstract individual. To liberals, being protected from arbitrary and capricious power and authority meant that the state had to treat all individuals as essentially the same. That is, no natural attributes of birth, such as social class, sex, or race, should matter. Much of liberal political theory during the twentieth century has been concerned with defining these extralegal principles on which the rule of law is seen to rest.

Liberalism and Democracy

It should be noted that liberals were not, at first, democrats in the modern sense of that word. Liberals came to accept democracy only reluctantly, because it was the best way to protect individual liberty from the growing power of the state. 15 This was the argument of utilitarians such as Jeremy Bentham (1748– 1832) and James Mill (1773–1836). For these liberals, the state was needed to maintain order and defense, as John Locke had argued, and in general to promote a condition of "the greatest happiness of the greatest number," the main principle of utilitarian philosophy. Utilitarians did not argue against the state, but for a state in which reason, in the sense of the efficient matching of means to ends, ruled. This sort of state would continue to exercise considerable power, especially police and military power, and would continue to promote a rational society, especially by providing education for all, even if it had limited power to regulate economic activity.

In his Essay On Government (1820), James Mill averred that the main end of politics was to permit people to become rational and mature individuals. This can be done, he argued, only when they are able to make decisions that affect their own lives. Even though a wise and benevolent absolute ruler might make better decisions than individuals could make for themselves, a limited representative state would be better, he argued, because individuals would be responsible for their own mistakes. Therefore, some form of representative state would be better than an absolute monarchy, even a benevolent one. The liberal idea of democracy, or liberal democracy as it has come to be called, advocates democracy not as a value in itself but as a way of checking the power of the state while subjecting it to rational debate among citizens. The most powerful defense of liberty of thought and discussion can be found in John Stuart Mill's (1806–1873) essay On Liberty (1859). In this essay, Mill, who was James Mill's son, argued that the real threat to liberty came from irrational citizens who unquestioningly followed social norms and prejudices. A rational and well-educated public was the best guarantee against the state's becoming too powerful and violating individual rights. Indeed, when Mill did advocate a universal franchise in his Considerations on Representative Government (1861), he coupled it with a system of weighted voting so that those who were highly educated and commercially successful, which he took to be evidence of their rationality, would cast more votes!

Liberals at first believed that the right to vote and to hold office should be restricted to those individuals who owned a certain amount of property. Such restrictions were justified by the belief that the ability to decide political issues in an enlightened and critical manner was present only in individuals who owned property. Thus, when liberals gained power, the right to vote was restricted to property owners.

Under pressure from the working classes and from women in the suffragette movements, liberals eventually began to accept the universal franchise, but they always did so within constitutional frameworks that limited the power the masses could exercise. John Stuart Mill was one of the first liberals to argue for the vote not only for the working classes but also for women. But nineteenth-century liberals like John Stuart Mill in England and Alexis de Tocqueville (1805–1859) in France worried about the general trend toward equality that democratization represented in modern states.

They believed that this would lead to mediocrity in the population and a loss of a communal spirit and solidarity among the people. Although women began to agitate for the franchise in the nineteenth century, women's suffrage in most liberal states was not granted until the twentieth. Even after having been enfranchised, women still faced barriers that prevented the equal exercise of their formal rights. Some barriers were legal, such as laws restricting the autonomy of married women and their rights to own property independently of their husbands.

Some were the persistence of customs and social prejudices regarding motherhood, women's bodies, and their "proper" roles in the family; these barriers prevented women from being considered citizens with the same rights as men. Mary Wollstonecraft (1759–1797), a philosopher who shared liberalism's commitments to the rational development of individuals, exposed many of these prejudices as well as how the state promoted them by denying equal education to women. She argued that only through a system of education in which men and women were educated equally and in a culture that was blind to gender difference would society realize its potential as a free society. Mill and his wife Harriet Taylor extended Wollstonecraft's argument in On the Subjection of Women (1869), which attacked the laws that restricted women's roles and positions.

Varieties of the Liberal State

During the eighteenth and nineteenth centuries, liberals challenged monarchical and parliamentary absolutists for control of the emerging European, territorial states. Liberalism flourished in Britain and its colonies in North America primarily because Britain had the largest bourgeoisie of all European monarchies, thanks to its early industrialization and the extensive commercialization of its economy. Liberalism spread more easily in Britain, too, because the absolutist parliamentary state that had emerged out of the struggle between the crown and the estates proved easier to capture than did the absolutist monarchies in Europe On the continent, absolutists were not definitely defeated and were able to resist the imposition of the liberal state for a considerable time. This resulted in prolonged and often bloody struggles between liberals and monarchists in these realms. It was in the English colonies in North America that liberalism achieved its greatest triumph.

Britain: A Liberal Parliamentary State

After the English civil war and the Act of Settlement, which forbade monarchical absolutism in Britain, two factions struggled for control of the state within Parliament based on personal, regional, religious, and family loyalties. One faction was known as the Whigs (meaning cattle thieves in Scots-Gaelic) and favored the gentry's commercial interests and such Protestant sects as the Methodists, Baptists, Presbyterians, and Congregationalists because they did not conform to the hierarchy and liturgy of the Anglican Church, the established Church of England. The other faction was known as the Tories (meaning Irish papist outlaws) and favored the interests of the traditional aristocracy and the Anglican Church. During this period seats in Parliament were controlled by powerful families and many were openly bought and sold. In the early 1800s demands by Britain's growing bourgeoisie for an end to the practice of buying and selling of seats and for admission to Parliament resulted in reforms in the way that members of Parliament (MPs) were chosen. The first reform was the Great Reform Act of 1832, which extended the franchise to 14 percent of the adult males, and made it possible for the Whigs, who thereafter became known as Liberals, to come to power. Note that the Reform Act conceded the right to vote only to those who had already accepted the tenets of liberalism, the new bourgeoisie. The Liberals were supported by the commercial and industrial bourgeoisie and adherents of the nonconformist Protestant sects, who favored minimal interference into economic and social life.

Tories, who became known as Conservatives, were supported by the traditional aristocracy and adherents of Anglicanism, who favored an absolutist monarchical state that would interfere with economic and social life to protect people from their irrational impulses. The Reform Act of 1867, which doubled the electorate by reducing property-owning restrictions for voting, allowed portions of the working class to cast ballots for the first time. The Reform Act of 1884 provided for a secret ballot and created universal male suffrage. These reforms co-opted not only the bourgeoisie but also segments of the emergent working class to pursue political aims through Parliament. England was thus peacefully and gradually transformed into a liberal parliamentary state based on the defense of private property, individual liberties, religious equality, and universal male suffrage.

The United States: A Liberal Federal State

A received truth of American politics is that the United States does not constitute a state. The Founding Fathers never used the word when speaking or writing about the new state that they were creating. Instead, they called it either a government, a republic, or a union. When they used the term state, they were referring to one of the constituent states of the new entity or to Britain. The founders were also compelled to avoid the term to more easily gain ratification for the new constitution among those for whom the term state conjured images of the all-powerful absolutist states of Europe. Despite the Founding Fathers calling it something else, a state was, in fact, what they created.

Moreover, its purpose was not fundamentally different from that of the absolutist states of the day, including the extraction of resources in order to maintain a standing army. The format of the state was, however, different because the Founding Fathers were imbued with liberal ideas about rational knowledge, toleration, natural rights, the rule of law, equality, and a free market economy. The movement for independence began as a protest against the extra taxes levied on the colonies by the British Parliament to cover extraordinary expenses incurred during the French and Indian Wars (1755–1763) and to pay for western garrisons to protect settlers against continuing attack by Native Americans. These new taxes included the Sugar Act of 1764 and the Stamp Act of 1767, which required that revenue stamps be affixed to all legal and printed documents. These taxes affected the two groups in colonial society with the most extensive commercial interests: New England merchants and southern planters.

Using the slogan "No taxation without representation," New England merchants and southern planters formed an alliance with shopkeepers, artisans, and small farmers to protest the new taxes and boycott British-made goods. In response, the British Parliament rescinded the new taxes; the New England merchants and southern planters, now satisfied, sought to calm a situation that had exposed the more radical elements of colonial society: shopkeepers, artisans, and small farmers. Mobilized over taxes, these elements asserted that British power maintained an unjust colonial economic and social structure; they began to agitate for independence, a state the New England merchants and southern planters did not want. 20 In 1773 the British granted a monopoly on the export of tea to the East India Company; this ended a lucrative trade for New England merchants. Colonial merchants sought to persuade the British to rescind the Tea Act. Meanwhile, the radicals led by Samuel Adams (1722–1803), who hoped to goad the British to take action that would alienate the New England merchants and southern planters, dumped tea from East

India Company ships into Boston Harbor. After the Boston Tea Party, as this event is known, the British Parliament took harsh measures: the port of Boston was closed to commerce, the colonial government of Massachusetts was changed, persons accused of crime were taken to England for trial, and movement west was restricted; this last measure especially aggravated southern planters, who were in constant need of new land for their main crop, cotton. A cycle of provocative actions by the colonists and harsh retaliation by the British resulted in the convening of the First Continental Congress in 1774. Delegates from all the colonies attended and called for a complete boycott of British goods and, prodded by the radicals, considered the possibility of independence from Britain.

The Declaration of Independence (July 4, 1776), written by Thomas Jefferson (1743–1826) and adopted by the Second Continental Congress (1776), began by stating the tenets of liberalism: natural law, social contract, inalienable rights, popular sovereignty, and limited government. These were followed by a list of grievances the colonial elite harbored against the British. By the end of the following year, the colonists declared independence and adopted a written constitution, the Articles of Confederation and Perpetual Union, which stayed in force until March 1789. The Articles created a confederal state —that is, one in which the central government enjoys only those powers the constituent member states are willing to give it. There was no national-level executive, and laws passed by the Continental Congress were to be executed by the member states. Although the Continental Congress could declare war, make peace, ratify treaties, coin or borrow money, and regulate trade with Native Americans, it could neither levy direct taxes nor regulate commerce among the member states. There was no standing army and each state maintained its own militia.

The Articles of Confederation, did not, then, create a state strong enough to promote the economic interests of New England merchants and southern planters. The newly independent states competed with one another for foreign commerce, and European states treated each state of the Confederation as a sovereign state. At the same time, the influence of radicals in the Continental Congress and the legislatures of certain states, such as Pennsylvania and Rhode Island, increased, threatening dominant economic interests. Faced with these threats, the Virginia state legislature called a conference of state leaders, which met in 1786 in Annapolis, Maryland, in order to organize a subsequent conference to revise the Articles of Confederation. In the meantime, Daniel Shays (1747?–1825), a former Revolutionary War army captain, led a rebellion of debt-ridden farmers against the state of Massachusetts to prevent foreclosures on their land. Although Shays's Rebellion (1786), as this event is known, ended peacefully when fourteen of the captured rebels were eventually pardoned and the state legislature met some of their demands, it demonstrated the weakness of state militias and the growing influence of the radicals. A conference was convened in May 1789 in Philadelphia for the purpose of revising the Articles. All states except Rhode Island sent a delegation.

The 55 delegates, representatives of New England merchants and southern planters, agreed upon the broad ideological principles on which the new state should be based. As adherents of liberal principles, they wanted a new state capable of promoting commerce and protecting property from radical state legislatures. The constitution produced by the convention in Philadelphia brought into being a state strong enough to promote commerce and protect private property, but not to become itself a threat to commerce and property as radical state legislatures had become. To accomplish both power and protection, the central government was separated into coequal legislative, executive, and judicial branches. The legislative branch (Congress) was subdivided into two houses: the Senate, appointed by state legislatures to six-year terms, staggered such that only one-third of the Senate would be appointed every two years, and the House, directly elected for two-year terms.

Power and protection were also accomplished by dividing governmental responsibilities between the central government and the constituent state governments. A strong, but not too strong, national state was imposed upon the preexisting states, which had been autonomous from one another under the Articles of Confederation and as colonies of Britain. The Constitution rescinded the right of states to maintain armies in peacetime, and gave the central state the power to conduct foreign policy and command the national army as well as the state militias (if called into national service). To Congress the Constitution granted the right to declare war, to call the state militias into national service, and to appropriate money to support the armed forces. In addition, Congress was given the responsibility of assisting commerce by making "internal improvements," such as building roads, bridges, and canals, creating a national currency, controlling patents, collecting tariffs, and providing subsidies. To the states were given the power to make law in a host of areas, including property, banking, business, family, public health, education, crime, elections, local government, occupation, and land-use. To ratify the new Constitution, it was necessary that a bargain be struck with those who believed that, despite separation of powers and federalism, the state was still too strong and might still threaten economic interests and individual rights. A Bill of Rights was adopted in 1791 in the form of amendments to the original document. In spite of the guarantee of individual rights to all persons, the Constitution maintained the Three-fifths Compromise, which stipulated that five slaves would be counted as three persons for purposes of apportioning seats in the House of Representatives. Thus, the purpose of the liberal federal state built by the drafters of the Constitution was to strengthen the national government ("form a more perfect Union") and create a national army ("provide for the common defence"), while at the same time making certain that the new state itself could not be easily taken over by radical forces.

France: A Liberal Republican State

The establishment of a liberal state was relatively easy in the former colonies of British North America, which were dominated by the commercial classes. The colonies never had a peasantry or nobility in the European sense. There was no deeply entrenched Catholic Church, and no traditional landed nobility. This was not the case in Europe, where, strong absolutist monarchies supported by the Catholic Church had been built. In France, liberals had a difficult time gaining control of the state and were not immediately successful. Although French liberals were able to overthrow the monarchy, a long and difficult struggle between liberals and conservative absolutists ensued in the years following the French Revolution. Even after successfully gaining control, the resultant liberal republican state retained many aspects of the previous absolutist state, especially its centralized, unitary character. As was shown in the previous chapter, the state-making process in France resulted in the most absolute monarchy for its day in all of Europe. In 1789, Louis XVI (r. 1774–1792) summoned the Estates General, its first meeting since 1628, to gain support and consent for new taxes to pay debts associated with France's recent war with Britain in North America.

The nobility and the clergy refused the king's request and challenged his authority by demanding a say in the governance of the realm in exchange for the relinquishment of their immunity from taxation. This challenge to the king's authority encouraged the Third Estate, that is, the bourgeoisie, which was already very heavily taxed, to make their own demands. The Third Estate declared itself the only true representative of the French people. Rioting and protests broke out in Paris and on July 14, 1789, a mob stormed the Bastille prison. Rioting and civil unrest soon spread to the rest of France; an attempt to form a constitutional monarchy was unsuccessful and France was proclaimed a republic in 1792. Louis was tried and executed as a traitor on January 21, 1793. Although in Britain and the United States civic republicanism had been transformed in ways supportive of property and capitalist commercial interests, in France a more radical republicanism gained influence and circulated in political writings, in theater, music, opera, and scientific circles. French radical republicans, who were called Jacobins (from the name of their meeting place, a former Dominican convent), placed the claim of equality for all citizens—an implicit element of liberal claims of individual rights, which moderate liberals more responsive to the concerns of the property-owning bourgeoisie avoided—above all else, even the protection of private property.

Drawing liberalism toward one of its possible poles, the Jacobins promulgated the Universal Declaration of the Rights of Man (August 26, 1789) and abolished provincial administrative units of monarchical France as well as serfdom and noble privileges. Important Jacobin leaders such as Maximilien Robespierre (1758–1794) and the Marquis de Sade (1740–1814) combined radical liberal individualism with an intense commitment to freedom and independence in republicanism; they argued for a widened sphere of individual liberty that would encompass all aspects of individual life, not only property ownership but also moral and sexual life. 26 Although France was declared a republic in 1792, the stiff resistance of the nobility and the clergy prevented liberals from gaining full control of the French state.

Moreover, France was invaded by several European kings, who saw the survival of the new French republic as a direct challenge to their monarchies. In order to deal with these threats, the republic ordered universal conscription (levée en masse) in August 1793. At the same time, all of France's economic resources were placed under the authority of the new republican government, called the Directory. These two actions were truly radical: for the first time, an army of citizen-soldiers loyal to the nation was raised and supported by mobilizing the vast resources of an entire national economy. To compensate for its weakness at home, the republican régime waged war against its absolutist, monarchical enemies abroad. As the cost of these wars in terms of blood and treasure began to rise, rioting against the new republic began; France plunged into turmoil. Internal disorder, military threats from abroad, and rising sentiments for a return to strong centralized rule encouraged Napoléon Bonaparte (1769–1821), the republic's most successful general, to seize dictatorial power in 1799. Napoléon sought to unify France around the liberal ideals of the revolution— liberté, egalité, fraternité (liberty, equality, and brotherhood)—and to restore order. Between 1799 and 1804, he reorganized the state's central administration, provided France with a constitution and a uniform legal system called the Code Napoléon (1804), and expanded territorial administration. He placed préfects under the absolute control of the central government in charge of the 83 départements into which France had been divided by the previous revolutionary government. Napoléon also revived the Conseil d'état, which since the time of Louis XIV had been composed of salaried counsellors—lawyers and administrators—who worked under the direction of the king. Napoléon sought not only to unify France but to unify Europe around French leadership, which he attempted to do by force.

He declared himself emperor of France in 1804, raised an army of 600,000 men, and, from 1804 to 1815, invaded and defeated monarchies across Europe from the German principalities to Portugal in what are known today as the Napoleonic Wars (1804–1815). Defeated in 1814 by an allied army of Austrian, Prussian, Russian, and British troops, Napoléon was banished to the island of Elba in the Mediterranean. Within nine months he had escaped from Elba and secretly returned to France, where he rallied liberals against the restored monarchy. After taking power, Napoléon once again raised a huge army and attempted to establish French hegemony over Europe. Once again he was defeated by a combined Austrian, Prussian, Russian, and British army at Waterloo in 1815. Napoléon was again banished from France, this time to St. Helena in the South Atlantic, where he died in 1821. After Napoléon's second banishment, the monarchy was restored with constitutional limitations and a parliament. A number of political groups appeared, which fought a seesaw battle for control of the French state.

On one side were the Royalists, conservative members of the aristocracy, who fulminated against the French Revolution and sought to reestablish the monarchy and to restore the prerogatives of the Catholic Church. On the opposite side were the Jacobins, or radical liberals, who continued to fight for a secular, egalitarian republic. Numerous moderate groups took positions between these two. The constitutional monarchy of Louis XVIII (r. 1815–1824) and Charles X (r. 1824–1830) was overthrown by Louis Philippe (r. 1830–1848), who reestablished absolutism. In 1848, liberals overthrew the monarchy once again and established France's Second Republic, which lasted only until 1851. During this short period, France was governed by a popularly elected president and a unicameral parliament. The Second Republic was overthrown in 1851 by Louis Napoléon, the nephew of Napoléon Bonaparte, who established the Second Empire, which he ruled as Napoléon III (r. 1851–1870) until his armies were defeated by the Prussians in 1870. In the wake of Napoléon III's defeat, in 1871 liberals established the Third Republic, which lasted until the Germans invaded France in 1940. The Third Republic had a two-house legislature. The Chamber of Deputies was elected by universal male suffrage and the Senate by indirect election by local notables. In liberal fashion, the terms of office were staggered: senators served longer than deputies and their age requirements were higher. The executive was divided between a president and a council of ministers headed by a prime minister. The president appointed all members of the council, including the prime minister, but it was collectively responsible to the legislature. The president was elected by a joint meeting of the two houses of the legislature for a seven-year term of office and was given the power to dissolve the legislature, a traditional monarchical prerogative. This basic format was carried over to the Fourth Republic, which was organized in 1945 and lasted until 1957, when it collapsed under the weight of the Algerian crisis, and to the present Fifth Republic, which was established in 1958 by General Charles de Gaulle (1890–1970).

SUMMARY

In this chapter we have concentrated on the formation of liberal states. Liberalism's ideas of popular sovereignty were deployed in different ways under different circumstances to transform absolutist states into ones more readily able to resolve the problem of the mutual dependence of sovereign and subject. Liberalism established the conditions under which the property of the bourgeoisie could be protected and expanded while maintaining the state's ability to organize for war and provide public justice. It is important to recognize that liberalism also created opportunities for critical movements to create a space in which working classes, women, slaves, and religious and racial minorities could organize politically and could claim access to and otherwise challenge state power.

7

THE ANTILIBERAL STATE

In this chapter the emergence of antiliberal states during the twentieth century is discussed. The focus is on the dilemma faced by liberal states as their economies became increasingly industrialized. In certain states, such as the United States and Britain, where liberals came to power with little difficulty, and where liberalism heavily influenced the organization and governing practices of the state, a form of the state has emerged in the twentieth century in which the distinctions between state and civil society are maintained but combine in subtle ways to manage jointly the social, economic, and political life within it. In other states, especially those with a long history of monarchical absolutism, such as Russia and Germany, two distinct varieties of the antiliberal state emerged: the progressively centralized communist state, which abolished the distinction between state and civil society, and the "reactionary modernist" fascist state, which combined capitalist modernization (i.e., belief in technological and scientific progress linked to utilitarian goals of organization, efficiency and productivity) with a reactionary imaginary of the volk, or "people," as constituting a historically homogeneous and "pure" nation.

INDUSTRIALIZATON, MODERNITY, AND THE CRISIS OF LIBERALISM

Remember that one aspect of liberal thought was a belief in progress, especially scientific progress. Liberals believed that science was based on a system of truth that would transform the world for the better by producing new technologies to make life more comfortable. Liberals also believed that science would perfect human morals and social life by providing a critique of all irrational belief systems and by eliminating all arbitrary power. The transformation of the world for the better through science was to be realized by giving free rein to individual initiative and acquisitiveness in civil society and by rationalizing the state, that is, subordinating government to the rule of law and reducing politics to administration. The tremendous increases in industrial production and trade that took place from the middle to late nineteenth century appeared to liberals to be the realization and validation of human ingenuity and rationality. Liberals tended to attribute such progress to individuals, rather than to the state, which they tended to view as a neutral protector of the private sphere of individuals rather than as a progressive force. Industrialization was, however, a double-edged sword.

On the one side, it produced an abundance of material goods, while on the other, it produced profound misery. One economist and social theorist, in summarizing the impact of the Industrial Revolution, puts the problem thus: "There was an almost miraculous improvement in the tools of production, which was accompanied by a catastrophic dislocation of the lives of the common people." Catastrophic dislocation was widely evident in the cities in which much industrial production took place, and to which increasing numbers of people looking for work moved. Cities were dark, dirty, dangerous, and congested. The living and working conditions of the proletariat, the label given to the working class in the nineteenth century (from the Latin, meaning the lowest economic class), were extremely bad. Workers, including children, were paid very low wages and were compelled to work long days, often 15 hours or more. They lived in crowded, dilapidated housing without heat or plumbing. Their food was extremely poor; this, together with the long hours of work in unhealthy conditions, made them susceptible to debilitating, chronic illnesses for which medical care was scarce and expensive, if available at all. Women were placed in especially difficult circumstances. After working in factories or doing "piece work" (i.e., work paid by the piece, not by the hour) at home to supplement their husband's or father's inadequate pay, they, and their unmarried daughters, had to perform hours of backbreaking household work for which they were not compensated.

Eventually, workers began to demand a living wage and better working conditions as well as a share of political power. At the beginning of the nineteenth century, the protest of the proletariat was manifested in a more or less militant campaign for the right to vote, which would give the proletariat some measure of indirect control over industrial capitalism by allowing it a voice in the affairs of the state. Early suffragette and feminist groups often took a leading role in such campaigns. Workers supported liberalism's commitment to individual equality and its emphasis on procedural democracy. Early feminists, such as Mary Wollstonecraft, were drawn to its emphases on individual merit and universal education; they argued that these were the prerequisites for the emancipation of both women and men. Nevertheless, liberal parties and politicians tended to become more apologetic of industrial capitalism in the nineteenth century and unwilling to go beyond modest political reforms. Liberalism came to understand industrialization in exclusively economic terms. That is, liberals thought that the free market would solve all the social problems created by industrialization.

They assumed that the horrendous social dislocation, gross inequalities of wealth, and urban squalor that it produced would be dealt with by the "trickle-down" effect, which would spread wealth from the wealthy through the middle class to the poor, and through the judicious application of minimally intrusive reforms. They also thought that the market would create a harmony of interests among all peoples engaged in global trade, which would put an end to war. For liberals, the state's role was limited to facilitating the workings of the free market by providing the people with the education they needed to make the industrial market economy prosper, guaranteeing the individual the right to accumulate private property, and encouraging economic competition by preventing monopolies. This way of thinking, which is known as a form of economism, failed to address the social and political concerns of workers, and liberals began loosing their support. Feminists also turned away from liberalism because the men who controlled liberal parties generally refused to extend to women the individual rights and respect their ideology promised. Feminist theories came to emphasize instead the cultural customs, traditions, and institutions (such as the nuclear family) that reinforced even liberal men's sense of their superiority over women.

Radical Working-Class Movements

By the end of the nineteenth century the proletariat turned to movements that sought to take direct control over industrial capitalism by overthrowing the liberal state and making all industry, business, and agriculture the property of the proletariat rather than the original owners. These movements were animated by ideologies, such as socialism, anarchism, and utopianism, that rejected, in often provocative ways, the managerial and rationalized forms of industrial capitalism. Anarchists, such as Mikhail Bakunin (1814–1876) and Pierre-Josèphe Proudhon (1809–1865), called for direct action to violently disrupt the social and political processes of industrialization.

The Luddites, a semiorganized group of workers opposed to the way industrialization continually put workers out of work, broke into factories and smashed machines. Various humanistic utopian socialists, most significantly Comte de Saint Simon (1760–1825), FrancoisCharles Fourier (1772–1837), and Robert Owen (1771–1858), developed socialist and communal alternatives to industrial life, sometimes creating experimental communities based on Christian or humanitarian values. The latter were often romanticist attempts to return to a pure, pristine, and humane human essence in harmony with nature and now obscured by industrialization. By far the most influential radical theory was that of Karl Marx (1818– 1883), a German economist, journalist, and political organizer.

Modern capitalist economies, he argued, forced the majority of the population to live under conditions in which they were powerless. Factory owners and finance capitalists owned the means of production, and workers had nothing but their bodies to sell. Wages were set by a market over which capitalists had complete power. Marx described the social effects of the production and consumption cycle of industrial capitalism as alienation, a process in which "the worker becomes a slave of the object" he or she produces. Specifically, "the object produced by labour, its product, now stands opposed to it as an alien being, as a power independent of the producer."

More generally, in his Communist Manifesto (1848), Marx characterized the general effects of the rapid changes brought about by industrial capitalism in the following way:

> Constant revolutionizing of production, uninterrupted disturbance of all social conditions, everlasting uncertainty and agitation distinguish the bourgeois epoch from all earlier ones. All fixed, fast-frozen relations, with their train of ancient and venerable prejudices and opinions, are swept away, all new-formed ones become antiquated before they can ossify. All that is solid melts into air, all that is holy is profaned, and man is at last compelled to face with sober senses, his real conditions of life, and his relations with his kind.

To Marx, the dependence of life on the circulation of commodities meant a life of enormous uncertainty, dizzying speeds of change, and the extreme exploitation of workers by owners of capital. But, in Marx's interpretation, industrial capitalism also opened up the possibility for people to organize and take control of the changes occurring in the areas that mattered most—the productive relations that, Marx argued, in reality governed their lives. Marx's critique of industrial capitalism was powerfully attractive to industrial workers because it blamed their economic plight not on themselves as individuals, as did the liberals, but on the capitalist mode of production. It appealed to some feminists because it traced the patriarchal domination of men over women to the structures of industrial capitalism, and promised that with the overthrow of capitalism, men and women would not just be politically equal, as liberal feminists argued, but equal in all aspects of life. 6 The role of the state posed difficult questions for Marx's analysis. Although he never wrote a systematic treatise on the state, Marx began to develop an account of the capitalist state through his criticism of the idealist German philosopher, Georg Friedrich Hegel (1770–1831).

Hegel had posed fundamental criticisms of the liberal conceptions of man and state. Unlike liberals, Hegel saw the state as an active agent of change; indeed, he saw the state as the supreme agent of rational transformation of human societies. For Hegel, the state embodied the spirit of human history and the realization of a rational society. He argued that liberalism's belief that separate, abstract individuals using only their own initiative could produce a rational and just society was mistaken. Civil society, the sphere of individualistic economic interaction and voluntary social organizations, Hegel argued, realized only a truncated version of human reason, one based on instrumental calculations of self-interest and the alienation of men from other men. A fuller realization of reason was embodied in a modern state in which men gave self-conscious direction to the organization of their shared ethical and social life. The state, to Hegel, represented an ethical unity; sovereignty became the medium between particular human communities and the universality of the human spirit. Therefore, the realization of human freedom was to be found in the struggles among sovereign states, leading eventually to the victory of the sovereign power that represented the most free and rational ethical life, that is, the state in which all forms of arbitrary power had been eliminated. Such a state was, for Hegel, the parliamentary state with a highly developed professional bureaucracy that administered justice fairly and universally. Although Marx shared Hegel's rejection of liberalism's idea that the individual in civil society was the agent of human progress, he rejected Hegel's idealist view of the state, and with it Hegel's entire conception of, and allegiance to, state sovereignty.

For Marx, the agent of historical change was class conflict, not the conflict between sovereign states, as it was for Hegel. Marx argued that the political order was a reflection of the class holding power. Under capitalism, the bourgeoisie created a state that promoted its needs and power. Police power kept the subordinate class of workers in check and was needed to keep order in the context of the misery and destitution caused by capitalism; the state's economic agencies ministered to the capitalist order, providing necessary infrastructure; its judicial system secured the rights not of everyone but of property owners; its wars opened markets and secured investments abroad. In a communist system, Marx argued, the state would become unnecessary: eliminate class conflict and the need for a coercive apparatus would likewise disappear. Sovereignty, then, for Marx was a myth, a form of false consciousness; that is, it led people to believe their society was rational, fair, and free when it was in reality a historical creation that served the particular interests of the capital-owning class.

Antiliberal and Antisocialist Ideologies

The first to resist liberalism's individualism and progressive rationalism were conservatives, that is, those who defended the monarchical state, the aristocracy, and the established church. In Britain, conservatives rallied behind Edmund Burke (1729–1797), whose Reflections on the Revolution in France (1790) defended the principle of monarchy in general and the British monarchy in particular against the excesses of the French revolution. In France, royalists sought to resurrect the monarchy and to restore the privileged position of the Catholic Church, which they were able to do from 1815 until 1871, except for the brief period of the Second Republic (1848–1851). In the German-speaking kingdoms and principalities, conservatives came to see the state itself as the embodiment of national culture and tradition. 8 Conservatives were no better than the liberals at dealing with the dislocations and social miseries of industrial capitalism.

Conservatives and some workers began to turn to fascist movements, which had arisen in the 1920s in many European states that were suffering the dislocations of capitalist industrialization. Fascism, a word coined from the imperial Roman symbol of authority (a bundle of sticks bound around two axes, or fasces), arose as an ideological antidote to the class warfare called for by socialism. It rejected liberalism because it thought that rational individualism and bourgeois civil society weakened the state. Fascists accepted industrialization and used science and technology to serve the needs of state power. 9 It appealed to those of the population who felt left out and exploited by rapid industrialization: the small farmer, shopkeepers, and some elements of the proletariat. It also drew support from the owners of big businesses and industrialists who were seeking a way to control the proletariat. It called for the creation of a single movement led by a single, charismatic leader possessed of natural gifts of "body and spirit . . . believed to be supernatural, not accessible to everybody."

Varieties of Antiliberal States

Industrial capitalism conditioned the organization and governing practices of states in the twentieth century. All twentieth-century states became more highly centralized and organized, using science to rationalize administration and intensify their role in social control. The organizational form a particular state took depended on its history, especially the way in which challenges emerged to absolutism and liberalism. Two prominent states in the twentieth century explicitly rejected liberalism and dissolved the distinction between the state and civil society; these were the Soviet communist state in Russia and the fascist state in Germany. Our consideration of these two states as antiliberal states takes issue with accounts of "totalitarianism," which ignore how the particular histories of Russian and German state-making have influenced twentieth-century forms of these states.

Russia: A Soviet Communist State

Russia's absolutist past set the conditions that allowed the emergence of the antiliberal Soviet communist state. An absolutist monarchical state had developed around the principality of Muscovy (Moscow), which, with the help of the Orthodox Church, was able to gain independence from the Tartars by the fourteenth century. During the principate of Ivan III the Great (r. 1462–1505), Moscow gained control over the neighboring Russian-speaking principalities, as well as its own nobility, and formed a powerful absolutist state. Centralization continued under Ivan IV, the Terrible (r. 1533–1584), who first used the title czar (Russian for Caesar), and Czar Alexei (r. 1645–1676), who enserfed the Russian peasantry. Peter the Great (r. 1689–1725), an energetic, ruthless, and cruel czar, strengthened Russia's army and navy by borrowing military technology from European states, especially Sweden, Holland, Britain, and France, and by employing western European technical experts in various departments of government. During Peter's reign, the bureaucracy was streamlined and the Orthodox Church was subordinated to the authority of the crown by making it into a governmental department. The state promoted trade, education, literature, science, and the arts. Peter also conquered Ukraine and acquired a stretch of the Baltic coast, where he built his capital city, Sankt Petersburg (St. Petersburg; later Petrograd, then Leningrad in 1924, and back to Sankt Petersburg in 1991).

Russian absolutism was eventually challenged by an emerging intelligentsia, which thought the monarchy stifled creativity, and pushed for a liberal constitutional monarchy. This challenge was encouraged by Russia's defeat in the Crimean War (1853–1856), which undermined the position of those who argued that a tyrannical absolutism was the key to Russia's military successes and future survivability as a state. In response to this agitation and Russia's defeat in the Crimean

War, Czar Alexander II (r. 1855–1881) introduced a number of reforms that he hoped would satisfy the demands of the intellectuals. Alexander abolished serfdom and initiated a system of local self-government under assemblies (zemstvos) chosen by a restricted franchise with limited powers at the provincial and municipal levels. He also reformed the judiciary to make it more independent of the crown, and expanded the freedom of the press and that of academic inquiry at the universities. At the same time, however, the czar's agents prevented Russian workers from creating unions, and ruthlessly crushed strikes. This attempt to impose liberalism from above by an absolutist monarchy collapsed when terrorist activities by revolutionary groups persisted. The czar responded by rolling back his reforms, censoring the press, and clamping down on the universities. These repressive measures only served to antagonize his opponents, who increased their terroristic activities. In 1881 the czar himself was killed by a bomb thrown under his carriage by a group who opposed absolutism.

The Expansion of Russia, 1462–1796

Alexander III (r. 1881–1894), Russia's penultimate czar, believed that more repression was the monarchy's only salvation. Therefore, he clamped down on the discontented even harder than had his father. When he died of natural causes in 1894, he bequeathed to his son, Nicholas II (r. 1894–1917), the most repressive and absolute monarchy in Europe. Industrial development lagged behind the economic powerhouses of Germany, Britain, the United States, and Japan. Much of Russian industry was controlled by foreigners, under contracts with the monarchy, and Russian capitalists often invested their profits abroad. Together, these limited the development of the bourgeoisie, who were portrayed as being in league with the czar as agents of foreign powers. Owing to the ruthlessness of the czar's regime, and the negative view held by many workers and peasants of the bourgeoisie, antiliberal political programs had gained considerable room for development. Thus, the particular version of absolutism that grew in Russia established the conditions that made the experiment with a progressively centralized, communist state possible. The Soviet communist state emerged in the context of World War I (1914–1918) and on the heels of failed attempts to transform a ruthless absolutist state into a liberal state in the second half of the nineteenth and early twentieth centuries. The war devastated Russia, as it did other states in Europe. During 1914–1916, over two million Russian soldiers were killed or wounded. The war imposed a heavy strain on the economy, which was industrially weak compared with other major powers in Europe. The economy eventually collapsed, and strikes broke out in Petrograd in 1916. Troops sent by the czar refused to suppress the strikers, and Nicholas abdicated on March 15, 1917. To develop war industries and to fight the war, much of the population had been mobilized, either as soldiers or as workers in the heavy industries necessary for the war effort.

This politicized the population, especially the urban working classes, which increased in size and importance as elements of the rural peasantry moved to the cities to take industrial jobs.

The absolutist monarchy could not sustain itself in the context of an increasingly politicized population that demanded justification for state policies and even a say in governing. Indeed, after defeat in the RussoJapanese War (1905), the czar experimented with a parliament, called the Duma, which failed. With the Duma, the czar attempted to mediate the maintenance of the old régime with the new demands of middleclass bourgeoisie and the working classes, both of which became mobilized in political parties. Although the Duma was divided into two houses—an upper house appointed by the czar from the nobility, the Orthodox Church, universities, and provincial councils, and a lower house elected from a fairly broad franchise—it failed to contain the political energies provoked by Russia's military losses and an industrializing economy.

The Bolsheviks (meaning majority in Russian), one of the working-class parties led by Vladimir Ilyich Ulyanov (later known by his revolutionary pseudonym Lenin, 1870–1924), took power on November 6, 1917, after a brief attempt by liberals and social democrats to establish a government. Their support came in part from radicals in the working class in important cities such as Moscow and Petrograd. But they drew more general support from other sectors of the population by promising, and delivering, a separate peace with Germany, thus ending Russia's involvement in World War I. The Bolsheviks called for a social and political revolution that would create a society based on equality through collective and national ownership and direction of the economy. All citizens were to have jobs; the nobility was to be abolished and land given to those who worked it; private ownership of industry was to be eliminated along with the vast inequalities of wealth, status, and influence it had produced. In part to respond to counterrevolutionary activity, in part to consolidate power against rival liberal and left factions, and in part to defend against invasions from outside powers (the United States, with British backing, invaded Siberia in 1919), the Bolsheviks established a political structure that consolidated power in the party leadership. The strategy was to penetrate the state apparatus, one of the defining features of the absolutist state, with loyal members of the party.

The party was built on the soviets (committees in Russian), ad hoc groups that sprang up in 1917 in order to coordinate the strikes of the workers, soldiers, and peasants. The Soviets elected representatives to the national councils, which would elect party leadership and set and oversee state policy.

The second national congress in January 1918 established the Central Committee of the Communist Party as the state's chief executive body and promised an impressive list of political and social rights, which were extended only to the working class. 15 In January 1924, after their victory in the civil war and the reconquest of territory originally comprising the Russian Empire, a new constitution was promulgated that extended this state structure into a federal Union of Soviet Socialist Republics (USSR). The supreme governing body was the Congress of Soviets, which was divided into a Council of the Union chosen on the basis of population, and a Council of Nationalities, composed of delegates from each union, autonomous republic, and province.

The Congress of Soviets selected a Presidium, which handled its business between sessions, and a Central Committee, which directed the activities of the federal ministries. Despite having created a formal state structure, real decisional power rested with the Communist Party, especially the Politburo and Central Committee. Decisions were taken according to a procedure known as democratic centralism, which allowed for full discussion of an issue but required absolute obedience to the decision once taken. Democratic centralism established a strategy of state construction that was modernist, that is, based on the same progressive character of science, technology, and rationalism that lay behind industrialization.

Modernists sought a vantage point and vision from which they could see and understand the entire social world as a whole, and put tremendous faith in large-scale organization directed from a central point to manage and coordinate the social world. Rather than persist in situating the agent of progress and modernity in civil society, as twentieth-century states influenced by liberalism did, the Soviet communist state located it in the state apparatus itself. The state would manage progress—scientific, economic, political, social, and moral—directly rather than relying on an independent civil society. Therefore, the entire Soviet economy, except for individual households, was directed and administered by the State Planning Commission for the USSR (GOSPLAN).

GOSPLAN determined production targets, wages, and prices. It determined what consumer goods (refrigerators, cars, clothes, etc.) would be produced, and where they would be produced. The goods produced were sold in state-run stores at prices fixed by the plan. These stores were often out of stock because GOSPLAN emphasized heavy industry and military production at the expense of consumer goods for the individual Soviet citizen. The state also provided a vast array of social and medical services. From the 1920s, Soviet citizens were guaranteed unemployment insurance, free medical care in state-run clinics and hospitals, old-age pensions, and disability pay. Housing, although often in short supply and poorly constructed, was provided at low rents. The political structure of the state together with the modernist ideology allowed the general secretary of the Communist Party to adopt extraordinary power. Iosif Vissarionovich Dzhugashvili (later known by his revolutionary pseudonym Joseph Stalin, 1879–1953), who became secretary-general in a power struggle after Lenin's death in 1924 and held this position until his own death in 1952, ruled the Soviet state with a ruthless despotism reminiscent of the czars.

In 1934, after the assassination of his likely successor, he unleashed a reign of terror over the Soviet Union, lasting until 1938, during which time he purged the Communist Party of the Soviet Union (CPSU) and the army of "unreliable" elements and arrested ordinary citizens for "anti-state" activities. The state secret police became omnipresent. Millions lost their lives by execution or overwork in labor camps in Siberia. 16 Stalin was followed in 1953 by Nikita Krushchev (1894–1971), a reformer who appealed to the humanitarian aims of communism. He was ousted by conservatives in the top organs of the party in 1964 because of his disclosures about Stalin's reign of terror, his pro-consumer, antimilitary policies, and the humiliation caused by his retreat during the Cuban missile crisis. This ushered in approximately 20 years of conservative, bureaucratic rule. Leonid Brezhnev (1906–1982) was designated secretary-general in 1965 and ruled the Soviet Union until his death in 1982. Brezhnev was cautious and conservative and governed in a consensusbuilding bureaucratic style.

During his years as secretary-general the Soviet state became increasingly corrupt, the activities of its political class resembling those of the Mafia. He was replaced in 1982 by Yuri Andropov (1914–1984), who died the following year of cancer. Andropov was followed by Konstantin Chernyenko (1911–1985), who died from emphysema in 1985. In 1985, Mikhail Gorbachev (b. 1931) became what subsequent events would prove to be the Soviet Union's last secretary-general. Gorbachev, who was influenced by the reforms of the Khrushchev years, instituted a comprehensive reform program that included democratization, public openness (glasnost), and restructuring (perestroika). Restructuring involved a radical decentralization of control and management of the economy to the level of factories and limited private ownership of retail stores and services. By democratization, Gorbachev meant reducing the monopoly over political power held by the CPSU, which involved the introduction, in 1989, of free elections for some seats in a new national legislature called the All-Union Congress of Peoples' Deputies. Public openness meant ending censorship of the media and arts.

His strategy was to introduce a civil society independent of the state while maintaining the political monopoly of the CPSU. This strategy unleashed powerful social forces that ripped the Soviet state apart in 1991. Disengaging civil society from the party apparatus left the way open for numerous possibilities. One was a nonstatist form of socialism, which anti-Soviet radicals in Eastern Germany and (in the mid-1960s) Czechoslovakia had explored. The Czechoslovakia experiments under Alexander Dubcek (1921–1992) were ruthlessly suppressed by Soviet armies in 1968. Western European and, especially, U.S. intervention in post-Soviet Russia has led to another possible trajectory: a liberal state with a civil society dominated by a capitalist economy fed largely by foreign capital and directed by international financial organizations. It is certainly possible that others will emerge.

Germany: A Fascist State

Although Germany developed an antiliberal state in the twentieth century, it did so out of a very different geostrategic position and according to a different history of state formation from that of Russia. However, several similarities exist: both states absorbed civil society and in both the state came to be identified with a single political party. Also, both committed unspeakable cruelties against their subject populations and those in neighboring territories whom they defined as enemies. But the German fascist state embodied a personalized rule driven by an ideology of ethnic purity and exclusion, which looked to the past for its identity and glory.

The fascists rejected the present in favor of an eternal past, whereas the Bolsheviks tried to remake the present into a more rational and egalitarian future. The particular history of absolutism and liberalism in the formation of the German state set the terms for the emergence of the fascist state in the 1930s. Most important was the dominance of Brandenburg-Prussia, one of a multiplicity of small city-states, minor kingdoms, duchies, and principalities that had come into existence in the German-speaking area of Europe since the time of Charlemagne's Holy Roman Empire. By the seventeenth century, Prussia, under the leadership of a powerful monarchy descended from the last grand master of the Teutonic Knights, Albrecht von Hohenzollern, and a landowning military aristocracy called the Junkers, became dominant by building a powerful absolutist state. In Prussia, like nowhere else in Europe, war made the territorial state and the state, once formed, made war. Prussia, a German-speaking tribal area that had been forcibly Christianized by the Teutonic Knights, did not evolve as England had into a state dominated by its parliament. Surrounded by strong neighbors—Sweden to the north, Russia to the east, and France to the southwest—and lacking protective geographical features such as mountain ranges, marshlands, or open ocean, the Prussians built an efficient military machine in support of a strong, centralized state. The relation of the landed nobility to the state also made possible their unconditional military service. As one historian put it: "Nowhere did the cult of mechanical military obedience . . . so come to permeate the landowning class."

The first attempt to build such a state was taken during the Thirty Years' War when Friedrich Wilhelm, the Great Elector (r. 1640–1688), imposed a tax to support a small army without the approval of the Ständestaat. Members of the Ständestaat, the Prussian estates, who disapproved, were arrested and imprisoned. After the war, such draconian measures were abandoned and feudal constitutionalism reasserted itself. The second attempt, and the decisive one, was taken during the First Northern War (1655– 1660), which involved Poland, Sweden, and Prussia, when Friedrich Wilhelm was able to persuade the Ständestaat to agree to a standing army. As the war progressed, he proclaimed his right to raise taxes without the approval of the Ständestaat and to use his army to collect them. Under Friedrich III (r. 1688– 1713) and Friedrich Wilhelm I (r. 1713–1740), known as the drillmaster of Europe, the crown continued to strengthen itself against the Ständestaat, which declined in power and importance.

The Hanseatic League and the Teutonic Knights

The decline of the Ständestaat was paralleled by the rise of the king's bureaucracy and increased centralization. The major institution in this process of centralization was the Generalkriegskommissariat, or General War Commission, which came to control all aspects of the recruitment and maintenance of the army. It created a three-tiered administrative structure that penetrated local government and was run from a central office in Berlin, the capital of Prussia. It collected taxes, administered justice, and controlled the police. Under the Generalkriegskommissariat, Prussia was gradually militarized. The Junkers formed the officer class and their peasants were forced into the army. The harshness of the state-building process in Prussia was aggravated because the region was economically backward and the population small. The economy was one of large estates owned by the Junker aristocracy upon which a multitude of landless peasants scratched a living from very poor soils. There was almost no bourgeoisie. Unity and identity with the state were fostered through respect for military virtues: obedience, discipline, and heroism.

Victories in battle justified continued heavy taxation to support a strong military. The building of a strong, centralized, militarized state and the concomitant glorification of martial values inclined Prussia toward aggressive actions against surrounding states. Under Friedrich the Great (r. 1740– 1786), the Prussian state fought and defeated the Austrians, Poles, Czechs, and the Russians. In 1806 Napoleon invaded the German-speaking kingdoms and principalities. He defeated the Austrians at Austerlitz (1805) and the Prussians at Jena (1806). Within 18 months, all the other smaller German principalities were defeated and occupied by French troops. The French Revolution had stimulated the development of liberalism in Germany, and, at first, many intellectuals and liberals welcomed Napoléon's invasion, which they viewed as an agent of progress against the absolutist regime. Note, however, that German liberalism was distinctive, and critical of its British and French versions.

As was the case with British and French liberals, Immanuel Kant (1724–1804), the most important German philosopher of the Enlightenment, opposed the absolutist state, but in a way that argued for a cosmopolitan republican state governed by the rule of law. Kant viewed reason as dictating moral imperatives and laws to men and women rather than seeing it as primarily the instrumental calculation of self-interests. For Kant, reason did not guarantee that states would be governed by the rule of law and would eschew arbitrary power, but it opened the possibility of a state that would function positively within a moral society. Therefore, Kant's liberalism was more sensitive to the role of the state in modern life, even if it considered the state as something of a Faustian bargain (i.e., a pact with the devil).

Brandenburg-Prussia, 1440–1806

The defeat and six-year occupation of the German states by the French stimulated the creation in 1815 of a confederation of 39 of these entities. It was reasoned that defeat and occupation by a foreign power could be avoided if German states were united into a single state. The idea of a unified German state was also fed by the historical and political philosophy that developed in Enlightenment Germany. Having rejected the individualism of English and French liberalism, German political philosophy contained a strong romanticist streak in which the social order was viewed as a living, organic unity in time and space that fed on a common language and common folk traditions, as in the work of Johann Gottfried von Herder (1774–1803), who propounded the idea that different cultures provided different answers to life's central questions.

Herder taught that the desire to belong to a culture was a basic human need. Over the next century, the German state came to be associated with its own unique German kultur, or culture. Liberalism was associated by many Germans with foreign states, especially Britain and France, and was seen as having been imposed on German culture. During the 1840s, the demand for more than a confederation was raised by German liberals, who were increasingly supported by the bourgeoisie. The overthrow of the monarchy and the establishment of the Second French Republic (1848–1851) by French liberals touched off popular disturbances in Vienna, the capital of Austria, and Berlin, as well as in other German cities.

Too weak to suppress these uprisings, the rulers of these states agreed to the liberals' demand for the election of a constituent assembly, which was given the task of writing a constitution for a unified German state. This effort eventually failed because of disputes about which German-speaking entities were to be included. Prussian victories in wars against Denmark (1864), Austria (1866), and France (1870–1871) assured Prussia's status as the most powerful German-speaking state. Prussia forcefully brought together less powerful German-speaking states into an empire led by Wilhelm I (r. 1861–1888) of Prussia, who proclaimed himself its kaiser (Caesar in German), or emperor. Although the empire-wide parliament, called the Reichstag, was elected on the basis of universal male suffrage, placating the liberal demand for representation, the real decisions affecting the functioning of the empire were made in the Bundesrat, which was composed of delegates from the länd (state) governments and presided over by the chancellor. The Reichstag was limited to dealing with nonessentials.

The creation of universal male suffrage stimulated the development of German political parties. The first party to appear was the Social Democratic Party (SPD), which was founded in 1875 and became officially socialist in 1891. The SPD grew very rapidly. In 1877 it received nine percent of the vote cast for the Reichstag; by 1890 its share of the vote was 20 percent; and by 1903 it had soared to 32 percent, which made it the largest party in the German Empire. By 1907, the SPD counted over one million dues-paying members and had a close relationship with Germany's trade unions, whose leaders had assumed key positions within the party. Otto von Bismarck (1815–1898), chancellor of Prussia from 1862 and the empire's chancellor under Wilhelm, attempted to suppress the party, though without success owing to the party's disciplined political organization and its strong support among the proletariat. Therefore, he attempted to attract workers away from the SPD by passing a series of laws that met the SPD's demands for the health, safety, and retirement of workers. In 1883 he passed a law that insured workers against sickness; in 1884 a law was passed that insured against accidents; and in 1889 a law provided for disability insurance and old-age pensions. Bismarck's strategy did not work, however, and workers continued to flock to the SPD.

The German Empire created by Bismarck was defeated in World War I, which led to the transformation of Germany into a liberal constitutional state called the Weimar Republic (1919–

1936). The Weimar Republic was imposed by the Allies upon a Germany that was deeply divided between liberals and socialists, who supported it, and conservatives, who preferred the old imperial state. This division made it difficult for the Weimar Republic to govern effectively and prevented it from dealing with the serious economic problems Germany began to experience in the 1920s: soaring inflation and massive unemployment brought on by the excessive war reparations that had been imposed on Germany by the Allies, and the worldwide economic depression. Saddled with an alien state, Germans began to be drawn in large numbers to parties that sought to destroy the Weimar Republic. One of these parties was the German Communist Party, which had been formed in 1919 by radical members of the SPD who supported the Russian Revolution and favored a dictatorship of the proletariat. The other was the National Socialist German Workers' Party (NSDAP) or Nazi Party, led by Adolf Hitler (1889–1945), which was a virulently racist and anti-Semitic fascist party. In the 1932 elections the Nazis became the largest party in the Reichstag. The Nazis and the Communists, who had come in third, formed an anti–Weimar Republic majority, which made it impossible for the prorepublic parties to form a stable government. As Germany's economic crisis continued, widespread rioting and street clashes between Nazis and Communists became a regular occurrence. Encouraged by conservative parties and many agrarian and industrial leaders, the president of the republic, Paul von Hindenburg (1925–1934), named Adolf Hitler chancellor on January 30, 1933. Once in power, Hitler proceeded to overthrow the Weimar Republic from within and erect in its stead an antiliberal and antisocialist state (the Third Reich) ruled by a "Master Race" of Aryans, united by its love for the Fatherland, who promised to protect Germany from the evil machinations of "lesser" races (especially Jews), "decadent" Western democracies, and "subhuman" Marxists. The Nazi Party did not recognize the constitution or any law save the will of the Führer. The Nazis destroyed the federal structure of the Weimar Republic and centralized all political and administrative power in Berlin, the capital of the Third Reich. Jews were expelled from the civil service and Nazi Party members were placed in key administrative positions.

The Reichtag was abolished and land governments were merged with national ministries. The governors of the länder, which were now, in effect, administrative units of the central state, were Nazi gauleiters (party leaders) appointed by Hitler. The judiciary was purged of "non-Aryan" judges and centralized under the Reich ministry of justice. Special People's Courts, dominated by Nazi Party members, were established to try those accused of political crimes. A vast secret police network, which included the Geheimestaatspolizei (GESTAPO) and the Schutzstaffel (SS), was created.

Under the Nazis, the state massively intervened into civil society. Hitler developed numerous public works projects in order to create jobs and achieve full employment; married couples with children were given family allowances; free holidays were provided for low-paid workers at state-run resorts; and factories were placed under state direction, if not ownership, as was agriculture.

As fascism considered the economy to be at the service of the state, workers and employers were required to join a single corporation called the National Labor Front, controlled by the Nazi Party, which regulated working conditions and wages. Independent unions were abolished, and strikes were outlawed. Professionals, such as lawyers and doctors, were required to join guildlike organizations under Nazi Party control. 26 In order to create the "Master Race," the Nazis instituted a policy of sterilization and extermination of what they considered to be undesirable elements of the German population: the incurably ill, the feebleminded, homosexuals, Gypsies, and especially Jews. Jews and others were systematically rounded up and put into work or extermination camps, where millions died, subjected to scientifically sophisticated techniques of mass murder and genocide. The roundups and exterminations were so routinized and bureaucratized that they appeared to the participants as "normal." In her famous accounts of the trial of Adolph Eichmann (1906–1962), a former camp commandant who escaped justice until 1963, Hannah Arendt described the process as the "banality of evil."

Hitler's belief that Germany needed Lebensraum (living space), which he sought to get from, in his view, the "racially inferior" Slavic peoples to the east, proved to be the Nazi state's undoing. In 1939 Hitler invaded Poland, an act of aggression that started World War II. Germany's defeat by the Allies in 1945 brought an end to the Nazi fascist state. After the war Germany was occupied and partitioned by the victors into zones controlled by the United States, France, Britain, and the Soviet Union. The Soviet Union was given land from Polish territory in the east for which Poland was compensated by giving it German territory, and from which Germans were expelled. Berlin, which was well within the Soviet zone, was itself divided into United States, French, British, and Soviet zones of occupation. In 1949, the British, French, and U.S. occupiers merged their zones into a new liberal democratic state, the Federal Republic of Germany (West Germany), with its capital in Bonn. In response, the Soviets transformed their zone of occupation into a new communist state called the German Democratic Republic (East Germany), with its capital in East Berlin. Thus, two rival German states existed until 1990, when the German Democratic Republic was absorbed by the Federal Republic and a single German state was created.

Summary

In the nineteenth century the relationship of the state to key features of modernity, especially industrialization, came under question. The traditional ways in which absolutism and liberalism had institutionalized sovereignty did not permit the newly industrialized state to play the role it was increasingly called upon to play. In this chapter, we discussed the emergence of antiliberal forms of the modern territorial state that abolished civil society in order to help the state meet the challenges posed by industrialization. The next chapter examines the emergence of another form of state, the managerial state, which sought to relegitimate liberalism and capitalism in light of the increasing role of the state in modern life.

8

THE MANAGERIAL STATE: SOVEREIGNTY

Neither the Russian communist state, the German fascist state, nor other antiliberal states such as Musollini's Italy, Franco's Spain, and Salazar's Portugal, rejected industrialization. Although all rejected capitalism in name, all retained key features of it. Fascists did not eliminate private ownership, and major corporations continued to play significant roles in fascist states. When the Soviet Union eliminated private ownership and many aspects of a competitive market, it retained key elements of the capitalist organization of work, including the concept of wage labor; it was the state rather than the market, however, that set wage rates and production targets. In this chapter we examine a form of the state that retains explicit commitments to capitalism and liberalism, although significantly modified and subordinated to a new form of state management. The formal organizational characteristics, internal operations, and basic purpose of the state have converged dramatically in the late twentieth century.

Indeed, a singular form, which we call the managerial state, seems to be the most prominent form of the state in the late twentieth century. While managerial states continue to rely on a liberal ideology to frame citizen understandings of the government and social world, this ideology does not adequately describe the character of state power and thereby hides the operations of state power, making it appear that managerial states either have no state at all or have one that is very weak and that "intervenes" in a civil society. Liberal ideology assumes that a private sphere—the economy, the family, the individual—is prior to the state. But as we will show in our discussions below of Fordism and the "consumerization" of citizenship, the relations of state and civil society, of public and private, are themselves constituted by the techniques, especially bureaucratization, through which the state promotes order. The managerial state continuously monitors, organizes, controls, and regulates the social, economic, and political activities within it. Unlike antiliberal states, the managerial state maintains the liberal distinction between the state and civil society. It does not seek to absorb the economy and national culture directly and completely into the state's bureaucratic apparatus. But the distinction between state and civil society in managerial states is a tenuous and fragile one because the state diffuses its power throughout civil society. In the words of one scholar, the managerial state "assumes responsibility for the entire condition of contemporary society—the condition of the air, the food and water; the relationship its citizens must be involved in; the habits they develop; their education; their health; and their ability to make a living."

RATIONALIZATION AND THE STATE

Early in the twentieth century, states began to develop mechanisms and strategies to gain some control over the contingencies of industrialization. One way to do so was to develop a knowledge of industrialization and its consequences; such knowledge facilitated direction and control. New social sciences—economics, sociology, political science—developed based on the idea that industrialization and societies in general comprised systems or structures; that is, they were wholes that were more than the sum of their parts. The individual parts could be understood and made somewhat predictable by understanding the laws of the whole. Systems came to be seen as coordinated through instrumental rationality ; that is, reason came to be seen as the efficient application of means, or the invention of new ones, to a given end. The end was given by the nature of the system: war/victory; economy/prosperity; polity/social order.

Viewing what were complex sets of contingent events as integral wholes that could be planned gave to those in power a new sense that the effects of industrialization could be mitigated and their outcomes controlled. In short, the rationalization of knowledge about politics and society helped to make the managerial state possible. What this meant for politics was that the state came to be seen as the coordinator of all of the complex systems that were said to compose society, such as the economy, polity, class structure, and value system. Intervention in each subsystem was limited to coordinating them with the others in managing the whole of the state. The greatest theorist, and critic, of the way this new form of knowledge transformed the state was the German historian, legal scholar, and sociologist Max Weber (1864–1920). Weber saw the rationalization of the state as inevitable because of the breakdown of the status-based solidarity of feudalism and the emergence of the industrialized and urbanized states of the late nineteenth century. The most important aspect of this development for Weber was the advance of bureaucracy because of its purely technical superiority over other methods of administration. Bureaucracy broke down the complex functions of organizations, such as governments and large corporations, into individual decisions, all coordinated in terms of laws and the instrumental rationality of the whole.

According to Weber, compared to other types of social organization, a bureaucracy is the most efficient means of exercising control over a large number of human beings. Bureaucracy, from the French word bureau, meaning desk or office, refers to the sum of individuals who are engaged in administering the public services that must be rendered each day if a state is to survive. The bureaucracy was developed by medieval monarchs in order to extract directly the men, money, and matériel necessary to fight wars and maintain a standing army. The first administrators, or civil servants, were from the king's household—his steward, reeves, chancellor, and constable—who collected his revenue, provided his justice, and maintained his peace. Gradually, two parallel sets of hierarchically organized institutions (financial and legal), staffed by individuals trained in the law and accounting, came into being. Within these institutions clerks and scribes developed and preserved routine ways of drafting orders and issuing instructions. Thus, a group of individuals appeared who spent their entire working lives in the service of the king. The development of a staff of full-time judges, lawyers, tax collectors, clerks, and scribes gave the medieval king not only the ability to rule his realm directly without the assistance of the aristocracy but also the ability to bypass the estates. Initially, those who occupied positions within the developing administrative structures regarded their offices as private property that they owned outright, derived income from, and bequeathed to their heirs.

In other words, offices were hereditary. During the nineteenth century a gradual rationalization of the administrative organization in every major European state took place, and the idea that such offices were private property gave way to the notion that they were public positions to be filled on the basis of ability and training. This rationalization involved organizational reform and the creation of a merit system for recruiting administrators. The novel idea developed that all of these offices and functions were related to one another in a complex system, a bureaucracy, and that state sovereignty was, in part at least, dependent on the ability to coordinate and manage these complex systems of relations. For this, a scientific knowledge of the laws of bureaucratic systems was necessary. For Weber the bureaucratic system was efficient because it rationalized human interactions in the following ways. First, it depersonalized them; that is, it treated all interactions without regard to the personal characteristics of the actors, such as gender, age, race, appearance, and ethnicity.

Second, it neutralized them; that is, it eliminated all emotional feelings of love, hate, desire, envy, and so forth, from nonfamilial human interactions. Third, it universalized them; that is, it disregarded social position, privilege, status, rank, and so on, in personal interactions. Fourth, it qualified them; that is, it eliminated friendship and family connections in interactions involving hiring and promotion. Finally, it organized them; that is, it arranged human interactions into a series of offices and roles with clear lines of domination and subordination between them. To Weber, bureaucratization and rationalization were systems of social control whose historical roots reached back to the Protestant Reformation. Although he was interested in questions of why they developed, much of his work explained how they worked as systems of domination, not why they came about. Although Weber's use of a methodology of ideal types may have led him to overstate the coherence and consistency of the bureaucratic system, and to ignore ways in which bureaucracies drew on noninstrumentally rational forms (e.g., personal loyalty, social prejudices), his idea that rationalization and bureaucratization constituted forms of subjectivity distinctive to the modern state and society, and legitimated the state on a new basis, is extremely important. The modern political subject has come to be constituted through the rationalizing systems of bureaucratic domination. People in the managerial state abhor rank, honorific preferences, and privilege because they come to know who they are as political subjects through the institutions of the state.

The managerial state, then, appeared to represent progress toward a political order free of domination because it was based on the rule of law and liberal ideals of individual rights and freedoms, but it came to exercise its control through familiar institutions and routine practices. In other words, the subject population of the managerial state came to accept domination by the state and willingly complied with it insofar as the state was perceived as legal and rational—that is, had been constructed by some rational procedure of which the subject was himself or herself a part. This was a far cry from the medieval state in which domination was accepted by reference to the personal status or position of the order-giver. Weber was convinced that the rationalization and bureaucratization of both state and civil society were necessary and inevitable. However, rather than a new realm of freedom, as liberals saw these processes, they represented for Weber a new mode of domination that gave the state, and other bureaucratized and rationalized organizations such as economic corporations, tremendous powers of control. According to Weber, modernizing the state and society comes with significant costs.

While rationalization eliminates personal and emotional elements such as love, hate, and desire from human interactions, it also results in widespread disenchantment and alienation manifested in various kinds of antibureaucratic activities and resistance, ranging from grumbling about "red tape" to violent attacks on administrative offices. Rationalization also separates means and ends, so that the determination of the latter was removed from rational judgment. For Weber, this amounted to the impoverishment of human spirituality and moral life. In a famous essay he argued that modern science, for all its methodological sophistication and explanatory power, could never justify the choices it had to make about the ends to which society ought to use its knowledge. The spiritual and moral guidance human beings once took from religion and culture was thoroughly disempowered by the rationalization and disenchantment of the world. What was left was an "iron cage," a neat, highly structured, law-governed, objective order that, by seeking to eliminate contingency, eliminated much of the human spirit that made life worth living.

The Consumerization of the Citizen

As the managerial state has expanded in the twentieth century, individual citizens have increasingly come to be treated less as bearers of rights, as in liberal states, and more as efficient contributors to and consumers of the outcomes of bureaucratic state practices. In the managerial state, the political consciousness of the citizen becomes that of the rational consumer, who looks at the state through the lens of a utilitarian calculus of costs and benefits. Taxes, for example, come to be seen less as necessary contributions to the public good and more as the price of government services. The managerial state becomes the "producer" of public "goods" ("good" slipping in meaning between a normative "good"—what should be done—and a "good" in the sense of a commodity) that are "sold" to the citizenry through the industrialized mass media. One of the most important political "goods" that the state "sells" to the public is a set of images of a homogeneous national identity sufficient to establish the individualized consumer/citizen as part of a unified, political, and moral community.

As we saw, in the liberal state political information circulated in a public sphere consisting of newspapers, magazines, clubs, scientific societies, commercial book publishing, and so on. Although the liberal public sphere was never as egalitarian or rational as it is often presented, liberal citizenship presupposed the public circulation of ideas and knowledge that managerial states transform in important ways. Although information continues to circulate in similar ways in managerial states, technology and the industrialization of media industries and the concentration of ownership have reconstituted the relation of citizenship to the public sphere. Political information is increasingly managed and mediated by (1) political parties, which are interested primarily in winning elections; (2) industrial capitalist media, which are interested primarily in profit; and (3) state bureaucracies, which are concerned with producing rational outcomes. In the liberal state of the late nineteenth and early twentieth centuries, political information and imagery were mediated by political parties in which organized elites set out interpretations of the state's needs and shared goals according to class affiliation, political ideology, or other group identities. As the industrialization of the mass media has increased during the twentieth century—especially through radio and television, which reach subjects in the "privacy" of their own homes—political parties have declined as mediators of political information and interpreters of political needs.

With the decline of parties, the public character of political discussion and debate has also declined. People in managerial states receive their information and interpretations of politics as spectators outside the forums for political discussion and debate, such as union or party meetings or civic organizations, through which citizens used to receive much of their political information. In the managerial state, political information and images are produced and circulated as industrial products like soap and cars. To be successful as capitalist corporations, television and newspapers must reach wide audiences and, therefore, seek to present images and information tailored to the "average" consumer of information. Increasingly, the attitude prevails that one can be a good citizen and gain the knowledge one needs to vote by "keeping up with the news," but not by actively engaging in political activity and debate; this attitude has routinized the citizen as a consumer and has caused political values and ideologies to become merely images to be consumed rather than subjects of political discussion and debate. The tenuousness and fragility of the distinction between the state and civil society are apparent in this industrialized construction of the citizen as consumer of media-presented information. The media are both public and private.

Although the state does not own and directly control the media, it does intervene to limit and at times direct the way in which information is presented. This is clearest in times of war, as was the case recently with the U.S. military's manipulation of information about the Gulf War. Election campaigns that take place primarily through the media adopt the same kinds of strategies for controlling the images of candidates, devising and strategically placing advertisements, and controlling the timing of statements. The aim of these efforts is to manage the electorate by carefully regulating, according to the expert knowledge of professional media consultants, the images and information it consumes. This new language of citizenship appears to reinvigorate a republican political imaginary insofar as information about government and society is made more widely available in the public media. But this mode of publicity actually deepens the passivity of citizenship, even as it allows some citizens to become more well-informed about public affairs. The language of citizenship in managerial states maintains the appearance of popular sovereignty while allowing room for the autonomous operations of bureaucratic and managerial structures under conditions in which the mediations of citizenship and power are opaque to most citizens.

One is either "inside" the system, the "insider" being a government official, a lobbyist, or some other functionary privy to and presumed to be knowledgeable about the inner workings of the system, or "outside," a consumer of the outcomes of a system that appears as an opaque box. Moreover, even those inside the state are subordinated to the logic of spectatorship. In other words, in the managerial state, citizenship is constructed in a new way. Most citizens must be outside the governing apparatus of the state for it to function smoothly according to the criteria of bureaucratic and instrumental rationality. Citizens who do manage to move inside participate only in those specific areas in which they can claim some special competence or some proprietary interest, such as lobbyists and "special interest groups." The managerial state must unify this distribution of insiders and outsiders, making them all appear as members of a single, territorial community. It does so through association with the "nation," a ritualized performance that invokes an abstract, imagined community created through public imagery in the mass media.

Corporatization of the Capitalist Economy

Perhaps the most important change that undermined the social conditions of the liberal state and encouraged the formation of managerial states was the reorganization of the capitalist firm, which brought about a shift in the form of capitalist individualism. Prior to the second half of the nineteenth century, the dominant form of organization of capital was the individual firm, that is, the business owned by an individual, a family, or a small partnership. In most cases, those who owned the business participated directly in it. From the point of view of enhancing profits in an industrial system, however, this individualist organization was quite restrictive. It limited the amount of capital that could be invested to that owned by the individual owner or family. It also entailed considerable risks for the owner: if the business went bankrupt or was sued, the personal assets of the individual owners were at risk. By the end of the nineteenth century, first in the United States and then throughout the industrial capitalist world, the individualist entrepreneur was replaced by the corporation. Incorporation was a highly useful tool that overcame the limits of individual or family ownership. Unlike the latter, the "corporation as a form severs the direct link between capital and its individual owner." 14 Risk of failure and loss of capital were now borne not by the owners but by the corporation. This made possible vast combinations of capital. One cultural historian of the post–Civil War United States describes the new economic form of capitalism this way:

The corporation embodied a legally sanctioned fiction, that an association of people constituted a single entity which might hold property, sue and be sued, enter contracts, and continue in existence beyond the lifetime or membership of any of its participants. The association itself was understood as strictly contractual, not necessarily comprised of people acquainted with each other or joined by any common motive other than profit seeking.

He goes on to assess the cultural significance of the idea of the corporation as follows:

With the corporate device as its chief instrument, business grew increasingly arcane and mysterious, spawning new roles intermediary between capital and labor, in middle management, accounting, legal departments, public relations, advertising, marketing, sales: the entire apparatus of twentieth-century corporate life was developed in these years and clouded the public perception of the typical acts of business. Organization and administration emerged as major virtues, along with obedience and loyalty. At the same time the rhetoric of success continued to hail the self-made man as the paragon of free labor, even as the virtues of that fictive character grew less and less relevant.

The idea of the corporation—the large hierarchical and bureaucratically organized combination of capital— would become the standard organization of private property and production during the twentieth century in managerial states; in some, however, the corporations were direct arms of the state and in others they were owned and managed by private capital. In many states, corporations were owned, either entirely or in significant parts, by foreign capital.

The corporation allowed for ever greater concentrations of capital, which dramatically increased productive capacity. During the first half of the twentieth century a new social system emerged in which workers were increasingly seen as consumers of the products of the industrial economy. Workers increasingly came to be seen as individual consumers whose identities as human beings were tied to the products they consumed, as participants in a consumer culture. In the early twentieth century the industrialist Henry Ford (1863–1947), founder of the Ford Motor Company, pioneered a new social system for an industrial economy. This system has become known as Fordism, and describes the network of political, economic, and social relations that dominated managerial states increasingly from the 1930s to the 1970s.

In his automobile factories, Ford improved techniques for mass production to the point where he could produce large quantities of identical automobiles at greatly reduced cost. The first automobile to be so produced was the Model T, which was the first "world car," a standardized product that would appeal to "ordinary" people everywhere. Of course, the "ordinary" person who needed or wanted his or her own automobile had to be created, in part through advertising but also through changing the rules of industrial society. Ford realized that he could improve profits by selling these cars to the very workers who produced them. This meant paying higher than subsistence wages, contrary to the norm of nineteenth-century capitalist firms. In effect, Fordism amounted to a class compromise in which workers accepted loss of control in the factories in return for sufficient wages to live a comfortable, private life. Of course, this only applied to workers in some factories and in industries in which higher wages could be wrested from often intransigent employers. Fordism was in practice inequitable, creating divisions within the working class. Nevertheless, after World War II, and in part because of the war, the Fordist reconstitution of the worker as consumer became the norm that determined the aspirations of even the poorest workers. For liberals, Fordism came to be seen as a worthy system of industrial relations, which the state should and could manage by manipulating economic policies. To Marxist critics, Fordism, although it produced certain isolated gains for some workers, entrenched the alienation of the industrial capitalist system deep into social life and relegitimized the domination of the bourgeoisie over industrial society.

In the Fordist compromise, workers became consumers who compensated for the loss of control over their work with consumption of material goods during leisure time. Increasingly, workers would be represented by labor unions—representation that led to increased wages, safer and better working conditions, and a shorter workweek. Unions and workers would turn to the state to guarantee the gains won in organized labor struggles. In return for legalizing unions and for the state's acceptance of its role as guarantor of labor's hard-won gains, unions gave up the aspirations of socialist and more radical workers' movements to redirect investments toward social needs rather than corporate profit, or democratizing control over the factories. Essentially, mid-twentieth-century labor unions, especially in the United States, accepted the class compromise of Fordism, and organized the patriotism and support of workers for a form of the state that managed the Fordist industrial system. Fordism became entrenched in the U.S. economy during the 1930s as an antidote to the Great Depression, and in the 1940s as a facilitator of the massive war production of World War II, during which vast numbers of people had participated as either workers or soldiers. After World War II, the consumer aspect of Fordism became deeply entrenched. This was in part for the economic reason of absorbing the tremendous productive capacity that the war had produced, and in part for political reasons: to control and pacify workers and soldiers whose expectations had been heightened by participation in the war. The state came to function as the instrumentally rational guarantor of the Fordist class compromise and the consumer society.

Gendering the Management of Economic Prosperity

One result of Fordism was that responsibility for ensuring the well-being and continued prosperity of the economy was transferred to the state. The working class looked to the state to cement the gains it had won through unionization and collective bargaining with private capital. Private capital looked to the state to oversee the general conditions of accumulation of wealth in the national economy, managing the money supply through its treasury and central bank, regulating the stock market, ensuring competition by regulating monopolies, and providing or guaranteeing investments in infrastructure such as roads, ports, electrical grids, and telephone systems. Of particular importance was the state's role in providing general security and stability through the police, the courts, the prisons, and the social services (at home) and through military interventions (abroad) to stabilize opportunities for investment and trade. Fordism also depended on a particular division of work between men and women. Early on, Ford required that workers in his automobile factories maintain a stable, healthy, and traditional family life. By this he meant that women would care for the children and do housework while men worked in the factory for wages (of course, women were not paid for their work), and that the family would go to church regularly and would avoid alcohol and drugs.

Antisocial or disruptive behavior, even in "private" life, could be cause for dismissal from the factory. Although unions were able to fight and defeat many of the social restrictions placed on male workers, they left the division of labor between men and women intact. The family, then, played a distinctive role in Fordist economies and in the regulation of the industrial citizen. It provided the "private" infrastructure of emotional support and organized consumption that kept men happy at work and, above all, self-disciplined. That is, they were disciplined to support the family, a responsibility that they accepted because of the services women provided for them outside the factory by taking care of household work, raising children, planning family consumption, and providing sexual and emotional satisfaction. World War II, paradoxically, deepened this divide; managing the division of labor between men and women became an important part of the managerial state. This was paradoxical given that during the war, as men went to fight, women took up industrial jobs. Rosie the Riveter became the symbol of a generation of women who ably demonstrated that they possessed the strength, intelligence, and character to do the "hard work" of mass industrial production, despite the contention of Fordist ideology that they were naturally unsuited to do so.

After the war, government programs guaranteed returning soldiers their old jobs and required women to return to "private" life. These programs not only managed the supply of workers by ensuring against the massive unemployment that might be expected to follow the demobilization of millions of soldiers, but they also reinstituted the structure of Fordist discipline. Government programs to aid education also helped manage the labor supply, giving male workers the skills for the next generation of industrial jobs by providing ex-soldiers with grants to attend college in programs such as the G.I. Bill in the United States. The return to domesticity in the larger culture of the 1950s and 1960s can then be seen as a strategy within the context of managerial states, which blended elements of state and civil society together in a diffuse network of regulatory power. To accomplish their objectives, twentieth-century managerial states have come to rely increasingly on experts in economics, law, psychology, organizational science, and various substantive areas of public policy. For women this meant the promotion of scientific approaches to "home economics" and the inclusion of this subject for girls in public schools. This has led not only to the retaining of professionals and experts within a state's own bureaucracy, but also to the development of close interconnections between experts in private industries and in universities, whether public or private. Lawyers still dominate in government positions, as Max Weber argued they would in modern states, but to manage late capitalist industrial economies, states have generated networks of experts and bodies of expertise that cut across the boundaries of state and civil society.

Managing National Economic Life

Under some circumstances, the managerial state would intervene directly in the industrial capitalist economy by nationalizing industries that failed as private enterprises but provided the public goods the system as a whole needed (for example, railroads and utilities); by subjecting private corporations to environmental regulations; by providing social services; and by energizing the economy with spending on the military. In some cases the state would manage the economy indirectly by adding incentives and disincentives to the tax code or by passing tariffs or subsidies to favor some industries or forms of investment over others. The specific strategies used depended on situational factors in specific states, such as the history of bureaucratization within them; the roles of war and the military in the development of state institutions; the strength, ideology, and character of political parties and unions; and the relative position of the national economy in the world economy. Even states that continued a strong ideology of economic liberalism, and professed allegiance to nonintervention by the state in markets, developed into managerial states. In France and Germany some of the institutions created to direct mercantilist economies provided fertile ground for the growth of managerialism.

In both cases, the state took responsibility for developing the infrastructure and pioneered national systems of education, in part to produce well-trained civil servants with managerial and engineering expertise. Both France and Germany have gone through periods when certain industries were nationalized, that is, taken over and managed by the state. In the nineteenth century, the German state continued to industrialize by importing British machinery, then the most advanced in the world, and British technicians to train German workers in their proper operation. During the period of the German Empire (1871–1918), industries owned by the nobility, such as breweries in Bavaria, porcelain factories in Meissen and Berlin, and cigarette manufacturing facilities in Strasbourg, were nationalized.

Agriculture and mining also came under state regulation and control during this period. After World War II, the West German state denationalized certain industries, relaxed economic controls, and gave market forces (supply and demand) more significance. Nonetheless, the West German state continued, and continues, to intervene very actively into economic life. Subsidies were made available in order to encourage postwar reconstruction, especially in housing. Tax exemptions were given in order to increase savings and reduce personal consumption. The state subsidized the production of fertilizer and controlled certain agricultural prices by regulating imports and exports. In general, the approach was and continues to be state intervention in order to manage market forces to achieve specific ends. In France, nationalization occurred after World War II and continued into the 1980s, when U.S.- and Britishinspired neoliberalism began to influence even the socialists away from state ownership of industry and toward more indirect forms of market management using tax and fiscal policies. In the late 1940s and early 1950s the railroads, electricity production, telephone communications, petroleum production, aircraft manufacturing, and some automobile manufacturing were taken over by the state because state ownership was seen as necessary for economic development or, as in the case of the Renault automobile manufacturer, a punishment for collaborating with the Vichy régime during the war. After the war, national economic planning was introduced.

It was not until the twentieth century that active state regulation and management of the economy began in Britain. As will be shown in Part 3, during the nineteenth century, Britain dominated the world economy as the strongest and most innovative capitalist economy. Liberal economic policies were a crucial factor in its dominance. During the 1920s, when Britain no longer dominated the world capitalist economy, the price of coal began to be regulated and industries were encouraged by tax-abatement schemes to locate themselves in economically depressed areas. During the 1930s, John Maynard Keynes (1883–1946), an economist teaching at Cambridge University, argued that the Great Depression could be overcome and prevented if the state actively intervened by using monetary and fiscal policy to encourage economic growth. The key to economic growth, he argued, was full employment to be attained by careful management of markets. After World War II, the British state began to nationalize certain industries, such as coal, steel, electricity, and transportation; institute a series of economic development councils that offered technical and financial incentives to key industries; and use Keynesian-inspired monetary and fiscal measures to attain full employment.

Systematic economic planning was introduced in the 1960s with the establishment of the National Economic Development Council (NEDC), which brought together representatives from government, industry, and labor to monitor the performance of the economy, consider plans to foster economic growth, and agree upon methods to improve economic performance. Other measures were taken to improve economic productivity and managerial efficiency. In essence, the British state guides a largely privately owned economy by manipulating market mechanisms. 24 In the United States, where liberalism has also had a significant impact, state management of the economy developed out of different historical conditions than those in Britain. In important ways the growth of managerialism in the United States owes much to direct mobilization for war by a state whose ideology and geographical location inclined it to avoid a permanent large military force, at least until after World War II.

The necessity of mobilizing economic resources in order to fight the Civil War (1860–1865) and reconstruct the South after the war marks the first significant intervention of the American state into the economy. From 1860 to 1877, the state became a major purchaser of iron, textiles, shoes, and meat. The state established and operated its own manufacturing facilities for clothing, pharmaceuticals, foodstuffs, and firearms. The state also instituted the first U.S. income tax, as well as other taxes, including excise, luxury, and inheritance, during this period in order to supplement revenues from customs duties.

Several acts of Congress passed during the Civil War were designed to encourage industrial growth and westward expansion. The Homestead Act of 1862 gave land in the western states to those who were willing to settle and farm it. The Morrill College Act of the same year granted land for the building of universities dedicated to the improvement of agriculture and mining. The Immigration Act of 1864 allowed millions of immigrants to flood into the United States in order to provide labor for the new factories serving its rapidly industrializing economy. The Union Pacific and Central Pacific railroads were founded as federally chartered companies and given land in the West in order to construct a transcontinental railroad. 26 During World War I, the U.S. state intervened in the economy in order to boost the production of war matériel. It regulated industries, imposed price controls, and involved itself in labor disputes. It set up a complex of boards and agencies that mobilized U.S. workers and industry for the war effort. The income tax, which had been abolished after the Civil War, was revived and made permanent with the passage of the Income Tax Amendment in 1913. The War Industries Board regulated industrial production according to wartime needs.

After World War I, the state did not significantly intervene in the economy until the Great Depression of the 1930s. Faced with the collapse of the economy, Franklin D. Roosevelt (1882–1945), who had been elected president in 1932, initiated a program called the New Deal, which sought to revitalize the economy by stimulating aggregate demand through government spending on public works and other types of projects. The National Industrial Recovery Act of 1933 established the National Recovery Administration and the Works Progress Administration, which, by means of price supports for agricultural products, bulk purchasing of manufactures, regulation of credit and interest rates, monetary controls, and jobs programs (which built roads, bridges, dams, schools, libraries, and houses), stimulated the economy to recover from the depression. During World War II, the U.S. state again intervened in the economy in order to mobilize it for the production of war matériel. Throughout the war the executive branch held unfettered control over the economy. The Office of War Mobilization, the Office of Price Administration, and the Office of Economic Stabilization together managed the economy by controlling prices, wages, rents, and profits, and by rationing consumption. After the war the U.S. state relaxed its grip on the economy but did not release it completely. As in other managerial states such as Britain, France, and Germany, state management of the economy has become permanent. The principal tools for this task were Keynesian-inspired monetary and fiscal policies and a host of regulatory agencies and commissions, such as the Federal Trade Commission (FTC) and the Interstate Commerce Commission (ICC). The state also subsidizes major sectors of the economy, such as agriculture.

As the dominant power on the Western side of the war, the United States engaged in massive military spending—which took the form of contracting for weapons from private arms producers. During the Cold War, military spending became a form of economic management, not unlike the way military spending during World War II had helped to pull the economy out of depression. The arms race during the Kennedy administration in the early 1960s and under President Ronald Reagan in the early 1980s became the main engine of economic growth and spurred technological development in the economy as a whole. A policy of military Keynesianism, which blurred the lines between state and civil society by generating a military industrial complex, remains central to managing the U.S. economy.

Managing Welfare

One of the most significant areas of state management of industrial capitalism is social welfare. Welfare programs such as health insurance, social security, unemployment insurance, and aid to the poor are important tools used by the state to manage prosperity and maintain public order. These programs are often used to channel money to consumers to ensure sufficient aggregate demand for the mass-produced goods of industrial corporations, and to redirect labor to the new jobs that the economy requires. They are also important components of the management of general social order by disciplining recipients of aid through stipulating program requirements and by ameliorating and confining the worst effects of the dislocations of the capitalist marketplace. Concern for the welfare for the entire subject population did not, however, begin with the managerial state. Such programs paralleled the development of the state in Europe. During the medieval period it was the duty of the Catholic Church to assist the poor and to provide education, which it did primarily to educate its own priesthood. Over time, these responsibilities and many others were gradually shifted to the state. Three epochs in the process of transference can be identified.

The first includes the period before the Industrial Revolution, when the primary concern was poverty among the rural peasantry. The second epoch begins with the Industrial Revolution, about 1750, and lasts until the the beginning of the twentieth century; during this epoch the social and economic problems created by industrialization and urbanization were addressed. In the third epoch, which began in the early decades of the twentieth century and extends to the present, the state has taken on the responsibility of maintaining the education, health, and safety of the entire subject population. 31 In the first epoch, the state sought only to rescue the rural poor from destitution. The most developed system for providing poor relief, as it was called, appeared in England during the Tudor period (1536–1603). During this time several poor relief acts were passed by Parliament. Under these acts every destitute person was to receive relief and each parish was to raise money in order to pay the indigent an allowance to supplement their meager wages. Poor relief programs were administered by county justices of the peace.

By the end of the eighteenth century this system of poor relief came under heavy criticism because it depressed rural wages and reduced the mobility of the poor, who could not seek better employment elsewhere without losing their allowances. Therefore, Parliament passed the Poor Law Amendment Act (1834), which removed poor relief from the justices of the peace and gave it to elected local boards operating under central authority. In 1929 the English Parliament passed an act that abolished poor relief and replaced it with a system of public assistance administered by county councils. In France, until the French Revolution, the king relied upon the Catholic Church to provide poor relief through its hospitals, outdoor relief centers, and other charitable foundations. The king provided bread (pain du roi) to the beggars and vagabonds of Paris, and each of his intendants was permitted to use a small share of the king's revenues to aid the poor in their généralités. The French Revolution abolished the charitable foundations of the Church and the royal revenues; hence poor relief fell to the new local authorities created by the revolutionary government (départements and communes). Préfects of the départements were required to deal with rural destitution and, after Napoléon seized power, undertook many public works projects, such as building roads, in order to provide jobs for the rural poor.

In 1871 the French National Assembly passed a law that required each départements to provide public assistance to all who were unable to work because of old age, mental illness, or sickness. During the second epoch the idea that the state's responsibility to provide poor relief as a temporary concession to the indigent, working poor was replaced with the idea that the state could regulate its workers by providing a panoply of social services. The new conditions that caused this change in thinking were industrialization, urbanization, and modern warfare. It began to be recognized that beyond the rural worker's basic right to life, which poor relief laws recognized, workers of a state's population had to be provided a minimum standard of health and physical well-being. This recognition was connected to the necessity of maintaining a healthy subject population for the dual purposes of providing recruits for the armed forces and boosting morale. Thus, the state began to concern itself with standards of sanitation in the new industrial towns, to regulate the conditions of employment in the new factories, and to guarantee a decent standard of subsistence by insuring against sickness, unemployment, and old age. These programs were designed to discipline or otherwise minimize the restlessness of workers and the poor as a first line of defense, so to speak, against radical political parties and movements as well as general social disorder, which would disrupt the industrial economy.

The first such regulation was initiated in Britain. In the nineteenth century, Parliament passed the Factory Act (1833), which created a system of factory inspection. The Mine Regulation Act of 1842 protected miners; the Factory Act of 1847 limited the workday to 10 hours; the Merchant Shipping Act of 1876 protected merchant seamen; and the Regulation of Railways Act of 1889 protected railroad workers. In 1848 Parliament passed the Public Health Act, which guaranteed minimum levels of sanitation in places of work and in dwellings. The first system of insurance against sickness, unemployment, and old age was started in Germany. In the 1880s, German Chancellor Bismarck pushed a series of laws through the Reichstag that he hoped would destroy the Social Democratic Party (SPD) by making the state responsible for the provision of social insurance for the working class. The first of these laws, which insured workers against sickness, was passed in 1883. Workers paid two-thirds of the cost and their employers the other one-third. These premiums were collected and paid by special insurance societies approved and regulated by the state. A second law, which insured workers against accidents, was passed in 1884.

Premiums for this insurance were paid by employers, who were permitted to form industrial associations to collect the premiums and pay claims. The third and last law of this series was passed in 1889 and insured workers against invalidity and old age. Workers and employers contributed equally to this fund, and the state made a contribution to the pension ultimately paid. The German system spread to other industrializing European states. In Britain, Parliament passed the Workmen's Compensation Act in 1897, which required that employers insure employees against the dangers of their employment. In 1908 the Old Age Pensions Act introduced a pension system paid for entirely by the state for workers over the age of 70 who were unable to support themselves. In 1909 Parliament passed the Trade Boards Act, which established a minimum wage for workers in jobs that did not provide trade union representation. In 1911 the National Insurance Act introduced a health insurance scheme to which workers, employers, and the state paid equal premiums. This act also provided for unemployment insurance in certain industries such as ironfounding and shipbuilding.

Social insurance for workers advanced much less rapidly in France. The first such act was not passed until 1905, when pensions were provided by the state for the aged poor and incurably ill. In 1910 the National Assembly passed the Old Age Pension Act, which provided pensions for wage earners from a fund contributed to by employees, employers, and the state. In 1913 the National Assembly passed an act that gave aid to families with more than three children in order to encourage population growth and to fight a high infant mortality rate. In the United States the advent of social insurance was even slower than in France. Although perhaps as much as 30 percent of workers had workmen's compensation insurance required by different states, only 2 percent had old-age insurance in 1915. Not until the depths of the Great Depression did the American state introduce accident, unemployment, and old-age insurance for wage earners. Industrial accident insurance was introduced in 1930. The Social Security Act of 1935 introduced retirement and unemployment insurance.

In 1950 the portion of the Social Security Act that provided aid to blind and needy children became an aid-to-children program called Aid to Families with Dependent Children (AFDC), which paid benefits to one parent in a family where children were beneficiaries. In the same year aid was extended to the totally disabled. In 1972 a uniform federal system of Supplemental Security Income (SSI) was set up for the aged, blind, and disabled. In the third epoch the idea that the state's responsibilities were to provide social services to the working class was replaced with the notion that the state was responsible for insuring the health, safety, and retirement of the entire subject population. Again the aim was to discipline and regulate the poor, to limit the political development of radical movements, and to promote general social order.

In Britain the Widows, Orphans, and Old Age Contributory Pensions Act of 1925 created a new social insurance scheme and extended unemployment insurance to cover most wage earners. A series of housing acts gave the state the responsibility of constructing housing. In 1928 France passed a compulsory social insurance law that gave sickness, maternity, invalidity, and old-age insurance to all citizens. During the Weimar Republic in Germany, unemployment insurance was expanded. After World War II, in Britain the Family Allowance Act, which paid weekly benefits to families with two or more children under the age of 15, was passed by Parliament. In 1946 the National Insurance Act was passed; it provided substantial coverage for sickness and unemployment as well as maternity benefits, widows' allowances, and retirement pensions for the entire population. The National Assistance Act, which was passed in 1948, required local governments to make accommodations available for the old, the infirm, and those in need of a place to live. Finally, also in 1948, the National Health Service was created; this placed all health services (private, local, and national) under the authority of the state and made it freely available to the entire subject population.

After World War II, the French state also strengthened and rationalized its social insurance scheme such that the vast majority of its subject population became covered by social insurance paid for by contributions from employers and employees. French social insurance covers sickness, disability, retirement, widowhood, and death. It also includes generous benefits for families. The larger the family, the greater the benefits. An additional allowance is paid to families if the mother does not work. In addition, large families receive income tax rebates, reduced fares on public transportation, and increased pensions. France also provides an extensive system of hospitals, orphanages, retirement homes, and asylums. Although the French state does not have a national health service, it does contribute to an individual's medical expenses under a fee reimbursement plan. Patients are free to choose their physicians, and the state insurance system reimburses the patient for 80 percent of the bill.

The German state has also broadened its coverage since the end of World War II. Social security legislation passed in 1954 allowed retired persons to maintain the standard of living they enjoyed during their working years by indexing pensions to reflect earnings and taking inflation into account. The Federal Unemployment Office makes payments and grants low-interest loans to workers to cover travel expenses incurred during their searches for new jobs, moving expenses, interview expenses, vocational retraining, and counseling. Since 1959 German construction workers have received subsidies from employment offices, known as "bad weather money," for rainy, snowy, or subzero winter days. In 1996, these payments were replaced with a system guaranteeing workers 75 percent of their gross pay per hour for inclement days during the months from November to March. Germany continues to provide health insurance through the system established by Bismarck in the 1880s, although it was overhauled in 1955. The scheme is still supported by joint contributions from workers, employers, and the state, and is still administered by welfare funds that pay the physicians of the patients' own choosing.

The U.S. state did not introduce health insurance until 1964 with the passage of the Medicaid program, which provides joint federally and state-funded health insurance for the poor, and the Medicare program, which provides federally funded insurance for the elderly that covers hospitalization and subsidized outpatient care. Unlike European states, the American state still does not provide health insurance for the general population. Contemporary liberals consider welfare programs as entitlements, that is, as programs justified in part because they are equally available to all citizens as individuals, regardless of race, class, or gender, and in part because they are seen as providing the prerequisites for all persons in the society to live a dignified life. All persons, liberals argue, are entitled to receive adequate medical care, to avoid destitution, to be able to provide for their own and their family's economic well-being, and to receive unemployment compensation when they are thrown out of work.

Entitlements, for liberals, then, are legitimate functions of the state in an industrial economy. But the liberal ideology does not fully recognize the extent to which these programs intervene in the recipient's private life. In other words, liberals want to maintain a clear and inviolable distinction between state and civil society and between public and private; but these programs actually render the distinction, at best, fragile. Conservatives who challenge the legitimacy of these programs also promote a sharp distinction between civil society and the state, public and private, which does not accord to the realities of welfare programs. In practice, the management of social services for the poor, the elderly, or the unemployed involves the state deeply in the regulation of people's everyday lives.

Moreover, in spite of the attempts to maintain the universality and equality of entitlement programs, wealthy and privileged groups have been able to avoid the more intrusive forms of intervention entailed by them. Feminists have recognized the disciplinary aspects of social services most clearly. Women and men become subjects of the state's management of social services in different ways and to different extents. This is especially the case in states, such as the United States, where women have been relatively unsuccessful in obtaining child-care programs, maternity leave, and equal pay for equal work, all of which would help make them equal to men in the public world of civil society and the world of work. Although all social service programs require recipients of benefits to conform to certain rules, some programs intervene into the private lives of their recipients more intrusively than do others. To receive unemployment insurance, for example, one of the few social service programs in which men participate more than women, one must actually be looking for work, going to school, or enrolled in a job-training program to receive compensation.

But the state relies on the recipient to provide evidence; it does not send an agent of the state out to follow the individual around to see if he is actually looking for work or going to school. On the other hand, the programs in which women participate in greater numbers than men often subject recipients to far more state scrutiny and intrusion into their lives. Single mothers receiving state aid for their children may be required to live with their parents, and those receiving food stamps are limited in the choices of what they can buy with them. More significant, women in these programs are often subjected to constant surveillance by social workers and other agents of the state, such as the police, who have the power under some circumstances to remove children from their mothers.

These programs fall disproportionately on women because of the traditional prejudices and social structures that see women as primarily responsible for the home and "private" life. As we mentioned above, these customary prejudices were an important part of Fordism. In practice, the man's private life in managerial states is more inviolable than is the woman's. The poor, which often includes high numbers of racial and ethnic minorities because of prejudice and structural inequalities in the provision of education and work opportunities, are also often subjected to intrusive forms of state intervention that blur the lines of public and private.

MANAGING POLITICAL PARTICIPATION

As we discussed above, the managerial state reconstitutes citizens according to a logic of insiders and outsiders, and relocates sovereign unity and indivisibility in the nation. This political distribution is managed by the formalization and routinization of procedural democracy. The principal way that people participate in politics in the managerial state is through regular elections, which channel participation away from unpredictable, disruptive, and spontaneous forms of participation such as demonstrating, rioting, and throwing bombs. Elections "domesticate" and pacify participation and transform it into a routine, peaceful public activity. Through rules that (1) regulate the composition of the electorate and (2) transform voters' choices into electoral outcomes, the managerial state controls when, where, how, and which individuals will participate. From the early nineteenth century in the United States, for example, the composition of the electorate was regulated by property-owning and tax-paying requirements, poll taxes, literacy tests, and franchise laws that denied women, blacks, and youths, the right to vote. Although these restrictions have been abandoned in the twentieth century, the inconvenience and expense of registering to vote (furnishing proof of identity, residency, and citizenship, and taking time off from work to appear at the registrar's office) still regulates the composition of the electorate by depressing the electoral participation of the poor and poorly educated.

Thus, in the United States, personal registration skews the electoral process in favor of better-educated, higher-income people. 43 In the managerial state, elections are increasingly understood as electoral "systems." Elections make sense, and are made sense of by the press and the academic discipline of political science, as part of a rational system of rules and regulations the aim of which is to produce predictable outcomes. Crucial to regulating this system is the manipulation of the outcomes of elections by regulating the way in which individual votes will be translated into seats in a representative body. Two sets of regulations are crucial to managing this system: (1) those that establish the criteria for winning and (2) those that define the electoral districts.

There are two ways to regulate winning. One is to award victory to the candidate who receives either a plurality or a majority of the ballots cast. Another is to award victory to competing political parties in rough proportion to the votes each has received of the ballots cast. For example, a party that received 40 percent of the vote would receive about 40 percent of the seats in the representative body. Systems of proportional representation are advantageous to small and weak social groups; majority and plurality systems are advantageous to large and powerful groups. This is because in an election to a representative body, proportional representation reduces the number of votes that a political party must receive in order to win seats; and majority and plurality rules increase that number. Thus, the choice of the rules that regulate winning will have a substantial impact on the number and nature of the political parties within the state.

Britain and the United States both manage the participation of their subject populations through regular elections for representative bodies such as Parliament, Congress, state legislatures, and city and county councils. Elections for Parliament must be held every five years, and elections for one-third of the Senate and the House of Representatives of the Congress every two years. Neither state controls the composition of the electorate through property-owning requirements, poll taxes and the like, although in the United States, residency requirements of varying amounts of time are still used by individual states. The composition of the electorate is regulated primarily through personal registration laws, especially in the U.S. state, where the political parties arc weak. Winning has been regulated by the use of plurality electoral systems, which favor large, powerful groups and have produced two dominant political parties both in Britain and the United States. Although other parties exist in both states, they have had difficulty surviving— especially in the United States, because the electoral system and state laws create difficulties for "thirdparty" candidates attempting to gain access to the ballot. In the United States especially, the outcomes of elections can be influenced by gerrymandering (manipulating the geographical boundaries of districts in order to increase one outcome over another), named after an early nineteenth-century governor of Massachusetts, Elbridge Gerry (1744–1814), who allegedly redrew the lines of a district in the shape of a salamander in order to increase the vote for his party. Because different distributions of voters among districts produce different outcomes, those who control the lines of the districts are able to manipulate the results. Gerrymandering has been used extensively in the United States to dilute the voting strength of racial minorities.

The French and German states have also managed political participation by regulating the composition of the electorate and manipulating the transformation of voters' choices into electoral outcomes. In the nineteenth century both used property-owning and tax-paying requirements and restricted the franchise to men. In the twentieth century the franchise has been granted to all individuals over 18 years old, who are, by law, required to register. From 1871 to 1958, France used proportional representation, which produced 10 to 20 parties, none of which was large enough to win a majority of seats in the National Assembly. When Charles de Gaulle came to power in 1958, he changed the electoral law to a majority system that requires a second ballot if no candidate, including in elections for the presidency, receives a majority on the first ballot. Germany has used both plurality and proportional systems. During the Weimar Republic proportional representation was used, which produced a plethora (about 40) of small parties. During the Third Reich only one party was permitted, the Nazi Party, and no elections were held after 1933. After World War II, the German state instituted a combined plurality-proportional electoral system. One-half of the seats in the Bundestag are elected by plurality from single-member districts and one-half by proportional representation.

The trend in managerial states has been toward fewer large parties that do not differ much from one another in terms of ideology. Such catchall parties seek to capture as many voters as possible by appealing to prudent administration, managerial ability, technical expertise, or personal morality, as well as appealing to what is good for the "nation" or "the people" as a whole. Thus, elections in the managerial state have become ritualistic confrontations between candidates and parties who claim to be able to manage the state more effectively and efficiently than their opponents, rather than occasions for serious public debate and discussion about pressing issues. Increasingly, parties control their images by employing the marketing techniques of consumer manipulation used in commercial advertising in order to mobilize or demobilize voters. Public opinion polling is also used extensively. Recent trends in such management of participation have produced significant political disenchantment among voters and a general apathy toward public affairs, which is reflected in marked declines in the percentage of eligible voters who actually vote in all managerial states.

SUMMARY

In the managerial states of the twentieth century the relation of subject and sovereign has been reconstituted, and the state has developed new powers of surveillance and social control. One of these new forms of control stems from the relocating of sovereignty in the nation, an imagined community of all citizens within a particular territory. Part 3 discusses nationalism and the nation as part of modern state practice and the spread of the state as the hegemonic form of political organization throughout the world. Part 4 examines the question of whether the recent trends toward neoliberalism—a revival of economic liberalism in the context of a globalizing capitalist economy—are transforming the managerial state or whether this trend can best be understood as a retooling of managerialism.

9

GLOBALIZING THE TERRITORIAL STATE

THE COLONIAL STATE: SOVEREIGNTY EXPANDED

As we already have discussed, the idea of sovereign political space depended on a new way of envisioning the world as a whole, as an infinite, empty space. The globe consisted of an infinite landscape given to men, and secondarily to women, to use to satisfy their needs and realize their purposes and wants. Over about four centuries European states carved this space into empires, jurisdictions, and spheres of influence over which each claimed absolute, sovereign authority. The legitimacy to rule within a territory was bound up with the recognition of that right by other states, who claimed the same sovereign rights over different territories, as well as the right to participate in practices of diplomacy. The existence of territorial states was deeply implicated in the construction of a world order that was economic and cultural as well as political and military. Indeed, it is impossible to understand the development of modern states without taking into account the way European states constructed an interconnected global order by means of conquest, trade, religious conversion, and diplomacy. In this chapter we look at the modern state as it was implicated in the construction of a global grid of imperial possessions. In the next two chapters we turn to the emergence of states within this grid.

European Imperialism

Imperialism refers to the process of "expanding a state's power and authority by territorial acquisition or by extending political and economic domination and control over other peoples." European imperialism differs from other historical empires such as the Roman, Chinese, Inca, and Zulu. These empires were not global and their internal dynamics did not construct their world as infinitely expandable. Despite being more decentralized, unplanned, and episodic than these empires, European states claiming sovereignty beyond their borders, individuals greedy for profits, and missionaries seeking souls for the universal Christian commonwealth produced the first global system of contiguous and interconnected empires extending across oceans and continents. The planet was thus enclosed in a grid of European colonial possessions. Very few portions of the non-European areas of the globe escaped European imperialism. Huge swaths of territory, all of the Americas, Australia and New Zealand, most of Africa and the Middle East, and portions of Asia were incorporated within the European imperial system. Those areas that escaped direct European hegemony— China, Persia (Iran), Japan, Korea, Siam (Thailand), and Abyssinia (Ethiopia)—were eventually reconstructed by indigenous elites using the state as it had emerged in Europe as the basic model and incorporated into the globalizing system of nation-states largely on European terms.

Typically, discussion of European imperialism begins with the voyages of discovery (1400–1600) by Europeans along the coast of North Africa, out into the Atlantic Ocean, and beyond. Actually, European expansion began much earlier. It is important to recognize that expansion overseas was essentially a continuation of internal expansion, which began with Charlemagne's conquests. The feudal politico-military practice of governing, was spread by conquest and dynastic marriage from the Frankish core of Europe to the peripheries of the continent and to the British Isles. The Normans conquered and colonized England, Wales, Scotland, Ireland, and southern Italy as well as the island of Sicily. Burgundian knights were a major force in the reconquest of the Iberian Peninsula. Teutonic Knights colonized Prussia after which they conquered and converted the Livonians. These conquests resulted in the political homogenization of Europe around feudal institutions and were not the creation of patterns of regional subordination and dependence associated with modern imperialism. In other words, Frankish culture and politico-military governing practices were spread by individual knights who replicated feudal institutions as they conquered new parts of Europe.

Thus, internal European expansion took place by a process of individualized "cellular multiplication" rather than according to an overall imperial plan organized and carried out by a centralized state. The primary reason for the internal expansion of Frankish politico- military practices was land. The knights who conquered the peripheries of Europe were usually second and third sons who were forced to find their own land in distant regions because the eldest son had, according to the law of primogeniture, inherited the family fief. A general scarcity of fiefs and an overpopulation of warrior-knights developed in the core of Europe during the eleventh century and sparked a scramble for new hereditary fiefs in areas of Europe not yet touched by feudalism.

Thus, the rise of a class of fiefless knights created expansionary pressures in the original Frankish core, which resulted in the spread of feudal institutions to the peripheries of Europe. Such expansionary pressures, combined with religious fanaticism and the desire for booty and trade, resulted in Europe's first attempt at external expansion, the Crusades. From the eleventh through the thirteenth centuries European armies, at the instigation of various popes, attacked the Muslim peoples of the "Holy Land" in order to establish a Christian kingdom in Palestine.

A Crusader state, the Kingdom of Jerusalem, which was divided into four feudal principalities (Jerusalem, Edessa, Tripoli, and Antioch), was established and existed for about 200 years (1099–1291). It was protected by the crusading military order of the Knights of the Hospital of St. John of Jerusalem (Hospitallers), which was created in 1099 after the First Crusade; the Poor Knights of Christ and the Temple of Solomon (Templars), which was organized in 1118 to protect pilgrims to Jerusalem; and the Knights of the Hospital of St. Mary of the Teutons in Jerusalem (Teutonic Knights), which, after the failure of the Crusades, was transferred to the eastern frontier of Prussia. Palestine was eventually reconquered by Muslim armies led by Saladin (1138–1193), the great Muslim ruler who had unified Egypt and Syria in 1187. The Crusades, and the religious differences they reinforced, helped to give rise to an increasingly European cultural identity that understood the world as divided between Christian and non-Christian civilizations, cultures, and religions. This imaginary was reinforced by the rise of the Ottoman Turks, Muslims who overthrew the Byzantine Empire in 1453. As one historian says:

> From the Renaissance onwards, indeed, European political thinkers in the age of Absolutism repeatedly sought to define the character of their own world by opposition with that of the Turkish order, so close and yet so remote from it; none of them reduced the distance simply or mainly to one of religion.

The voyages of discovery, then, can be seen as Europe's second external expansion. It was motivated by the same goal as was the internal expansion two centuries earlier, more land. By the fifteenth century, European agricultural production had reached its maximum output, given the level of technology and arable land available. At the same time, the advent of large standing armies, brought about by the military revolution, sharply increased the revenue requirements of medieval monarchs. More land, which was at the time the primary source of wealth, was needed to expand agricultural production in order to increase revenue.

The emergent modern states, each with its own economic base and centralized political institutions, were the chief vehicles for Europe's second external expansion. Unlike China, where a single politico-military authority prevailed over the entire empire, limiting Chinese expansionism, no such authority existed in Europe. But this did not lessen the impact or culturally specific character of European imperialism. European states, although sovereign entities, were linked through an interlocking set of economic, political, and cultural relations. This situation was historically unique and engendered a vast global quest among rival European protostates for political, economic, and military power. This quest, which had been confined to the European continent, began to spill over into the oceanic sphere in the early fifteenth century. The result was the European hegemonization of the globe and the replication of the state through colonization.

Before European Hegemony

Before discussing Europe's second expansion in more detail, we need to discuss briefly the global economic situation before European hegemony. Europe, after a period of isolation following the disappearance of the Roman Empire, had gradually become integrated into an economic system of exchange that stretched across Eurasia from northeastern Europe to China. This economic system involved merchants, traders, and producers operating from key cities who exchanged agricultural goods (mainly spices) and manufactures (mainly silk cloth and other textiles). During the Middle Ages, Europe was the least developed of the regions of the Eurasian world economy and China the most advanced. Neither Europe nor China was hegemonic over the other. Although linked together by sea lanes and overland caravan routes, Europe and China were distinct from each other in terms of language, religion, and culture. This trading system was composed of three major commercial regions: Western Europe, the Middle East, and the Far East. The Americas, the Pacific Islands, Japan, and the Antipodes (Australia and New Zealand) existed independently of this system.

Western Europe formed a region bound together by three trading networks, each with its own center. The first was the Champagne fairs, which were held in the east-central French cities of Lagny, Provins, Troyes, and Bar-sur-Aube. These cities had year-round commodities markets established by local counts who wanted to make profits and become independent of their overlords. They rented halls, stalls, and stables to traders for whom they provided protection and safe conduct. Fair guards appointed by the counts policed the fairs, heard complaints, enforced contracts, collected fines, and punished cheating. Six fairs were held annually. They started in one city and moved to another, in a predictable circuit, according to religious feast days. The second network was in Flanders, where favorable soils and terrain for sheep-raising, and an ancient tradition of weaving, resulted in Europe's first major industry: woven woolen textiles.

Ghent and Bruges were the two key commercial and financial centers of this network. The third was northern Italy, which linked the western European region to the rest of the world trading system through the port cities of Genoa, commanding the western Mediterranean, and Venice, commanding the eastern Mediterranean. These port cities were linked to the Champagne fairs by overland routes and to the Middle East through the Kingdom of Jerusalem in Palestine. Shipping and shipbuilding had become major industries in these cities, especially Venice, which built ships to carry Crusaders and their equipment to the Holy Land. Long-distance trade between Flanders and the Italian port cities was dominated by Italians, who introduced banking, credit, and bookkeeping into Europe. The major items of trade were spices and silks from the Far East. The Middle East was the core of the Eurasian economy in the thirteenth century. It connected the western European region to China by way of three routes. A northern route, called the Silk Road, went eastward from the Kingdom of Jerusalem via Constantinople across the Asian landmass to China. A central route connected the Mediterranean with the Indian Ocean via

Baghdad and the Persian Gulf. A southern route linked Alexandria and Cairo to the Red Sea, which was linked to the Arabian Sea and the Indian Ocean. The Indian Ocean formed a region between Western Europe and the Far East that was divided into two sailing circuits. In the western portion, Muslim shipowners sailed from the Arabian Peninsula to the Malabar Coast (the southwest coast of India). The eastern portion was dominated by Hindu shipowners who sailed from the Malabar Coast to the Straits of Malacca. These two circuits were produced by the natural forces of the monsoons, which created two sailing seasons, west to east in the spring and summer, east to west in the autumn and winter. Arab traders were the intermediaries between the western Mediterranean and India, and Indian traders were the intermediaries between India and the Straits of Malacca. Trade beyond the Straits of Malacca was dominated by Chinese shipowners. The Malabar Coast was the central exchange point where the western European region via the Middle East and the Far Eastern region via the Straits of Malacca converged. When the three routes through the Middle East fell under the control of the Ottoman Turks, Europeans began to seek a new route to India.

Europe's Second Overseas Expansion

Europe's second overseas expansion succeeded because of political and technological developments as well as the religious zeal, economic greed, and adventurism with which it was pursued. Advances in maritime technology, especially the magnetic compass, the astrolabe (an instrument for observing the position of celestial bodies), and portolans (navigation charts), enabled sea captains to find their positions in open ocean and encouraged voyages out of the sight of land. The oared galleys of Roman design, which had evolved in the relatively placid waters of the Mediterranean, were replaced by the more maneuverable lateen-rigged caravels, which had greater cargo capacity and could sail efficiently across expanses of rough, open ocean, with or against the wind. These new maritime technologies shifted the geographical locus of power and economic accumulation from the Mediterranean Sea to the Indian and Atlantic Oceans, and to the general exploitation of the wealth of Asia and the Americas. They opened vast new opportunities for the accumulation of wealth and expansion of the European state's power in both its domestic and international spaces. Increasingly, European religious, political, and cultural practices and institutions, such as Christianity, private property, and the territorial state, appeared as hallmarks of a universal human development, the markers of advanced civilization. By spreading their institutions and practices throughout the world, Europeans constituted and maintained a sense of their own superiority over peoples outside Europe, whom they considered "primitive" and "savage."

The first thrusts outward from Europe were made by the Genoese, who sailed out of the Mediterranean through the Straits of Gibraltar and into the Atlantic Ocean in order to establish a sea route from Genoa to Flanders. The Genoese were eventually successful in diverting the overland trade between northern Italy and Flanders onto their own ships and thus ruined the economic viability of the Champagne fairs, which went into economic decline and closed. In the fifteenth century, the Genoese were replaced by the Portuguese and Castilians. Of the two, the Portuguese led the way owing to their geostrategic location on the southern edge of the European landmass, their experience in long-distance maritime trade, and their strong and centralized protostate. The first Portuguese discoveries were the Madeira Islands in 1419 by Gonçalves Zarco, and the Azores Archipelago in 1427 by Diogo de Silves. Both island groups, uninhabited when they were discovered, were quickly colonized. Madeira, initially a source of timber, later became one of Europe's chief sources of refined sugar. These discoveries and the profitable trade in sugar that they created encouraged additional voyages into the Atlantic and along the western coast of Africa. After 1460 the pace of exploration slowed, resuming only after the pope settled a conflict between the Portuguese and the Castilian crowns over which monarchy had the right to explore Africa and the Atlantic. The Treaty of Alcoçaves (1479), which settled the dispute, gave the Portuguese a monopoly of fishing, trade, and exploration along the coast of Africa and allowed the Castilians to keep the Canary Islands. The Portuguese, therefore, devised a plan for opening a sea route to India, with the crown taking 20 percent (the Royal Fifth) of the profits of these explorations, which it conducted in secret in order to safeguard Portugal's lead in maritime technology and geographical knowledge. In 1483 Diogo Cão discovered the Congo River and sailed south as far as 22 degrees south latitude.

In 1487 Bartolomeu Dias (c. 1450–1500) rounded the Cape of Good Hope. In 1497 Vasco da Gama (c. 1460–1524) left Lisbon with a large fleet and sailed up the east coast of Africa to Mombassa, where he secured the services of an Arab pilot who guided him across the Indian Ocean to the Malabar coast of India in 1498, thereby circumventing the Ottoman Turks. Following da Gama's voyage, the Portuguese sent large fleets to Asia on a regular basis. One of these, led by Pedro Álvares Cabral (1468–1520), accidentally discovered Brazil in 1500. Afonso de Albuquerque (1453– 1515), who was made viceroy of India in 1509, extended Portuguese hegemony by defeating the Turks, Malays, and Moghuls. He captured the port cities of Ormuz and Muscat from the Arabs and built forts in Sumatra, Timor, the Malaccas, and Ceylon. His captains sailed to the mouth of the Mekong River in Vietnam and arrived on the coast of China at Canton, and then Japan, in 1542. Portugal had established its hegemony in Asia and control of the entire spice trade to Europe.

When Christopher Columbus (1451–1506), sailing for Spain, landed in Lisbon in 1493, the Portuguese king laid claim to his discoveries in the Americas, arguing that they were his under the terms of the Treaty of Alcoçaves. The Spanish appealed to the pope, who drew an imaginary line on the globe 100 leagues (about 1,000 miles) west of the Azores and granted to Spain all discoveries west of that line and to Portugal all discoveries east of it. The Treaty of Tordesillas was signed in 1494 and allowed Portugal to maintain control of the sea route around Africa to India and to keep Brazil. Columbus made several additional voyages to the "New World," during which he found no gold or spices. Other Europeans followed, such as the Florentine Amerigo Vespucci (1454–1512), who explored the southern coast of South America to Patagonia; the Castilian Vasco Nuñez Balbo a (1475–1519), who crossed the isthmus at Panama and sighted the Pacific Ocean in 1513; and the Portuguese Ferdinand Magellan (c. 1480–1521), who in 1519 found the strait at the southern tip of South America that now bears his name and sailed up the west coast and into the Pacific and to the Philippine Islands. Magellan's voyage, completed by one of his captains, was the first to circumnavigate the globe and, in the process, found the westward sea route to India sought by Columbus. However, Magellan's strait was never used as a regular channel of trade with the East.

Globalizing European International Society

The expansion of European protostates spread European society throughout the world. The processes through which European political, economic, and cultural norms and practices became the norms for all states and peoples made those states into what they became. By the hegemony of European society, we mean not only the dominance of specific actors or institutions, but the routinization of specific sets of social relations through which peoples inside and outside Europe were integrated into the European imperial system. The principles of these social relations were economic (private property and capitalism), political (rule associated with the modern state, especially pressures of militarization), and cultural (Christianity and humanism). The specific processes of European expansion and the encounters with non-European peoples were multilayered and multifaceted experiences that fundamentally changed both conqueror and conquered alike. Economic gain, military and diplomatic competition, and religious mission all provided important motives for the expansion of early European protostates. It is important to remember that developments inside and outside Europe were closely connected. English and Dutch advances in weaving produced cloth not only for home markets but for foreign trade; the development of credit instruments in Venice and other Italian port cities was motivated by foreign trade, as were numerous important technologies.

Sovereignty inside became dependent upon conquests outside; that is, the ability to realize the sovereign identity European states claimed for themselves came to depend upon the colonial possessions over which they exercised control. Sovereignty inside European states, then, became dependent upon denying sovereignty to other peoples. Imaginaries of non-European peoples were constructed (through travel literature, for example), which justified treating non-Europeans as not worthy of sovereignty. It is important to recognize that these imaginaries constructed what was meant to be "European" as well, marginalizing groups such as Gypsies, Jews, and Muslims living in Europe. Europeans considered non-European peoples either as inferior by nature or as primitive and unable to take on the responsibilities of sovereignty. What Europeans did not question was the universality of state sovereignty and their right to spread it throughout the world. They generally failed to recognize, however, that this portended violence toward peoples within as well as outside Europe. European lawyers and statesmen came to understand the international society being created as a global civitas, a global city or "republic of all mankind."

The dualistic political and moral structure generated by the way European statesmen, lawyers, and clergy came to imagine non-European "others" can be seen in slavery. Long after slavery was outlawed in Europe, European states continued to promote it in their colonies and supported it in world trade. Even after the slave trade was outlawed, colonial states continued to use strategies not unlike slavery (such as forced labor), which, too, were unacceptable in their home states. Europeans used coercive labor discipline in their colonies long after such practices had generally disappeared in Europe, having been replaced by wage labor. In large part, the reasons for continuing forced labor were economic. Slavery and other directly coercive labor regimes produced extremely large profits. These practices also persisted and were legitimated, even when they were not so economically profitable, in part, for geopolitical reasons, especially the military-political competition among European states. Colonies came to be regarded by European states as pawns in strategic and economic competition with other European states. Therefore, keeping order and creating allies among colonized peoples led to treatment of those peoples that would be unacceptable toward Europeans. By the nineteenth century, colonialism also took on a certain psychology in which the colonies were portrayed and treated according to paternalistic attitudes and practices. Regularly, native peoples were associated simultaneously with paternalistic possession and with the feminine in European culture.

Colonized peoples were often seen as children in need of the domination of the colonial master. One scholar has shown how, in India, the experience of colonialism masculinized the subcontinent's traditional culture by accentuating the character traits, attitudes, and practices associated with male dominance over women that had been secondary within traditional India. In this paternalistic psychology, race and gender overlaid each other. The dualistic structure created by the hegemony of European society can also be seen in diplomacy. As we discussed in earlier chapters, the institutions of modern diplomacy first emerged primarily in the struggles over Italy during the late fifteenth and early sixteenth centuries, when institutions of diplomacy developed as a strategy to gain information and influence about the motives and movements of rival city-states and potential allies. The papacy was the initial object of such strategies, given its central position in the network of Italian city-states, over which Spain, France, and the Habsburg Empire (later the Austro-Hungarian Empire) struggled during this period.

As a result of this struggle, European states created the institutions of resident embassies, extraterritoriality, and congresses of states to produce treaties. These became the central institutions of modern diplomacy among states. But diplomatic practices with regard to non-European peoples emerged in a somewhat different way and created similar tensions with the system of diplomacy as had developed in Europe. First, Europeans did not initially understand the languages of the peoples they encountered. Also, because non-European peoples did not organize their societies around the principles of private property, especially with respect to land, misunderstandings and miscommunication frequently occurred. Usually in such cases, either Europeans assumed that indigenous peoples understood what the Europeans meant by treaties and agreements (assuming that certain behaviors by the natives constituted agreement with the Europeans on their terms), or they simply imposed their "agreements" on them. This can be seen in the way Europeans went about giving their discoveries European names as a way of taking possession of them.

The dualism in European-created global order is exemplified in an early weapon of mass killing, the machine gun. Invented during the nineteenth century, the machine gun seemed to European militaries to violate all the norms of war (as the crossbow had been considered during the Middle Ages), which they still considered a noble enterprise in which soldiers were to conduct themselves honorably and to demonstrate their valor on the battlefield. The machine gun was simply a weapon for mass slaughter, and many types of machine guns were invented. In 1862, the American Richard Jordan Gatling (1818–1903) patented a machine gun that could reliably fire 200 rounds per minute. Although not used in the American Civil War, the Gatling Gun was used extensively against Native Americans during the conquest and colonization of the West by the American state. During the 1860s and 1870s various European states and the Ottoman Empire bought Gatling Guns and used them, together with various types of machine guns invented by others, in their colonies, especially in Africa. Here racism intersected with the other motifs of colonialism. It is helpful to quote from one history of the machine gun in Africa:

Whatever the general causes, or the personal motives of the individual colonizers, the whole ethos of the imperialist drive was predicated upon racialism. Attitudes to the Africans varied from patronizing paternalism to contempt and outright hatred, but all assumed that the white man was inherently superior to the black. . . . Clearly, working from such a theory of human development, it was easy, even natural, to go on to regard superior military technology as a Godgiven gift for the suppression of these inferior races.

Emergence of European Colonial Empires

In this section we review cases of expansion by specific European states into the non-European world, linking hitherto isolated peoples and areas within a grid of political, economic, and cultural relations. We then conclude the chapter with a discussion of the institutions of these colonial states as extensions of European territorial sovereigns. In the Americas, the Spanish organized a series of conquests of native peoples and empires into an imperial administrative system. Balboa, the first conquistador (conqueror), achieved hegemony over the indigenous Americans of the isthmus by military force, terror, and diplomacy. Hernando Cortéz (1485–1547) conquered the Aztecs of Mexico by military force and diplomacy (1519–1521), establishing his capital at Mexico City, the former Aztec capital. Francisco Pizarro (1475–1541) defeated the Incas in 1532 and established his capital in Lima, not Cuzco, the Inca capital, which was too high in the Andes for Europeans to live comfortably. Hernando de Soto (1500–1542) explored and conquered the American Southeast (Florida), and Juan V´squez de Coronado (1525?–1565) explored and conquered the American Southwest. Conquests were aided by the spread of epidemic diseases carried by the European conquerors.

Small pox, measles, influenza, and typhus wiped out 95 percent of many Native American populations because they had no natural immunities to such diseases. In addition to having established themselves on land, the Spanish were able to create a monopoly of seaborne trade between the Americas and Europe, much as the Portuguese had done between Portugal and India. These trade monopolies were eventually challenged by other European protostates during the latter part of the sixteenth century. England, under Elizabeth I, tried to break the Spanish monopoly but was unsuccessful. In 1604 the English signed a peace treaty with Spain (the Treaty of London) that recognized Spain's right to dominate the Caribbean trade in exchange for England's right to colonize coastal areas of North America. Although the eastern seaboard of North America had been originally explored in 1534 by a Genoese, Giovanni de Verrazzano (1485?–1528), and a Breton, Jacques Cartier (1491–1557), in 1536, both of whom were sailing for the king of France, the area was colonized by the Dutch and the English in the 1600s. Settlement was encouraged by the English because it was the only way to prevent the Spanish from challenging their claims. The English were able to dislodge the Dutch from the city of New Amsterdam (renamed New York) and to establish a string of settlements along the coast.

In the Far East, the seaborne empire established by the Portuguese was challenged by the Dutch, who sought to create an alternative trade in spices by controlling both the supply and the shipping. The Dutch began to acquire territory in the East Indies (especially on the island of Java) and founded a colony at the Cape of Good Hope in 1652, which functioned as a way station for Dutch ships involved in the spice trade. The Dutch established a direct trade, controlling the source and carrying the spices to Europe by sailing a southerly route around the Cape of Good Hope. Gradually, the Dutch replaced the Portuguese and the spice trade shifted from the Red Sea and Persian Gulf to the area around the Straits of Malacca. A Dutch captain, Abel Tasman (1603?–1659), charted New Zealand and Australia in 1642–1643. By the early seventeenth century the Dutch had become, arguably, the dominant colonial power on the globe in part by using their advanced capitalist financial institutions. In Brazil the Dutch challenged the Portuguese-controlled market for Brazilwood (which was used for dying cloth) and sugar, which had been brought by the Portuguese from Madeira. In 1623, the Dutch invaded Brazil and captured Bahia; in 1643 they occupied Pernambuco. However, in 1645, Portuguese settlers rebelled against the Dutch and had expelled them by 1654.

Despite having had its coast explored very early by Europeans, Africa remained relatively isolated from the emerging global trading system until the 1800s. Large indigenous African empires, small states, and smaller stateless societies existed side by side and interacted with one another. Like the indigenous systems in the Americas, these societies had their own histories of war, conquest, and peaceful coexistence. For several hundred years after the beginning of Europe's second external expansion, Europeans and Africans had contact with each other only along the coasts. The Portuguese established trading forts at various places, where they traded for gold and slaves. Africa was first integrated into the global order when the demand for labor increased dramatically in the Americas, where labor-intensive crops such as sugar, cotton, and tobacco were being grown on ever-expanding plantations. In the 1780s, the decade when the greatest number of slaves were taken from Africa, 88,000 Africans per year were carried across the Atlantic. One-half of these went to the Caribbean, one-third to Brazil, and the remainder to the English colonies in North America.

Many thousands perished en route because of the horrible conditions under which slaves were transported. During the 1800s European adventurers, Christian missionaries, and explorers began to penetrate the interior of Africa. Africa's isolation was finally ended in the latter decades of the nineteenth century, when global rivalries among the major European states led to the penetration, pacification, and occupation of the African hinterland. A dispute between Portugal and the king of Belgium over ownership of the mouth of the Congo River led to a conference in Berlin in 1884–1885, known as the Berlin Conference, at which France, Britain, Portugal, Spain, Germany, and Italy presented colonial claims. They negotiated among themselves and, without regard to the wishes of Africans or knowledge about boundaries among African peoples, partitioned Africa among the attending states. The boundaries they mapped at the Berlin Conference became the boundaries of their colonial possessions in Africa. The doctrine of effective occupation, advanced at the conference, impelled what has come to be called the "scramble for Africa." Europeans, with the aid of military force, began to penetrate the interior in order to conquer and pacify African peoples; thus they could effectively occupy their colonial claims. Conquest was quickly followed by occupation and the establishment of colonial administration.

Within a couple of decades, all of Africa was enclosed within a colonial grid. In addition to Africa and the Western Hemisphere, other parts of the globe were enclosed within the grid of European imperial domination. As the Portuguese were displaced from the Straits of Malacca and Sundra by the Dutch, the East Indies became a Dutch colony. The instrument of colonization was the Dutch East India Company, which built forts at various places. The company used military means to take and hold several of the archipelago's islands and to dominate the Straits of Malacca. The company's rule was consolidated over Java. In the 1800s the Dutch government began to penetrate the interior of the islands, then known as the Netherlands Indies. The process of enclosure was complete by 1909. Plantations were laid out and planted with coffee, sugar, tea, tobacco, indigo, cinnamon, and cotton.

British and French rivalries in Asia and southeast Asia brought about the enclosure of other areas. The British East India Company occupied India in 1700 and controlled it until 1857, the year of the Sepoy Rebellion, when the British government took it over from the company. Threats from the French encouraged the British to invent a pretext to start a war with the king of Burma in order to occupy his kingdom; the occupation was completed in 1852. The Dutch, who had replaced the Portuguese in Malaya, were themselves replaced by the British; the most important place occupied was Singapore, an island at the tip of the Malayan Peninsula that was easy to defend and gives easy access to the Straits of Malacca. Malaya was initially administered by the East India Company, and later by the British India Office. The French conquest of Vietnam began in 1857, with Saigon becoming the site of the new colonial government after its capture in 1859. Vietnam, Cambodia, and Laos were ruled as French Indochina. The Philippines, long a colony of Spain, became a colony of the United States after Spain's defeat in the Spanish-American War (1898–1899). China and Japan were never directly colonized by the European states. Japan was able to isolate itself from direct foreign control. China, on the other hand, although not occupied, was forced to conclude a number of treaties, known as the Unequal Treaties, which effectively denied Chinese sovereignty by allowing the major European states to establish spheres of influence over large sections of Chinese territory along the southern coast.

The United States, itself the creation of British imperialism, expanded its sovereignty westward, enclosing and destroying indigenous native peoples in the process. In 1803 it bought the Louisiana Territory from Napoléon and in 1819 acquired Florida from Spain. The Republic of Texas, which had broken away from Mexico, was admitted to the Union in 1845. During the Mexican-American War (1846–1848), the United States seized what is now the American Southwest and California. After the Civil War, the United States bought Alaska from Russia, and after the Spanish-American War in 1898 it acquired Puerto Rico and the Philippines. The United States also seized Hawaii, Guam, and other Pacific islands. The Middle East was incorporated into the global order after World War I, when it was the empire of the Ottoman Turks. At its height in the seventeenth century, the Ottoman Empire included the Middle East, the Balkans, North Africa, and parts of southern Russia and Ukraine. After World War I, the empire, which had fought on the German side, was replaced by the Turkish Republic in 1923, and its Middle Eastern provinces were given to France and Britain to administer under League of Nations mandates.

COLONIAL RULE

The Portuguese empire took shape before ideas about colonial rule were well developed. European protostates did not have well-developed plans for ruling and managing colonial possessions. They expanded their sovereignty by extending their principles and practices of administration, which were based on their conceptions of colonies as their private property, and on their imaginary of the non-European peoples they took it upon themselves to rule.

Portuguese sovereignty penetrated inland only in Brazil, where Portugal established captaincies ; these were ruled by individuals who received hereditary delegation of royal jurisdiction and a percentage of the royal tithes and rents in return for securing and settling horizontal strips extending indefinitely inland from the coast. In the rest of their empire, the Portuguese were content to occupy outposts on the coasts. They established a viceroyalty at Goa from which they extended a network of outposts throughout the Indian Ocean and Straits of Malacca. It was from such coastal settlements that Portugal was able to dominate the sailing routes of the Indian Ocean until challenged by the Dutch. The Spanish, on the other hand, expanded their sovereignty by constructing a territorial rather than maritime empire. Unlike the Portuguese, who were content to confine themselves to the coasts, the Spanish sought to impose themselves on land and people. Once the exploration and conquest of the Americas were completed, Spain set up a centralized administrative structure. Spain's absolutist governing practices were then transferred to Spanish possessions in the Americas.

The empire in the Americas was initially divided into two viceroyalties, New Spain (Mexico) and New Castile (Peru); each was headed by a viceroy, who ruled in the king's name. Viceroys, who were without exception born in Spain, were instructed to enforce colonial law, maintain order, and collect revenue. They were assisted by advisory and judicial bodies known as audiencias. Audiencias were established at Santo Domingo, Mexico City, Panama, Lima, Guatemala, New Galicia, and Bogotá. They were further subdivided into territorial units administered by an alcalde, who handled legal matters, and a corregidor, who executed colonial law and collected taxes. 26 The Spanish system was highly centralized, and little colonial self-government was allowed. All important decisions were made in Madrid. The wealth produced by the colonies in the Americas encouraged Spanish absolutism at home because it gave the crown an independent source of income that allowed the king to ignore his own estates (cortes) when money was needed to pay for his armies and wars. The expansion of English sovereignty took a different form. English possessions along the eastern seaboard of North America were of three types: crown colonies, which were owned by the king and governed by an appointed governor; property colonies owned by individuals such as Lord Baltimore and William Penn, who appointed their own governors and high officials; and charter colonies owned by joint-stock companies, which elected their own governors and officials.

Eventually, the crown made all the English colonies in North America into crown colonies; their governors and high officials were appointed by the king. These colonies were then grouped together under a governor-general. The English colonies were the only colonies in the Americas where locally elected assemblies played a significant part in the governance of the colony. This was a result of Parliament's new power as a governing institution in England. The joint-stock company was a common method of English and Dutch imperial conquest and administration. Privately owned mercantile companies, such as the British East India Company, Hudson's Bay Company, the Royal Africa Company, and the Dutch East India Company, were granted full sovereign powers. In addition to the monopoly on trade in a given region or commodity, these companies were allowed to raise armies, build forts, make treaties, wage war, govern, and coin money. They fought wars against non-European native peoples in the name of trade.

The Dutch East India Company, from its birth in 1602, had as its objective the capture of the spice trade in nutmeg, cloves, pepper, and cinnamon. It later fought a five-year war in the Malaccas in order to suppress a revolt of local people that had broken out in 1649 over the Dutch policy of uprooting trees to control the production of cloves. Eventually, the Dutch East India Company, from its stronghold in Djakarta, acquired territorial control throughout the entire East Indies archipelago. In effect the company became a colonial state. The British East India Company took Bengal by military force in 1764. It fought four wars with the rulers of Mysore in 1769, 1780, 1790, and 1799, who after their defeat became dependent on the company. After three wars between 1775 and 1817, the company established its rule over Maranthas. Nepal was conquered between 1814 and 1816. The company took the Punjab and Burma in the Anglo-Sikh wars (1848–1852) and the Anglo-Burmese wars (1824–1826), respectively. By the 1830s practically all of India was under the direct control of the British East India Company. 28 Although Portugal, Spain, and France used mercantile companies to further their imperial ambitions, the companies chartered by these states were for all intents and purposes state-run enterprises, not joint-stock companies organized by private commercial interests.

The French crown forced its merchants, bankers, and financiers to invest in its various East India companies. Eventually, all such companies were taken over by the state and their colonial holdings were integrated into the administrative structure of the imperial European state. 29 In Africa colonial rule reached its apogee. By the time of the scramble for Africa, the doctrines of colonial administration of non-European peoples had been developing for 500 years. At the end of the nineteenth century, the European state had acquired the administrative capacity to extract resources and coerce its subjects well beyond that of the early modern protostates, which had carried out the initial phases of European expansion. Thus, the subjugation of Africans was more systematic and exploitive than the subjugation of other peoples had been. By the end of the nineteenth century there existed basic premises about how colonial states should be organized and administered; these were ruthlessly applied to Africa. The first was effective occupation. This premise, which originated in the sixteenth century (when the English and French were challenging Spanish and Portuguese imperial claims in the West Indies based solely on the doctrine of "discovery," and reaffirmed at the Berlin Conference), required that a colonial claim be occupied physically in order for the claim to be valid.

Effective occupation extended the principle of sovereign territoriality to the colonies. The second was economic self-sufficiency. This premise required the colony to generate enough revenue to pay the costs of its administration and development. The third premise was metropolitan advantage ; colonies always had to be of some use to the European imperial state, be it economic or political. The fourth was beneficence. It was assumed that the colonial state was beneficial for the subjugated African peoples within it. This assumption was based on the universal belief that colonialism, no matter how oppressive, was better than the "savagery" and "barbarism" of African peoples. The fifth premise was permanence ; that is, it was assumed that the colonial state would last forever.

The Partition of Africa

Two methods of colonial administration developed in Africa. One was indirect rule, which used existing African rulers to administer the colony, especially in places where there was a clear pattern of African hierarchical authority that acquiesced to European conquest and made no demands. Indirect rule was favored by the British, who saw it as an inexpensive way to administer their colonies, and a means to avoid the social and political disruption that would be caused if indigenous institutions were destroyed. The other method of colonial administration was direct rule, which removed existing African rulers and substituted European administrators in their stead or made the African chief a part of the colonial administrative hierarchy. This method was favored by the other colonial powers, especially France, which minimized the importance of existing African institutions and attempted to incorporate local chiefs into the administrative apparatus. The incorporation of indigenous chiefs and the minimalization of existing African institutions was motivated by the more "positive" imperial mission of the colonial powers who employed direct rule. The French, Italians, Portuguese, Belgians, Spanish, and Germans maintained the fiction that their colonies were an integral part of their states. This positive imperial mission was mostly favored by the French, who sought to create Black Frenchmen out of their African colonial subjects and never contemplated giving them independence.

Whether ruled indirectly or directly, the most important premise of colonial rule in Africa was economic selfsufficiency. Because indigenous African economies were not monetarized, the labor of African peoples had to be converted into cash in order to meet the financial needs of the colony. This was done by forcing Africans into the money sector of the colonial economy created by the imperial power. Africans were forced into the money sector in several ways. First, a tax, which had to be paid in cash, was levied on each hut or individual. In order to earn the money to pay hut or head taxes, Africans had to work for a period of time in the European sector of the colonial economy. Such taxes, which became routine in the 1920s throughout Africa, were the chief source of colonial revenue and increased in amounts as more and more Africans were incorporated into the money economy. Second, Africans were forced into work gangs to build colonial outposts, roads, bridges, and railroads, and into portage gangs to carry supplies. The colonial authorities justified such forced labor by arguing that work was an ennobling obligation that every ablebodied African male had to fulfill. Third, colonial officials forced Africans to grow cash crops, such as peanuts, cotton, coffee, tea, and palm oil, on their own land or by forcing them to work on European-owned plantations that grew such crops. Thus, African farmers were coerced into devoting a certain amount of their own land and labor to the raising of cash crops for export, often to the detriment of the production of food for themselves, a pattern that continues today throughout the world economy.

Summary

In this chapter we addressed the construction of a global grid of European colonial possessions created though conquest and colonization. European imperialism lacked a central, directing authority, as was the case for previous empires. European imperialism was driven by economic, political, and cultural forces, which were universalizing. In the next two chapters we discuss how this interlocking global grid of European domination constructed new states, and effected the reconstitution of European sovereignty itself.

10

THE NATION-STATE: SOVEREIGNTY REIMAGINED

Through colonialism European states transferred the idea of the state to their colonies, which laid the foundation of the present global system of sovereign territorial states. A strong congruity exists between the boundary lines of the present system of independent, sovereign states and the boundaries of the administrative units of the European colonial empires, most of which were fortuitous and arbitrary markers of the limits of European conquest. A crucial force that transformed the world of colonial empires into the world of independent territorial states was nationalism, which arose in connection with popular sovereignty and liberalism and helped generate independence movements in the colonial empires. Nationalism began to connect states with "nations" by inscribing the sovereign territorial state as the dominant form of political organization throughout the world and by generating a variety of particular experiences of nationhood, depending on specific historical situations. In short, nationalism re-formed the state in an ordering of the political world that was nearly global, and created a range of challenges to European supremacy and dominance within the emerging global grid of territorial states.

IMAGINING NATIONHOOD

Originally, the word nation (from the Latin natio, meaning birth or place of origin) was a derogatory term that referred to groups of foreigners from the same place whose status was below that of Roman citizens. During the Middle Ages, the word was used to designate groups of students from the same geographical locations attending Europe's medieval universities. Because students from the same regions often took sides as a group against students from different regions in scholastic debates, the word nation came to mean an elite community of scholars who shared an opinion or had a common purpose. The medieval state was stratified into the estates of the realm and other corporate groups that did not see themselves as belonging to a common people. Medieval monarchies were ruled by kings and nobilities who spoke languages and lived lives that were quite different from those of the ordinary people they governed. This was also true of the clergy. The king and nobles of the medieval monarchy had a common outlook and culture that they shared with the king and nobles of other monarchies, despite the dynastic wars they fought against each other. The ordinary people took no part in governance, which was the affair of the king and nobility, often spoke different languages from them and the clergy, and strongly identified with their locales. The medieval state was culturally and linguistically heterogeneous. Its subjects did not share a common monarchy-wide identity. In the words of one historian, Medieval Europeans were conscious of belonging to their native village or town, and to a group possessing a local language whose members could communicate without recourse to Latin or Greek. They were aware of belonging to a body of men and women who acknowledged the same feudal lord; to a social estate, which shared the same privilege; above all, to the great corporation of Christendom.

During the early sixteenth century, the word nation began to be applied to a whole population of people from a particular geographical locale rather than to a student elite. Entire populations were elevated and made into the bearer of sovereignty, the basis of political solidarity, and the ultimate object of loyalty. One's national identity, therefore, came from being a member of a certain people, which was defined as homogeneously distinct in language, culture, race, and history from other peoples. Thus, nation came to have its contemporary meaning: "a uniquely sovereign people readily distinguishable from other uniquely defined sovereign peoples who are bound together by a sense of solidarity, common culture, language, religion, and geographical location." Scholars once thought that national identity was a natural human emotion and that the world was fundamentally divided into nations based on common cultures, languages, religions, and histories. These scholars saw nationalism as the awakening of long dormant feelings of national identity. In this understanding of nationalism the nation is awakened by its irrepressible desire for freedom, self-government, and a state of its own.

Such "Sleeping Beauty" views of nationalism have served the function of justificatory ideologies. On the contrary, we follow recent scholars who view nations not as natural and primordial but as created, imagined, and invented. 5 We view the nation as consciously invented in order to create the cultural, sociological, and psychological conditions necessary to sustain the sovereign territorial state. The development of a full-blown national identity that overrides regional, class, and religious loyalties requires the systematic effort of the state. Creating a sense of nationhood requires the breakdown of the individual's attunements to local languages and cultures in order to create a common national culture (language, values, norms of behavior) that inculcates in the state's subject population a common national frame of reference across space (i.e., territory) and time (i.e., a single national history). Therefore, creating a national identity is closely connected to the formation of territorial states. Moreover, nationalism not only re-creates the local as the national, it mediates the local and the global. Nationalism, therefore, could only have arisen in the context of the globalizing of the European state. Historically, the process of nationalizing the subject population began, as one scholar puts it, at the very time in which Europe was torn apart by the War of the Atlantic, that is, the visceral struggle between Britain and France during the long eighteenth century. . . . States were forced to extract historically unprecedented amounts from their societies.

During the eighteenth century, creating a common national community to which all subjects of the state belonged—that is, a nation bound together by a common language, culture, religion, and shared history— enabled states to raise huge armies without creating a threat to the state. Thus, the process of state formation in Europe in the eighteenth century created nations where none had previously existed in order to mobilize resources and survive in a world of competitive states. The French Revolution formally fused the idea of the nation to the state. Article 3 of the Universal Declaration of the Rights of Man, which was written by liberal revolutionaries, declares that all sovereignty resides with the people.

This declaration heightened feelings among the French that they were a unique people who had liberated themselves from the tyranny of absolute monarchy and were destined to liberate the rest of Europe as well. Napoléon's armies spread the radical ideology of liberalism and the idea of the liberated nation as they marched across Europe. The peoples that the French defeated and occupied in the Napoleonic Wars (1804–1815), such as Germans, Russians, Spanish, and Portuguese, grew to hate the French occupiers and developed feelings of national consciousness of their own. These feelings were encouraged by aspiring state-makers, who saw them as a way of mobilizing their people more easily. Initially, monarchs were reluctant to encourage nationalist sentiments, because they could subvert the existing order. Already in the seventeenth century in England claims of "the rights of Englishmen" by the gentry and commercial class were used to establish the supremacy of Parliament against the king. In the colonies, rising national sentiment was linked to challenges to the supremacy of the central monarchy and even led to calls for independence. However, kings gradually learned how to separate nationalist feelings from liberalism's claims of popular sovereignty. Therefore, states could remain monarchies and still retain sentiments of national identity, and armies loyal to the monarchical state for which they fought could be fielded.

Nations and Intellectuals

The process of creating nations was assisted by the rise in all states of a class of intellectuals who began to imagine and propagate the idea of a historically unique people conjoined to its own state. Nationalism, a self-conscious discourse of unitary national identity, was a central element of the liberal public sphere, which we discussed in Chapter 5. Although the creation and sustaining of a nation require the systematic activities of the centralized, territorial state, the specific idea of a particular nation materializes out of the preoccupations of a small number of educated elites. Nationalist intellectuals often paint a heroic picture of the nation's past and present and hide the inequalities, exploitation, and patterns of domination and subordination that the creation and maintenance of a state inevitably involve. 8 Intellectuals in general had become important with the rise of ideology in the liberal state and with the development of printing, which, by making widely available mass-produced books, magazines, and newspapers, created an audience for the discussion of ideas among the general population. Early forms of nationalism appeared in the arts, such as opera, which became a popular form of entertainment throughout Europe during the eighteenth century. Nationalism was, then, an important element in the rise of mass markets. Initially, at least, it was compatible with, and even partly responsible for, the spread of the liberal state, inscribed, as it were, as a central element of the "marketplace of ideas." It is as difficult to imagine the nation emerging without the creation of a mass market in literature, news, and culture as to imagine the mass market emerging without symbols of national identity through which its products could be sold. Moreover, the nations envisioned by nation-imagining intellectuals, the vast majority of whom have been men, have been invariably familial in form, and representations of nationhood have been ordered around conceptions of masculinity and femininity, such as "Uncle Sam" in the masculinized U.S. version, and "John Bull" in the British. In feminized versions, women are praised and revered as objects to be protected, but not as equally participating citizens.

Women appear as mistresses, rape victims, "pinup girls" on patriotic calenders, wives, girlfriends, and daughters waiting dutifully at home. In these versions, women are a subordinated and disempowered national commodity needing protection. In masculinized versions, women appear as conquerors and soldier-heroes, such as "Marianne" in the French version. Both types of representations of nationhood involve subtle and complex relationships between gender politics in the state in question and how men and women properly belong to the nation. By the middle of the nineteenth century, intellectuals across Europe were defining nationalism as the highest human value and the source of all that is good. Nationalism became an ideology in its own right. Its basic tenet was the idea that a state should share a common culture and be governed only by individuals of the same culture. The invention of a nation required hard intellectual work: dictionaries of national languages had to be compiled; a body of national poetry, literature, theater, music, opera, painting, and popular festivals had to be created; and, most significant, a distinction was necessary from other national cultures as well as "deviant" cultures within the state that resisted identity with the nation as intellectuals had fashioned it. National rituals, symbols, and insignia, such as flags, seals, and commemorations of heroic events, had to be designed. Although the task of inventing the nation rested with intellectuals, it was by propaganda and systematic political education by the state that the local identities of the subject population were shifted to the newly imagined nation.

Types of Nationalism

It is useful to distinguish different types of nationalism in order to show how nationalism helped generate and undergird different states. Three different types can be distinguished: liberal nationalism, ethnic nationalism, and anticolonial nationalism. We will discuss each of them in turn. Liberal Nationalism As we saw above, the Enlightenment imaginary of liberalism and popular sovereignty along with the French Revolution and its aftermath were crucial catalysts for the development of nationalism, both in Europe and in Europe's overseas colonies. Although not all nationalists were liberals, liberal intellectuals began to organize nationalist movements. In certain cases, liberal movements demanded changes in such extant absolutist states as France, Portugal, and Spain. In others they demanded the creation of new unified states based on liberal principles where none had previously existed, as in Germany and Italy. In still others they demanded independence from a colonial power and the formation of a republic, as in the Americas. Thus, initially, nationalism went hand in glove with the spread of liberalism. Liberal ideas spread from Europe to the Spanish, Portuguese, and English colonies in the Americas, where they were accepted by educated, locally born elites. When combined with local conditions and circumstances, they produced nationalist movements.

The first nationalist movement for independence was born in the thirteen British colonies along the eastern seaboard of North America. A colonial elite composed of locally born, prosperous New England merchants and southern planters, who had been strongly influenced by the principles of liberalism and were strenuously opposed to the taxes that had been levied on their commercial interests by the British parliament, took the opportunity created by the war in the Atlantic and organized a movement for independence that produced the first new sovereign states in the Western Hemisphere: Massachusetts, Rhode Island, New York, Pennsylvania, Maryland, Virginia, and the rest of the original 13 colonies. Although the Constitution of 1789 brought these states together into a single federal state, it took nearly a century more for the American "nation" to be created. From the Founding to the Civil War (1860–1864), ordinary people of the United States primarily identified with their respective states or regions. It was only after the Civil War that individuals became loyal to a national political community beyond their states and began to think of themselves as Americans. This American identity was bound up with Protestant ideals of an exceptional people with a unique mission in the world, which in turn convinced Americans they had the right to conquer the entire continent.

Eventually, this new nation-state itself became an imperial power that imposed its sovereignty across the landmass of North America and beyond: to Puerto Rico in the Caribbean Sea and to certain islands in the Pacific Ocean, such as Hawaii, Guam, and, eventually, the Philippines. Spain's colonial holdings in the Americas were divided into viceroyalties, which were subdivided into audiencias. Viceroys were always peninsulares, individuals born in Spain, and audiencias were staffed by locally born administrators of Spanish descent known as criollos (creoles). Gradually, the elongated shape, variation in topography and climate, and communications difficulties of Spain's vast land-based empire imparted to the criollo elite in each of its audiencias a sense that they were inhabiting distinct communities. Encouraged by the success of the independence movement in the British colonies to the north, criollo elites formed a broad movement for independence from Spain.

Discontent with and resentment against Spain was mostly economic. The colonies were a source of gold and silver and were a market for Spain's manufactured goods. Both markets were monopolized by Spaniards, who overcharged for imports and underpaid for exports. The spark that ignited rebellion was struck by Carlos III (r. 1759–1788), who in an effort to modernize the administration of the empire introduced new senior officials from Spain, whose task was to execute colonial policy more efficiently and improve the collection of taxes. The better-educated criollo elite resented the new administrators and were particularly aggrieved by the policy of promoting the importation of goods manufactured in Spain by Spanish merchants to the detriment of goods locally produced.

Napoléon's occupation of the Iberian Peninsula (between 1807 and 1810) encouraged criollos in Caracas, Buenos Aires, Bogotá, Santiago, and Mexico City to take up arms against Spain. Unlike the short, relatively bloodless war fought by the North American colonies, the war for independence from Spain lasted 20 years and produced heavy casualties. The war was not a united effort by a single army. Rather, it was fought by various armies commanded by regional leaders such as Simón Bolívar (1783–1830), who liberated most of the viceroyalty of New Granada; José de San Martin (1778–1850), who liberated the viceroyalty of La Plata and, with the help of Bernardo O'Higgins (1778–1842), defeated the Spanish in the audiencia of Chile. San Martin and Bolivar also liberated the viceroyalty of Peru. Numerous risings against Spain in the viceroyalty of New Spain, beginning in 1810, resulted in Mexico's independence in 1824.

These events sparked the creation of the United Provinces of Central America in 1823, which separated into five independent states, Costa Rica, Guatemala, Honduras, Nicaragua, and El Salvador, by 1838. When the wars for independence were over, all that remained of the Spanish empire in the Americas were Cuba, Puerto Rico, and Santo Domingo in the Caribbean. 16 In its stead were 15 new sovereign territorial states, the boundaries of which conformed very closely to the empire's original administrative subdivisions. The commitment of the criollo elite to the ideals of liberalism was limited, however, by its social conservatism, which was based on its fear of insurrection from below. The criollo elite governed large Native American and slave populations that, if imbued with liberal values and mobilized politically against Spain, would have in all likelihood revolted against criollo domination as well. The massive and bloody Indian revolt led by the Inca descendant Tupac Amurú (1742–1781) in 1780, and the slave rebellion in 1791 on the Caribbean island of Santo Domingo (which created the new state of Haiti) led by Toussaint l'Ouverture (1743–1803), were very much in the minds of many criollos as they challenged

Spanish rule. Therefore, nationalist movements in Latin America vigorously avoided mobilizing nonelites, a pattern of politics that continues to this day in the states of the region.

In contrast to Spanish America, the nationalist movement in Portugal's only colony in the Americas, Brazil, remained unified. A territory-wide mentality was present among the colonial elite because the Portuguese required their locally born administrators to circulate throughout Brazil, which prevented them from developing a strong identification with a particular locale. Unity was also favored by the displacement of the Portuguese crown to Brazil during the invasion and occupation of Portugal by Napoléon's armies from 1807 to 1810. After the Portuguese, with British help, expelled the French from Portugal, the Portuguese king stayed in Brazil until 1820. When the king finally departed for Portugal, he left his son Pedro behind to rule Brazil as regent. Pedro, who because of his long years in Brazil had been imbued with the liberal nationalism of the local elite, decided not to return to Portugal. On September 7, 1822, he declared Brazil independent and made himself constitutional emperor, Pedro I (r. 1822–1831). Brazilian independence was recognized by Portugal and no war of independence was necessary.

Brazil became a republic in 1898. 18 In Europe, liberal nationalism animated the creation of a new sovereign state, Italy, and played a role in the creation of another, Germany. We have already seen in Chapter 6 that the German-speaking region of Europe was fragmented into a multiplicity of small kingdoms, principalities, duchies, and free cities. The defeat and occupation of these entities by Napoléon's armies produced a reaction by German intellectuals, who began to demand a unified German state that would be able to defend itself against foreign foes and be based, paradoxically, on the liberal principles that the French had helped to spread. For German liberals, the demand for unity could not be separated from the demand for political rights. Because nationalism and liberalism were intertwined, German kings and princes initially resisted the demands for unity and discouraged feelings of national consciousness from developing among subject populations. This resistance was overcome to some degree during the early nineteenth century, however.

The accession to the Prussian throne of Friedrich Wilhelm IV (r. 1840–1861), who was sympathetic to nationalism and liberalism, and the establishment of the short-lived Second French Republic (1848–1852), encouraged the formation of liberal governments in a number of German states. As we also discussed in Chapter 6, the dream of a unified German constitutional monarchy failed, having been disabled by the dispute between those who wanted a greater Germany that would have included all the German-speaking territories of the Habsburgs, and those who were satisfied with a lesser Germany, which would have excluded Austria. Germany was eventually unified by Bismarck, the Prussian chancellor, in 1870, who proclaimed Germany an empire. Nationalism in Germany became increasingly antiliberal and exclusionary, considering Germans to be a unique people defined by race and culture. The Italian movement for national unity was, like the German, the result of foreign occupation. At the Congress of Vienna (1815), which concluded the Napoleonic Wars, the victors placed the many small Italianspeaking kingdoms, principalities, duchies, and city-states of the peninsula under Austrian domination and protection.

Owing to the presence of French troops in Italy during the Napoleonic Wars, liberal ideas had spread among Italian intellectuals and professionals. An Italian nationalist movement, organized primarily by liberals, began to agitate against Austrian domination and for the creation of a unified Italian state. A series of insurrections against the Austrians and for a unified constitutional state took place during the 1820s and 1830s.

These were successfully suppressed by Austrian troops. In 1848, inspired by the Second French Republic, Italian liberals were able to persuade the rulers of several of the peninsula's kingdoms and duchies (Naples, Piedmont, Tuscany, and the Papal States) to grant constitutions. A liberal uprising in Vienna (the capital of Austria) that same year sparked liberal uprisings and rebellions against foreign rule along the length of the peninsula, which, after achieving some military success, were again eventually suppressed by the Austrians. During the next 20 years, Austrian hegemony over the peninsula waned and a unified Italian state was created, with French assistance, by Piedmontese armed force and diplomacy. The Risorgimento (Resurgence), as Italy's unification is known, did not, however, produce the republic desired by the liberals, but a constitutional monarchy instead.

Ethnic Nationalism In contrast to liberal nationalism, ethnic nationalism imagines a sovereign territorial state based on a shared culture, which is assumed to be primordial. Ethnic nationalism appeared within the great multilingual and multireligious empires of the Ottomans, Habsburgs, and Romanovs during the nineteenth century, and was made possible by a notable increase in literacy as well as by industrialization, which destroyed traditional ways of life and caused a massive movement of people from the countryside to the cities. Pasts were imagined and reimagined as singular cultures. Religion, language, and history were fused together in the minds of nationalist intellectuals, who made their respective communities within these empires appear to constitute nations deserving of their own sovereign states.

Within the Ottoman Empire (1453–1918), Greek, Bulgarian, Albanian, Romanian, Armenian, and SerboCroatian-speaking intellectuals, along with merchants, priests, teachers, and university students, became interested in their own languages. They wrote dictionaries and began to publish poetry and histories of their communities, creating a national identity among the literate elements of these communities. Eventually, such sentiments were transformed into a political demand for independence. Many achieved success, however, only when forces outside of the empire intervened on the side of the nationalists. Thus, Greek intellectuals who had demanded an independent Greece as early as 1798, and had instigated numerous uprisings in subsequent years, were eventually successful in 1828 thanks to Russian intervention. Bulgarian Orthodox priests, who were, in effect, nationalists in ecclesiastical robes, achieved a separate Orthodox Church, with a Bulgarian-speaking oxarch as its head, after a decade of effort.

A nationalist uprising in 1876 was savagely put down by the Turks. Two years later, Russia went to war with the Ottomans, which resulted in the creation of the sovereign state of Bulgaria. The empire was finally dissolved by the Allies after World War I, the Ottomans having sided with imperial Germany and the Austro-Hungarian Empire. Turkey, the core of the Ottoman imperial territory, became a sovereign state in 1923. The Middle Eastern provinces of the empire were placed under British and French control and were ruled under mandates granted by the newly organized League of Nations.

The Austro-Hungarian Empire, which had been gradually built up by the Austrian branch of the Habsburg family through war and dynastic marriage, was a polyglot realm that stretched from Gibraltar to Hungary, and from Sicily to Holland. Within it, the idea of nationality was officially rejected, the unity of the empire being maintained by the principle of loyalty to the emperor, who was seen as above ethnic differences. In 1784, a decision to conduct all of the empire's official business in German instead of Latin suddenly placed non-German-speaking intellectuals from among the Czech, Slovak, Hungarian, Polish, and Italian communities at a disadvantage with regard to social, economic, and political advancement within the imperial system. This disadvantage engendered nationalist movements throughout the empire.

The strongest nationalist movement was in the Magyar (Hungarian)-speaking provinces, where a Magyar language movement was already well developed. Budapest, with its university and parliament, was the center of intellectual and political life. There, Hungarian nationalists agitated for a public education system in which instruction would be in Magyar. In the 1830s and 1840s, the Hungarian parliament passed laws that made Magyar the language of government, administration, and public instruction within the province. Defeated by the French in 1859 and the Prussians in 1866, the emperor was forced to relax his rule, and in 1867 Hungary essentially became a semisovereign state within the empire, hence the name AustroHungarian empire. Nationalist forces representing other linguistic communities steadily gained ground within the empire. The assassination of the heir to the Austro-Hungarian throne, Archduke Franz-Ferdinand (1863–1914), while on an official visit to Sarajevo, the Bosnian capital, by a Serbian nationalist in June 1914 precipitated World War I.

After being defeated by the Allies, the Austro-Hungarian Empire was broken up into five sovereign states: Austria; Hungary; Poland; Czechoslovakia, which brought together Czechs and Slovaks; and Yugoslavia, which was composed of Slovenians, Croatians, Bosnians, Serbians, Montenegrans, and Macedonians. The overthrow of the czar in Russia, the turmoil caused by the Bolshevik revolution of 1917, and the subsequent civil war created conditions that permitted a number of territories within the Russian Empire to become independent states: Finland ; the Baltic states of Latvia, Lithuania, and Estonia; Georgia ; and Ukraine. The last two were reincorporated into the Soviet Union after the victory of the Bolsheviks in the civil war as were the Baltic states with Hitler's consent in 1940.

Anticolonial Nationalism

A third type of nationalism that demanded independence arose in the large number of anticolonial nationalist movements in the twentieth century. Independence was often granted without the need for armed struggle, although there were many exceptions. For 30 years or so after the end of World War II, a flood of new sovereign states appeared on the globe in Asia, Africa, and the Middle East. The legacy of World War II and the subsequent Cold War enabled the achievement of independence by many colonial states. First, European states had been weakened significantly by the war, making maintenance of colonial empires expensive and logistically difficult, especially against increasingly organized nationalist opposition. Second, the determination of the United States to rebuild a capitalist world economy favorable to its own economic expansion led it to support independence, provided the new states would remain open to U.S. influence and investment. The hegemonic position of the United States in the world economy enabled it to informally dominate postcolonial states. When nationalists threatened to forge real independence in states that the United States considered economically or strategically important, it installed more compliant indigenous rulers, often through direct military intervention.

Third, nationalism in colonial states itself was a "derivative discourse."

That is, having originated among Western-educated elites in the colonies, it was reflexively incorporated into the local experience. This resulted in political programs among the revolutionaries that sought to build states along the lines of European models. Hence, nationalist revolutionaries sought to build states suited to the conditions of their own societies and cultures as they saw them, but usually within the territorial boundaries and conceptual parameters of the European system. Creating independent states in colonial areas according to nationalist programs involved a particular dilemma that led to attempts to produce highly centralized states. On the one hand, newly independent states had to ensure their autonomy from former colonial powers and to counter attempts to both reassert the direct colonial control and to assert more informal dominance that would render independence and sovereignty moot. This led not only to a central role for the military in the new states, but to politico-military strategies needed to confront the often overwhelming military forces of the former colonial powers. Insurgencies, which included political organization of sympathetic civilian populations, charted not only new rules of military engagement but also conditioned new forms of state power. The most significant such case was in Vietnam, where nationalists first defeated French attempts to reassert colonial control after World War II, and then U.S. attempts to impose de facto control over a nominally independent state.

Once imagined, the nation had to be promoted and maintained against alternative imaginaries of social and political life that did not self-consciously stake the future to a centralized nation-state or participation in a world order of nation-states. In Asia the first colony to become independent under these terms was British India, where Mohandas Gandhi (1869–1948) became the first post–World War II nationalist leader to attract a mass following. Educated in London in law, he initially practiced in South Africa, where he organized the Indian community against British racial policies.

Upon returning to India in the 1920s, he began to agitate for independence. Using campaigns of nonviolent, passive resistance, hunger strikes, and peaceful protest marches rooted in a particular blending of Hindu and Western ideas and practices, his movement forced the British to quit India in June 1948. As a parting gesture of colonial power, and in an attempt to limit widespread ethnic bloodshed, which the British had earlier encouraged in order to divide Hindus and Muslims, the British partitioned India into two new states: the northwest and most of Bengal in the east becoming Pakistan, led by its own nationalist leader, the Western-educated Muslim lawyer Muhammad Ali Jinnah (1876–1948), and the remainder becoming India. 26 In southeast Asia nationalist movements appeared in the British colonies of Burma (now Myanmar), which was granted independence in 1948, and Malaya, which contained a sizable Chinese population that had immigrated to the colony during the nineteenth century and had concentrated themselves in the city of Singapore.

The Chinese were linguistically and culturally distinct from the indigenous Malays, spawning two rival nationalist movements that nevertheless cooperated with each other in ousting the British in 1957. Independent Malaya did not initially include Singapore, which remained under British rule. But six years after independence, in 1963, a new and larger state was created, called Malaysia, which included Singapore and two former British territories on the island of Borneo. This arrangement lasted only until 1965, when Singapore, led by Lee Kuan Yew, seceded and became an independent state.

The forerunners of the nationalist movement in the Philippines were Spanish-educated, liberal intellectuals who lobbied for the Philippines to become a regular province of Spain and for certain civil liberties and reforms of the civil service. The leading light among this group, known as the Propagandist, was José Rizal (1861–1896), a physician, sculptor, novelist, and poet. His execution in December 1896, after being falsely accused by the Spanish of leading an armed uprising, sparked rebellions in several provinces, which the Spanish suppressed. The nationalist uprising continued after the United States defeated Spain in 1898 and took control of the Philippines. Fighting between the United States and Filipino rebels lasted from 1899 until 1901, when the nationalist leader Emilio Aguinaldo (1869–1964) was captured.

The United States began to prepare the Philippines for independence, ensuring that an independent regime would be favorable to U.S. interests. Although progress toward independence was interrupted by Japanese occupation from 1942 to 1944, the Philippines became a sovereign state on July 4, 1946. In the Dutch East Indies several small nationalist groups appeared in the 1920s, led by Dutch-educated Javanese. The most outstanding of these was

Ahmed Sukarno (1901–1970), who was imprisoned by the Dutch but released by the Japanese when they occupied the Dutch East Indies during World War II. After the war, the efforts by the Dutch to restore their rule were vigorously resisted. Sukarno established a stronghold on the island of Java and defeated Dutch attempts to reunify the islands. Indonesia, including all the islands of the Dutch East Indies, became independent in 1950.

The nationalist movement in French Indochina began among French-educated Vietnamese intellectuals between World War I and World War II. Encouraged by the Vichy regime in France, the nationalists resisted the Japanese occupation of Indochina in 1940. The leader of this resistance was Ho Chi Minh (1890–1969), who had been educated in France and had lived many years in various European states and the United States. When the Japanese were defeated, the Vietminh, as the Vietnamese nationalist movement was known, were in a strong position, especially in the north, which they controlled. The French hoped to create a federated Indochina composed of Vietnam, Laos, and Cambodia. Negotiations failed to produce an agreement, however, and in December 1946 the Vietminh attacked French military forces.

After seven years of war, which culminated with the defeat of the French at Dien Bien Phu, an international conference, which met in Geneva in 1954, granted independence to Cambodia and Laos, and divided Vietnam at the seventeenth parallel. This division produced two rival governments in Vietnam: a communist one in the north, led by Ho Chi Minh and supported by China and the Soviet Union, and an authoritarian one in the south, led by Ngo Dinh Diem (1901–1963) and supported by the United States.

Although the Geneva Conference called for reunification of north and south in an internationally supervised election, this election was never held because of the active opposition to it by the southern government, which was almost certain to lose. In 1958 the Vietcong, a southern communist and nationalist group wanting unification, rebelled against the government of the south, whose armed forces were lavishly supported by the United States. In 1964, fearing a collapse of the southern government, the United States sent its own armed forces to Vietnam. Despite a massive military effort, the United States was unable to defeat the combined forces of the Vietcong and the North Vietnamese.

In 1973 the United States abandoned the southern government, and two years later, in 1975, the whole of Vietnam became independent under the government of the north, which had successfully linked communism to the idea of Vietnamese nationhood. In Africa south of the Sahara, nationalism was influenced by pan-Africanism, a movement initiated by welleducated blacks from the West Indies, such as Marcus Garvey (1887–1940), George Padmore (1902?– 1959), and the black U.S. scholar and academic W. E. B. DuBois (1868–1963). Pan-Africanism encouraged pride in African heritage and organized a number of conferences in the 1920s, which brought together African American and African intellectuals, writers, poets, and painters to discuss common concerns. Aimé Césaire, a poet from Martinique, developed the concept of Négritude around which an impressive literature and poetry developed in French-speaking colonies.

The sixth Pan-African Conference held in Manchester, England, in 1945 was attended by many African intellectuals, such as Kwame Nkrumah, Jomo Kenyatta, and Léopold Sédar Senghor, who were destined to lead nationalist movements in their respective colonies. In 1945 three independent states existed in Africa south of the Sahara: Ethiopia, Liberia, and South Africa. Ethiopia had never been colonized; Liberia had been founded in the 1840s as a haven for freed American slaves; and South Africa, which had come under British hegemony at the beginning of the nineteenth century, had been granted independence in 1931.

It was subsequently led by a minority, racist government of elite descendants of Dutch colonizers. The first effective African nationalist movement in the postwar period appeared in the Gold Coast, a British colony, which had a relatively large class of well-educated Africans. The movement for independence in the Gold Coast was led by Kwame Nkrumah (1909–1972), who, inspired by Gandhi in India, launched a campaign of civil disobedience and passive resistance in 1950.

Nkrumah's movement won the elections held in 1951 called for by constitutional reforms instituted by Britain in 1949; these reforms had allowed the Gold Coast to prepare itself for independence by becoming internally self-governing. In March 1957 the Gold Coast became the first African colony to become an independent state, and its name was changed to Ghana. Within a few years nationalist movements in other British African colonies achieved independence.

In Nigeria, three regional and ethnic nationalist movements had appeared: one founded by Nnamdi Azikiwi (1904–1996) with support from educated Ibos in the colony's southeast; another, founded in 1951 by Chief Obafemi Awolowo (1907–1987), drew support from the Yoruba people in the west; and the third was supported by the Muslim Hausa-Fulani people, located in the north. In October 1960 Nigeria became independent as a federal state. Additional British colonies in West Africa followed: Sierra Leone in 1961 and The Gambia in 1965.

In the East African British colony of Kenya the nationalist movement was blocked by resistance from a large European settler population, which owned large plantations situated on land taken from the Kikuyu people.

The nationalist movement, which was founded by educated Kikuyus such as Jomo Kenyatta (1894–1978), who had earned a doctorate in anthropology in Britain, began to agitate for the return of their lands. In 1952 a Kikuyu uprising, known as Mau Mau, broke out. The resulting crackdown led to the imprisonment of Kenyatta, a ruthless policy of repression, and the forced resettlement of native peoples into Britishcontrolled villages. Such "pacification" continued until 1959, when Kenyatta was released from prison; he became president of a newly independent Kenya in 1963.

The other British colonies in East Africa also achieved independence: Tanganyika, which the British had taken over from Germany after World War I, became independent in 1961 under the leadership of Julius Nyerere, a Western-educated Methodist minister; Uganda followed in 1962. British colonies in southern Africa included three territories—Northern Rhodesia, Southern Rhodesia, and Nyasaland—which had been joined in 1953 in the Central African Federation. A substantial number of European settlers in the Rhodesias bitterly opposed the African nationalist movements that had sprung up. In Nyasaland, where there were few white settlers, the U.S.-educated physician Hastings Banda won widespread African support.

Despite white resistance, Britain yielded to the demands of the African nationalists: Nyasaland and Northern Rhodesia became the sovereign states of Malawi and Zambia, respectively, in 1964. Southern Rhodesia remained a colony and the African nationalist leader, Joshua Nkomo, was jailed. The whites in Rhodesia, from whose name "Southern" was dropped, were determined to maintain themselves in power, whereas the British government insisted on independence under African majority rule.

In November 1965 the leader of the white community, Ian Smith, unilaterally declared Rhodesia independent from Britain and under white rule. The British and the international community imposed economic sanctions, which lasted for 11 years. At the same time African nationalists, now led by Robert Mugabe, took up arms and waged a low-grade guerrilla war against the white minority regime from sanctuaries in the newly independent states of Tanzania, Zambia, and Malawi.

Finally, in September 1976 the Smith government capitulated and agreed to constitutional revisions designed to give Rhodesia an African government within two years. In 1980 Robert Mugabe became president of the sovereign state of Zimbabwe. In the Congo, little had been done to prepare the African population for independence, which had never even been contemplated by the Belgians. By the end of the 1950s there was only a handful of universityeducated Africans in the colony.

In 1959 riots, organized by various nationalist groups, broke out. The Belgian government reacted by attempting to rapidly prepare the colony for independence. Elections were quickly held for rural and town councils. In 1960 the Belgians hastily granted the Congo its independence, but the Congo fell into civil war as various nationalist leaders, aided and abetted by rivalry among the European states, fought to gain control of the central government. Eventually, Joseph Mobutu (1930–1997), the commander of the Congolese armed forces, achieved ascendancy over the others and in 1965 changed the former Belgian colony's name to Zaire. (We will have more to say about Congo/Zaire in the next chapter.)

Although the French never considered independence for their African colonies, the situation after World War II made their cultural position untenable. During the 1950s, elections were held for assemblies in the eight territories of French West Africa : for a territory-wide assembly located in Dakar and for deputies to the French National Assembly in Paris. In 1958 the French offered the territories of French West Africa the choice of complete independence or membership in a new confederation of French-speaking states tied to France.

Initially, only the territory of Guinea accepted the offer; it became independent in 1958. By 1960 six additional territories— Senegal, Mali, Niger, Upper Volta (now Burkina Faso), Benin, and Côte d'Ivoire — followed Guinea's lead and became independent. Mauritania, the eighth territory, chose independence as well, although formal recognition was delayed by a claim by Morocco that it had been historically part of Moroccan territory. Togo, a former German colony governed by France under League of Nations' and United Nations' mandates, was given independence in 1960.

The island of Madagascar, which became the Malagasy Republic, and the four territories of French Equatorial Africa, which became Chad, Central African Republic, Congo, and Gabon, were also given independence in 1960. Cameroon, also a former German colony governed by the French under League of Nations' and United Nations' mandates, was also granted independence in that year. Portugal was the last European imperial state to leave Africa. Portugal steadfastly clung to the doctrine that its colonies in Africa were an integral part of Portugal and refused to contemplate independence. Nationalist movements led by well-educated African elites sprung up in every Portuguese colony. Faced with Portuguese intransigence, these movements had to take up arms in order to achieve independence.

In Mozambique, the U.S.-educated college professor Eduardo Mondlane (1920–1969) led the armed nationalist struggle from sanctuaries in Tanzania until he was killed by a letter bomb sent by the Portuguese secret police in 1969. His death did not deter the African nationalists, who continued the struggle. In Angola three rival elite-led nationalist movements sprung up, each drawing support from different ethnic groups. One was led by José Eduardo dos Santos, and was supported by the well-educated intelligentsia in the capital city of Luanda; another was led by Holden Roberto and was supported by the Bakongo people; and the third was led by Jonas Savimbi and supported by the Ovimbundu. All three movements waged war against the Portuguese and each other from safe havens in neighboring Zaire and Zambia.

In Portuguese Guinea the nationalist movement was led by the agronomist Amílcar Cabral (1921–1973). His assassination by the Portuguese in 1973 did not deter the nationalists, who continued the armed struggle under new leadership. Despite the commitment of 200,000 troops, the Portuguese were not able to stamp out the independence movements. Eventually, war-weariness in Portugal and discontent within the armed forces resulted in the overthrow of the authoritarian civilian government in Lisbon on April 25, 1974. Portugal's new democratic government granted independence in 1975 to Guinea (Bissau), Mozambique, and Angola. Angola was plunged into a civil war as fighting continued among the above-mentioned rival nationalist movements, which, aided and abetted by outside states, has continued to the present, despite the imposition of 12,000 Cuban troops from late 1975 to May 1991, and several truces brokered by the Portuguese.

All but a handful of the newly independent African states contained a medley of different ethnic groups lumped together into new political units, the boundaries of which paid no heed to indigenous ones.

The only cases where the territorial boundaries of the new African states conformed to the traditional boundaries of ethnic groups were Swaziland, Lesotho, and Botswana, all three of which had been British colonies and achieved their independence in 1967, 1966, and 1966, respectively. One new state, Somalia (1960), which had been an Italian colony, also contains only one ethnic group; this group, the Somalis, also live in neighboring Ethiopia and Kenya. In Africa north of the Sahara and in the Middle East, only Iran (Persia) had never been colonized and only the Kingdom of Saudi Arabia, Egypt, and Iraq, which we will examine in more detail in the next chapter, had achieved independence between World War I and II, the last two under treaties with Britain that greatly restricted their sovereignty.

The basis of nationalism in North Africa and the Middle East was rooted in the idea of a single Arabic-speaking nation transcending the borders imposed by European colonization, which was articulated by a small elite between World War I and II. The idea of a pan-Arab nation was strongest in Syria, Iraq, and Egypt.

During this period, pan-Arab nationalism was intensified by the conflict between Arabs and Jews in Palestine, caused by the Balfour Declaration of 1917, which had called for the establishment of a Jewish homeland in Palestine, and where Jewish immigration from Germany was on the rise because of Hitler's anti-Semitic policies. Arabs saw their lands being taken and given to European settlers. With the outbreak of World War II, Arab nationalists looked to the fascist states of Italy and Germany as future liberators. In the immediate postwar period, pan-Arab nationalism became even stronger owing to the partitioning of Palestine by the United Nations into two states, one Jewish and the other Arab. The Arabs rejected this decision and attacked the Jewish state of Israel when its independence was proclaimed in 1948. When the Israelis defeated the Arabs, an armistice was concluded in 1949 under United Nations auspices. The Arabs never accepted this settlement and refused to recognize Israel, which they attacked again in 1967 (the Six-Day War) and 1973 (the Yom Kippur War).

The defeat of the Arabs by Israel accelerated the spread of pan-Arab nationalism. In Egypt the Free Officers Movement led by Lt. Colonel Gamal Abdel Nasser (1918–1970), who supported pan-Arabism, toppled King Farouk in 1952. In North Africa in the early 1950s, the French attempted to stop the spread of Arab nationalism by taking repressive measures. In 1951 they arrested Tunisian nationalist leaders and in 1953 they deposed Morocco's sultan, who was sympathetic to the pan-Arab cause. As these measures did not bring about the desired results, the French were forced to grant independence to Tunisia and Morocco in 1956. In Algeria, which the French considered to be an integral part of France, an insurrection led by the nationalist Ben Bella broke out in 1954. A savage guerrilla war, intensified by the presence of nearly a million French settlers, many of whom had been born in Algeria, raged until 1958. Algeria was granted independence in 1962. In 1962 the British abandoned the South Arabian Protectorate, which became South Yemen; in 1971 they unilaterally abrogated the protective treaties with the southern Persian Gulf states of Bahrain, Qatar, and the United Arab Emirates, which became sovereign states.

Summary

Nationalism can be a progressive force, supportive of liberal rights and independence. It should not be mistaken as an "emotional" response to European colonialism; it arose as part of rational and often scholarly discourses about language, history, and law; it was transferred to non-Western states by Western-educated elites who viewed national independence as a rationally grounded right of their people. The creation of new states out of colonial empires created a new ruling class of nationalist elites, usually educated in Europe, who promoted the state as the logical consequence of national autonomy.

11

THE POSTCOLONIAL STATE: REFLEXIVE SOVEREIGNTY

The idea of the territorial state as it had evolved in Europe was imposed on the globe. Remember that the territorial boundaries of the vast majority of non-European states were defined by the imperial states of Europe as they colonized the planet. The anti-European nationalist movements led by indigenous elites promised a reversal of external domination, a recovery of the past, and a chance to construct an independent future. In their drive toward independence, indigenous nationalist elites in non-European states either accepted the institutions of direct rule imposed by the colonial power or created their own. In effect, indigenous elites used the instruments of direct rule as they had evolved in Europe to reimagine the state in order to achieve economic independence and political sovereignty within a global system of states.

AGAINST MODERNIZATION THEORY

Outside Europe, nationalism was bound up with programs to transform colonies into modern sovereign states. This entailed viewing indigenous peoples as living in "traditional" societies and European peoples as living in "modern" societies. Modernization theory developed in European social science to explain the process of transformation from traditional to modern societies. Traditional societies were defined as those characterized by small villages, subsistence agriculture, simple social structures, and particularistic behavior. Modern societies were defined as those characterized by cities and towns, commercial agriculture, industry, complex social structures, and universalistic behavior. Modernization scholars believed that the transition to modernity, the condition of being modern, would recapitulate the European experience. It was supposed that the former colonies would undergo the same developmental processes that European states had experienced, and would, eventually, end up looking much like them. This way of understanding modernization assumes that all states would, over time, pass through a single, universal process of state formation. Further, it assumes that the original European states had reached the end of the process.

The end point toward which all non-European states were supposedly evolving, albeit at different rates, was the industrialized, democratized, urbanized, bureaucratized, and culturally cohesive nation-states of Europe. Such a view is, first of all, ahistorical; that is, it sees the creation of the state as a universal, inevitable process rather than as a result of historical conditions and actions. Second, such a view is ideological in two ways. First, it hides from view, and implicitly justifies, the power, violence, exploitation, and racism through which Europeans imposed the state in non-European areas. Second, it considers the state's positive features as a gift of a modern, rationalist European civilization to the non-European world, and its negative features as the result of the inability of non-European peoples to live up to advanced European standards. Again, the result is to justify a European global order that either eliminates or co-opts non-European ways of life, transforming them so that they reinforce the global order. We saw that the original states emerged from a more or less common feudal and medieval basis, but owing to different situational factors, different outcomes of political struggles within them, and different pressures and influences from other states, they followed different trajectories that resulted in different forms of the state. State sovereignty is a modal feature of the modern world, that is, a model that migrates and is taken up and reworked by indigenous peoples according to particular circumstances and conditions.

Modernization theory's effect as a discipline of knowledge about states is to mark non-European states as always lagging behind the more "advanced" states of Europe. This reinforces the dualistic political and moral structure of European-created international society, although in a way that allows for a degree of independence of those states, but which "regulates" their sovereignty. That is, this way of thinking about non-European states encourages and sanctions behaviors that limit the sovereignty of non-European states, both by European states and by indigenous elites seeking to "modernize" them. This is not to deny that many non-European states, especially postcolonial states, have been ruled by ruthless civilian dictators and military strongmen. It is to say, however, that modernization theory prejudges these states by declaring such regimes as normal, natural, and even necessary in the "young" or "politically immature" states outside of Europe. Paradoxically, then, modernization theory sanctions intervention by "more advanced" or "more developed" states while simultaneously justifying military regimes and dictatorships, with all their horrors and cruelties, as necessary to these "undeveloped" states.

REFLEXIVE DEVELOPMENT

Non-European states must be understood not in terms of a presumed universal process of modernization exemplified by the original European states but, rather, in terms of how the sovereign state as a political form of hierarchical domination was constituted reflexively in the context of local cultures, power struggles among contending elites, the colonial experience, and race relations produced by the encounter between European and non-European peoples. In addition, we must take into account the global system of states, as well as the world economy, both of which have pressured non-European states to develop in specific ways. European states, and the global order their colonial activities generated, influenced and controlled developments within non-European states. Sovereignty, then, in non-European states has been both contested within and limited from without. The colonial encounters complemented and clashed with local conditions, generating certain spaces in which sovereignty was contested. One of the most important was the space occupied by ethnicity. Ethnicity provided an alternative identity around which political life could be organized in and against the new territorial state. 6 Ethnicity should not be thought of as a given attribute of people; it is an identity that people come to adopt under the conditions set by the struggles for independence, and just as with nationalism, its specific features, such as language, racial characteristics, shared histories, and religion, are constructed under modern circumstances.

In many cases, competition among contending elites for control of the institutions of the state and direct rule came to be organized around ethnicity, with different leaders drawing their support from particular ethnic groups whose solidarity they constructed and played upon. Thus, control of the state has been fiercely contested by strong individuals connected by patron-client networks to particular clans, tribes, social classes, or regions. These struggles to control the state and the concomitant ability to extract resources for oneself and one's supporters from the enclosed subject population, fragmented into rival ethnic groups, has created much turmoil in non-European states, especially those created by direct European conquest. This turmoil has legitimized military rule as well as the frequent intervention of former colonial powers in the name of "stability." Some states outside of Europe were created by the mass migrations of Europeans to non-European areas of the globe, such as in North and South America, Australia, and New Zealand. In these states, the local peoples, such as the Iroquois and other tribes in North America, Incan peoples in South America, Mayan peoples in Mexico, and Aborigines in Australia, became what we can call internal exile s, "others" within a territory that was ruled by a state that kept them out by pushing them off the land they occupied. Other states outside Europe were made according to two different but not unrelated reflexive processes. The first such method of reflexive state formation was by direct conquest of non-European peoples and their domination by European states. In this situation, the idea of the state was directly imposed on tribal, often nomadic, peoples whose politics were not oriented to a formalized, territorial space.

Direct conquest created new politicized spaces within which complex social hierarchies based on race (white over black), religion (Christian over pagan), and ethnicity (tribe over tribe) generated new practices of domination and submission. Nationalist elites in these directly created and dominated states sought to reverse the hierarchies of dominance and submission through independence. However, nationalist elites in such states were not able simply to reject the state imposed by direct conquest and return to some precolonial past. The second method of reflexive state formation in non-European areas of the globe was by external inducement. In this situation states developed from indigenous systems of politics in areas that were never directly conquered by European states. Externally induced states, such as Japan, which we will discuss further below, were produced through the ability of certain non-European peoples, for various reasons, to resist direct European hegemony and survive into the present by adopting the institutions and practices of the European state and grafting them to indigenous systems of rule.

INSTITUTING SOVEREIGNTY IN NON-EUROPEAN STATES

For European states the right of one state to be sovereign implied the right of all others to be sovereign as well. The states-system invoked background understandings of freedom, autonomy, rights, and equality, which were taken to be universal even as they justified and authorized particular states. This meant that the gaining of sovereignty by non-European states was, in effect, a direct challenge to European global domination. The right to self-determination, then, although an important constitutive rule of the sovereign state and states-system, created a significant dilemma: the global system has come to depend simultaneously on the universal principles of sovereignty for all and the maintenance of dominance and control by major powers. The solution that has emerged we describe as the regulation of sovereignty. European states (including the United States) have sought to regulate the sovereignty of non-European states as a condition of the latter's independence. Non-European states, although nominally independent, have been continuously subjected either to direct military intervention or to a panoply of less dramatic measures to ensure that they developed and maintained a particular form of sovereignty that followed the prevailing norms of the European-created system. We have already mentioned the role of modernization theory in such regulation. More important, the integration of non-European states into the world capitalist economy has fostered the regulation of their sovereignty. It has opened non-European states, and increasingly all states, to surveillance in order to ensure compliance with the norms and principles of capitalism as set by the international economic system.

It has also subjected them to daunting pressures to manage their economies and societies in ways consistent with integration into the world capitalist economy, such as conditioning loans on the adoption of deregulatory policies and reduced state subsidies and social benefit programs. NonEuropean states are the objects of enormous data gathering and analysis. The World Bank annual development reports, for example, are used as the basis for aid and investment decisions by European states, banks, major corporations, and investors. Subject states are constrained to do what is necessary to produce "good" reports in order to encourage investment and to enable broader access to markets for their own exports. The regulation of sovereignty through the global capitalist economy has increasingly become the case for all states. From the non-European point of view, instituting sovereignty required constant wariness against direct European military intervention designed to structure sovereignty to the former colonial power's liking, and/or toward the global agencies of the regulation of sovereignty, such as the World Bank, International Monetary Fund (IMF), the United Nations, and foreign aid programs.

It should be kept in mind, first, that for many of the former colonial states the "outside" pressures from former colonial states were already "inside" at the time of independence. That is, the act of colonization established boundaries and created state institutions that constrained and conditioned the sovereignty of postcolonial states at the outset of independence. Civil service institutions and militaries, which were initially formed as direct appendages of colonial rule, remained the backbone of the state apparatus after independence. Military advisers from the former colonial power often remained after independence to train the armies and police of the new states.

Second, nationalist leaders generally accepted both the basic principles and outlines of the European concept of territorial sovereignty, leading them to create states within the territorial borders arbitrarily established by the colonial powers and to comply with the norms of an international system that limited their sovereignty. Third, economies of the newly independent states usually remained dependent upon the economy of the former colonial power, which controlled the value of their money, provided the markets for their exports, supplied investment capital, and owned much of their land and national assets. It should also be kept in mind that sovereignty was contested, actually and potentially, by numerous forces within these states themselves. The identity of these forces depended upon the history and circumstances of the particular state. In some cases, conservative and reactionary nationalists sought to revive precolonial kings or emperors as heads of modern states. As we will see, this was the case in Japan, where during the nineteenth century Japanese nationalists influenced by the Prussian model sought to build a militaristic state that looked back to a presumed glorious imperial past. In many non-European states, nationalist leaders imported Western models of sovereignty (usually socialist but on occasion liberal), which they sought either to meld with or to replace local traditions. It should be remembered that "local traditions" had already been modified and reconstituted by colonialism, as, for example, in the spread of Christianity, which fused with native religions.

The efforts of nationalist elites to create sovereign states were contested, then, both by forces that sought to constitute sovereignty differently from those in power and by numerous forces that resisted the imposition of sovereignty altogether, preferring indigenous ways of social organization and political practice. And, of course, these internal struggles were not isolated from "outside" influences that limited and regulated sovereignty: European powers sought to influence the outcome of these struggles in part by manipulating what remained of the colonial structures, such as the church, the military, civil service, landowner organizations, and corporations, and in part by giving military, financial, and diplomatic aid to various factions in local struggles. Under such circumstances, a written constitution generally plays a different role in instituting sovereignty than it does for European states, but not because non-European peoples are too immature or politically undeveloped to appreciate constitutionalism, as modernization theory once argued.

Rather, this differing role was due to the distinctive historical circumstances that condition the emergence of non-European states. In Europe, constitutions establishing the basic institutional form of the state served to unify the subject population in time and space, as the American Constitution did for the diverse colonial society of southern planters, New England merchants, yeoman farmers, and urban artisans. Because the modern European nation-state emerged in the context of developing capitalism, constitutions served as focal points of national unity by providing the framework of laws that, above all, stabilized commercial relations and reinforced the political and social order necessary to a market economy. In many states, however, especially postcolonial states, the constitution does not perform the same function. In such states, the linkages between local and national were not established primarily by capitalist markets. In so-called patrimonial states, for example, individuals seek to acquire power through patronage (from the Latin patron, or a person chosen as a special guardian or protector)—that is, through connections with strong individuals and a particular family, clan, tribe, village, or region within the state. In many nonEuropean states, the political links between local and national are made by patron-client networks through which powerful politicians in the capital city (patrons) have close personal connections to less powerful politicians (clients) among certain families, clans, tribes, or villages.

The relationship between the patron and clients is reciprocal. Patrons receive political support from their clients in exchange for access to government jobs, contracts, assistance with the state's bureaucracy, and government spending programs. Clients provide loyalty and political support. In such states, then, the tremendous power and authority of sovereignty is manifested in the personal rule of the strong leader. It is significant that such a form of rule establishes spatial linkages and identities that do not necessarily conform to the territorial boundaries of the state, especially of those drawn by European colonial powers; that is, tribal, clan, ethnic, racial, religious, and other such networks and identities either do not fill completely or they overflow the borders of states. It should also be noted that personal rule and the patron-client networks it engenders have become political forces only as the result of the imposition of the state from outside and are not a given consequence of indigenous peoples' being organized into families, clans, or tribes. It is not surprising, given the historical circumstances of their emergence, that non-European states have often been ruled by the military. The military was the strongest institution in most non-European, postcolonial states at the time of independence. The military and the police were the European institutions of direct rule and thus had been in existence for an extended period prior to independence; parliaments, presidencies, and prime ministerships were usually created only on the eve of independence.

Moreover, the military was reasonably well trained, well equipped, and well versed in the techniques of controlling civilians and putting down rebellion. The strength of the military as an institution was also enhanced by the fact that it was often supported with training and equipment from European states (usually the former colonial power). The military has often been able to establish itself as the "real" unifier of the nation, as the necessary bulwark against the outside dominance of European states.

Varieties of Reflexive State Formation

We now turn to three cases of reflexive state formation, Japan, Iraq, and the Republic of the Congo, in order to show in detail how their sovereignty was instituted, regulated, and conditioned by forced participation in the European state system, including the world capitalist economy, as well as by indigenous cultures, conditions, and political struggles. Japan: Externally Induced State Formation The Japanese archipelago consists of four main islands: Honshu, which is the largest; Kyushu and Shikoku to the south; and Hokkaido to the north, as well as numerous smaller islands. The original inhabitants of these islands were the Ainu, an ancient Caucasoid people. The Ainus were gradually displaced to the northern island of Hokkaido by successive waves of Mongoloid peoples, who entered the islands from the Asian mainland through the Korean peninsula. Governance among them was clan-based. Each clan consisted of a number of households that claimed to have descended from a common chieftain. Eventually, one of these chieftains, Yamato, became dominant over the others.

In the fifth century A.D., Japan fell increasingly under the influence of imperial China. Chinese religion, Buddhism, and the Chinese system of centralized territorial rule were imported. The chieftain of the dominant clan was proclaimed emperor, and a bureaucracy selected according to competitive examination was created to assist him in governing. Centralization was resisted by the chieftains of the clans, especially the richest and most powerful. Gradually, large areas of the archipelago fell under the rule of powerful chieftains, who gathered around themselves groups of armed retainers who helped protect their domains. These armed retainers eventually formed a warrior caste, known as the samurai, which rendered faithful service to the chieftains in return for payments of rice. The samurai, not unlike the warrior nobility of the European feudal "state," developed a code of conduct, called bushido, which emphasized good deeds, bravery, and unswerving loyalty.

Japan, 900

Japanese feudalism sparked a long period of civil war among powerful chieftains. Finally, in 1600, Tokugawa Ieyasu (r. 1603–1616) won a decisive victory and became the most powerful chieftain in the Japanese archipelago, and assumed the title shogun, or military governor. From 1603 to 1867 the Tokugawa family ruled Japan as military dictators. The family itself directly controlled about 25 percent of the archipelago's land; the other 75 percent was ruled by the Tokugawa shogun's vassals. Although Japan was theoretically governed by the emperor, his position was purely ceremonial. Actual rule was in the hands of the shogun and his vassals, each assisted by armed retainers of samurai. In the 1500s the Japanese began to encounter Europeans. Portuguese explorers contacted Japan in 1542 and were quickly followed by Jesuit missionaries. When the Tokugawa shogunate was established in the 1600s, contact between Japanese and foreigners, primarily Europeans but also Chinese, was forbidden, except for carefully regulated trade at the port of Nagasaki. The shogunate's policy of isolation was based, first, on the fear that Christianity, which was seen as a subversive doctrine, would spread if Europeans were allowed to enter Japan in large numbers and, second, on the fear that certain of the shogun's vassals could become powerful enough to challenge his dominance if they had access to European military technology.

The strategy of isolation succeeded for about 100 years. However, chronic financial difficulties eventually weakened the shogunate. The currency was debased and taxes were raised in order to raise revenue. Gradually, the situation of small farmers became precarious as more and more rice had to be given to the shogun's tax collectors. Riots became common. By the middle of the nineteenth century, Japan was under great pressure by European states—such as Britain, Russia, and the United States—which wanted to topple the shogunate and enter the archipelago. The shogunate faced a difficult dilemma. It could no longer resist the European states, which possessed superior military technology; therefore, it signed treaties with Russia, Britain, France, and the Netherlands, states that regulated trade and diplomatic relations. For this the Tokugawa shogun was castigated by primarily low-ranking samurai from western Japan assisted by certain nobles from the imperial court and by wealthy merchants. When the shogun was overthrown in 1868, governing authority returned to the Emperor Meiji.

Although the Meiji Restoration, as the overthrow of the shogunate is called, transferred authority back to the emperor, he remained a ceremonial figurehead. Those who toppled the shogunate moved the emperor's court from Kyoto to the palace of the Tokugawa shoguns, established Tokyo as the capital, and thus strengthened the central government. 16 The young samurai who led the Meiji Restoration realized that Japan's survival as an independent entity depended upon the formation of a European-style national state. They imagined a state with a well-trained army and navy equipped with the best modern weapons available and supported by a modern industrial economy. Soon after the restoration, Japan's new elite began to invite European experts to Japan to teach new industrial and military techniques, and Japanese students were sent abroad to acquire European scientific and engineering knowledge. Railroads were constructed and a telegraph system was created. Factories were set up and strategic industries were subsidized. Schools and universities were built and compulsory education was decreed. A banking system was established.

A conscripted standing army that replaced the samurai was created. The state was reorganized: feudalism was abolished and, inspired by France's centralized system of internal administration, the Japanese archipelago was divided into prefectures. A standard coinage was adopted and internal barriers to trade, a legacy of feudalism, were eliminated. A legal code and a system of courts were copied from those of European states. The resources needed to build a European-style state were extracted by borrowing and from taxing the subject population, especially farmers. Farmers began to resist the heavy burden of taxation, which they saw as primarily benefiting the urban industrial sector, and resorted to armed uprisings. The restoration elite responded by suppressing these uprisings militarily, jailing the leaders, and censoring newspapers. The ruling elite eventually struck a bargain, promising to grant a constitution and establish a parliament. A commission was sent to Europe to study constitutions and returned most impressed with Imperial Germany. With the assistance of Prussian advisers, a constitution was drafted in 1889. It created a legislature, called the Imperial Diet, composed of a House of Peers and a House of Representatives, the numbers of which were chosen by a very small electorate defined by high tax-paying status. It met for the first time in 1890.

If Japan was going to compete successfully with its European rivals, a sense of nationhood also had to be developed. A national imaginary was created by nationalizing certain Japanese institutions and practices, especially those focusing on the emperor, as well as Buddhist ethics. In 1890 a law was passed that called upon all subjects to practice filial piety, to be loyal to the emperor, to obey the law, and to offer oneself to the state. By the end of the nineteenth century, the Meiji elite had built a European-style state with Japanese characteristics. Evidence of the Meiji elite's success came in 1904–1905, when Japan defeated Russia, the first time in modern history that a non-European state had defeated a European one. This victory enhanced the prestige of the military, which, during the 1930s, began to play a major role in Japanese politics. The military took indirect control of the state and launched a massive military buildup in order to counter the effects of the worldwide economic depression. They justified these policies by pointing to threats from other states to Japan's geostrategic position in northeast Asia, such as U.S. efforts to choke the flow of oil to Japan. The Japanese state thus became expansionist. The eventual result of this expansionism was defeat in World War II and occupation by the United States, a consequence that, ironically, the state-building project from its beginning was designed to avoid.

After World War II, the United States forced upon the Japanese a constitution that eliminated much of the military and gave the United States access to military bases on Japanese soil. Under the tutelage of the United States, the Liberal Democratic Party has dominated Japanese politics and succeeded in developing a managerial state in which large corporations oriented toward economic control of world consumer markets work closely with state technocrats, especially the

Ministry of Technology and Industry (MITI), to manage an export-led economy. Within major companies workers are guaranteed a job for life in return for nearly absolute loyalty to the company, but the majority of the workforce is subject to the precariousness of the world capitalist economy. Wages remain fairly low, although the state, together with major corporations, provides significant social benefits, and consumer markets are tightly restricted to limit imports. Japan has become one of the most powerful states in the current world order.

Some see Japan as a future hegemonic state, leading an Asian bloc in the world economy in competition with the United States and Europe; this view has, ironically, forced the latter two to remake themselves according to Japan's own distinctive state institutions and practices. During the 1990s journalists and scholars in the United States argued that in order to successfully compete in the global capitalist economy, the United States had to borrow from the Japanese state its distinctive forms of economic and worker management. 19 Whether the Japanese will turn the institution of the state against Europe and the United States remains to be seen. Let us note that we are skeptical of this characterization of the Japanese as the "other" and enemy of Europe and the United States.

Iraq: State Formation by Semi-Direct Conquest

Until the end of World War I, the territorial space that eventually became Iraq existed as three administrative regions of the Ottoman Empire. In 1916 Britain conquered these and other districts, dismantled Ottoman administration, and substituted their own system of indirect colonial rule developed in India. The British governed Iraq through tribal shaykhs, or chieftains, who, in exchange for grants and privileges, collected taxes and maintained law and order. 20 In 1920 the League of Nations assigned the mandate for Iraq to Britain, sparking a revolt among the shaykhs that the British put down by force. The British decided to end indirect rule through the shaykhs and imposed a provisional government made up of Iraqis friendly to them, which they replaced in 1921 with a constitutional monarchy. The British selected Faysal (r. 1921–1933), the third son of Sharif Husayn of Mecca, to be king. Faysal, after a well-managed plebiscite produced a 96-percent approval rating for Britain's choice, was enthroned on August 27, 1921.

Relations between Britain and the new Iraqi monarchy were formalized in a treaty that allowed the British to be closely involved in Iraqi internal affairs. An Iraqi army was established with the advice and assistance of British officers, and British advisers were placed in the government's ministries. Military and other types of aid were provided. Although a parliament was created, political life revolved around the king, a foreign monarch dependent upon the British; the British, who wanted their supporters in the king's cabinet and parliament; and Arab politicians, who had no deep roots in constituencies outside of parliament, except to tribal shaykhs, and who formed parliamentary coalitions based on personal ties. In 1929 negotiations between the Iraqi and British governments produced the Anglo-Iraq Treaty, which would remain in effect for

25 years. According to the terms of this treaty, the British were to promote Iraq's membership in the League of Nations, provide help to the Iraqis if attacked, maintain close cooperation in foreign affairs, be allowed to maintain two air bases on Iraqi soil, and continue training and equipping the Iraqi armed forces. The political instability engendered by Faysal's death in 1933 led to a military coup d'état in 1936, which was carried out by Bakr Sidqi, an Arab nationalist officer influenced by European fascism who favored an efficient authoritarian state strong enough to reverse British domination. A series of coups followed from 1937 until 1941. Elements of the indigenous officer corp had become the main site of Iraqi nationalism and resistance to the British. They jockeyed for power with pro-British governments until the British occupied Iraq militarily after a coup by a group of pro-fascist nationalist officers in March 1940.

Under a new treaty in 1947, British troops were withdrawn and the two air bases were returned to Iraq, although the armed forces were still to be armed and trained by the British, who would also still have a say in Iraqi defense planning. Widespread demonstrations against the new treaty led to a declaration of martial law and to the installation of a pro-British military government in 1952. Arab nationalist opposition to the government went underground and spread within the army, which had become dissatisfied with the proBritish elite. On July 14, 1958, the Iraqi army overthrew the Hasimite monarchy and, on July 14, the proBritish government. The coup was engineered by Abd al-Karim Qasim and Abd al-Salam Arif, members of the Free Officers Movement, which opposed the British-installed monarchy and its foreign policy. After a power struggle between Qasim and Arif another coup was staged by Arab nationalist army officers. They were supported by the Ba'th Party, which had originated in Syria, was strongly pan-Arab, and advocated radical social change. Initially, moderates led by Arif in the Revolutionary Command Council (RCC), as the new government was called, took control of the state in a bloodless coup in November 1963.

After a period of weak rule and growing social discontent, a strong group of military men and Ba'thist politicians deposed Arif in July 1968. After this coup, the Ba'th Party established a one-party state. An internal power struggle for control of the state ensued between civilian and military Ba'thists, eventually won by one of the civilian leaders, Saddam Hussein. On July 16, 1979, Hussein became secretary-general of the Ba'th Party, chairperson of the RCC, commander in chief of the armed forces, and president of the republic, all of which were approved by a newly elected national assembly in which delegates were either loyal Ba'th Party members or favorable to Ba'th Party principles. The conditions of Ba'thist rule are complex. It should be remembered that Iraq was a legacy of borders imposed on a variety of groups that the British forcibly integrated into a state. Colonialism generated two fundamental forces, not only in Iraq but throughout the Middle East, which defined the possibilities and limits of sovereignty. One was Arab nationalism, a multilayered movement that politicized an ethnic identity as an anticolonial force. It emerged in part among army officers who sought control of the armed forces against the colonial advisers and officers, as well as complicitous procolonial generals. This aspect gave Arab nationalism a statist form. More generally, Arab nationalism became an anticolonial force in reaction to colonial domination of the regional economy, especially oil, and the formation of the state of Israel in Palestine by the British, the League of Nations, and European Zionists.

These together politicized Arabism in complex ways. The other force, by no means completely separate from but not reducible to Arab nationalism, was Islam. In Iraq, Islam had developed considerable complexity, offering different forms that could be translated under conditions of colonialism into various political movements. Within Iraq, sharp divisions between Shiites (primarily in the south) and Sunnis threaten to break the state apart. In the north the Kurds have struggled for their own sovereign state, often with significant aid from foreign powers. At times colonial powers used Islamic clerics to bolster their domination. On the other hand, Islam provided a moral and spiritual basis, as well as a well-established social organization, for the political mobilization of the poor and oppressed. In some forms Islam saw in colonial domination a threatening modernizing and secularizing trend. Other forms of Islam embraced modernization.

Note that neither Arab nationalism nor Islam pointed unambiguously to the nation-state as the most appropriate form of political organization. Hussein reconstituted the state in Iraq by successfully manipulating these political forces, sometimes through repression, sometimes through accommodation. Initially drawing on the Ba'thist ideology of radical social reform, based in a largely secular socialist program although tailored to the conditions of Arab societies, and pan-Arabism, which called for close alliances among Arab states, he buttressed his control over Iraq's formal institutions through a vast network of kinship and personal ties built up since he joined the Ba'th Party in 1957. This in good part insulated the state apparatus from the conflicting social and political pressures of rival political forces, nationalist and Islamic. Iraq's position in the world economy and the states-system also conditioned state sovereignty. The British had established an economy in Iraq that was dependent on oil exports, which the British controlled first through direct ownership and then through its monopoly of technology for extracting and refining the oil. It also, along with giant U.S. (and one Dutch) oil companies, controlled the markets. Economically, this severely constrained the Ba'thist Party's programs of social reform. Also, the type of state organization Hussein created, dependent on networks of personal contacts and loyalties, funneled money into the personal bank accounts of Hussein and his ministers. Lacking the industrial base to build and maintain an advanced military, Iraq remained dependent on European powers and on playing off the superpowers during the Cold War.

Considerable sums were used to purchase weapons from abroad, which entailed taking on debts to foreign banks. From the end of the Cold War, Hussein has struggled to hold Iraq together as a centralized state. Congo: State Formation by Direct Conquest The area of Africa now occupied by the state known (since May 1997) as the Democratic Republic of Congo was settled over many centuries by small bands of Bantu-speaking peoples who engaged in subsistence agriculture. They encountered pygmy peoples who lived by hunting and gathering. Later, non-Bantuspeaking peoples penetrated the area from the north and settled on the fringes of the tropical rainforest. Except for contact with the Portuguese along the coast around the mouth of the Congo River during the period of European expansion, and Afro-Arab slave traders from the east coast of Africa, the peoples of what was to become the Congo lived isolated from outsiders until the 1870s, when agents of King Leopold II (r. 1865–1909) of Belgium established a rudimentary colony called the Congo Free State, which was recognized by the Berlin Conference (1884–1885) as the private domain of King Leopold.

In 1908, the Congo Free State was taken over by the Belgian government and renamed the Belgian Congo. The Belgian Congo was divided into 15 administrative districts without regard to African political authority, each headed by a commissioner. An army, called the Force Publique, was organized. It was officered by Belgians and its ranks filled with Africans. The Belgian government deliberately created rifts between neighboring African peoples and established administrative hierarchies of African chiefs, who supplied the Belgians with porters, soldiers, and food. As with other colonized areas, the process of creating a colonial state politicized tribal and regional identities, turning them into social forces around which political loyalties could be organized against others. This set a pattern for the future: to participate in the state, indigenous Africans had few options but to organize themselves around tribal identities.

Ethnicity as a political force was both created and politicized by the colonial state. In the 1890s King Leopold had opened one-third of the Free State's "unknown" territory to private companies, which were given long-term concessions to exploit resources, such as copper, in return for payments to the king. The concessionary companies ruthlessly exploited Africans by forcing them from their villages to work on plantations and in mines, beating them and executing them if they refused, and setting impossibly high work quotas that frequently resulted in death from physical exhaustion. Accounts of the extremely harsh treatment of indigenous Africans raised humanitarian concerns, especially in the United States and Britain, but nothing came of halfhearted attempts to eliminate the forced labor. After taking formal control in 1908, the Belgian government reduced the power of the concessionary companies and ruled the colony indirectly through African chiefs, whom they appointed and paid.

Often the individual appointed as chief over a particular people was not a chief in the eyes of those people. Later, these chieftaincies were grouped together into sectors, and one of the chiefs was appointed to head the sector. These heads were usually individuals who had worked for the Belgians as low-level clerks in the colonial administration or who had served as soldiers in the Force Publique. Thus, an administrative hierarchy was established that was loyal to the Belgians and that simultaneously politicized ethnicity and generated ethnic divisions. Despite formal Belgian prohibitions against the exploitation of Africans, labor was recruited by force with the assistance of the Belgian colonial administration, which often worked closely with the labor recruiters from the concessionary companies. The colonial authorities in Leopoldville and Belgium turned a blind eye to this practice, justifying it through the racist belief that Africans could be civilized only through regular labor.

The colonial authorities also forced Africans to cultivate cash crops, such as cotton, which were difficult to grow successfully in poor African soils but which settlers or foreign markets demanded. After World War II, the significant number of European-educated Africans in the Congo, known as évolués (French, meaning "evolved ones"), began to demand jobs in the colonial civil service commensurate with their level of education as well as equal pay for equal work. They began to organize professional, educational, mutual-aid, and ethnic societies and clubs. By the 1950s they began to demand independence. The first demands came in 1956 from a group of prominent Ngala évolués from Leopoldville. Nationalist political parties began to take shape, based on the already existing mutual-aid and ethnic associations. Only one of these parties, the National Congolese Movement (NCM), led by Patrice Lumumba (1925–1961), a prominent évolué from Leopoldville, claimed to be a colony-wide party. In June 1959, the Belgian government announced that it was going to "prepare" the colony for independence, suggesting that Africans were not capable of governing themselves. This racist language would provide the Belgians and others with justifications for continued intervention to regulate Congolese sovereignty.

Three nationalist leaders, each with a different imagining of the future structure of the independent state, emerged: Lumumba and the NCM were in favor of the establishment of a unitary state for the independent Congo. Joseph Kasavubu (1910?–1969) and his party, the Alliance of the Bakongo (ABAKO), and Moise Tshombe (1919–1969) and his party, the Confederation of Katanga Associations (CONAKAT), which was strongly supported by Belgians with a financial interest in the copper-rich Katanga province, were in favor of autonomy for their regions within a federal state. Elections were held in May 1960 for a national parliament and provincial assemblies. Lumumba's NCM won a plurality but not a majority of seats in the Chamber of Deputies, the parliament's lower house. Lumumba became prime minister and formed a coalition government. In June, Kasavubu was elected president. The tranquility of the first months of independence was broken on July 5, 1960, when the Force Publique mutinied against its Belgian officers. Belgium flew in paratroopers to restore order and evacuate Europeans. Lumumba replaced Belgian officers with Africans and appointed his uncle, Victor Lundula, to be commander in chief and Joseph Désiré Mobutu to be chief of staff. The army's name was changed to the National Congolese Army (NCA). We need to note here the important role of the military in the independent Congo, one of the legacies of colonialism that defines and limits the possibilities of politics in the Congo and elsewhere in postcolonial states.

The military was the element of the state apparatus that the colonial power often most highly developed. Soldiers were well trained, equipped with modern weapons, organized, and disciplined. The independent Congolese state initially maintained Belgian officers, depended upon supplies and training from Belgium, and cultivated a pro-Belgian officer corps. This officer corps enjoyed access to European ideas and was socialized to consider itself as members of the Congolese state with a distinctive responsibility to maintain order and stability. It is not surprising, then, that civilian leaders would turn to the military for key allies and would give officers important political roles in their governments. This was especially the case given the combination of continued dependence on foreign arms supplies and the willingness of foreign states to back one party against another.

Political success came to mean choosing between military patrons. Moreover, the combination of the politicization of tribal identities and the repression of alternative sources of political energy (unions, working class, or democratic civic organizations) that might challenge forced labor, foreign investment, or the practices of major property owners (especially copper mining by the foreign-owned copper companies) meant that mass support for military and nationalist leaders came to be based in often divisive, exclusionist visions of the state and politics. The crisis of the early 1960s and General Mobuto Sese-Sekou's rise to power illustrate this legacy. Tshombe, who had established a one-party government in the province of Katanga, declared it independent of the Congo on July 11, 1960. The Belgian government landed paratroopers in the Congo in support of Tshombe. Lumumba and Kasavubu, who feared that the Belgians were seeking to reoccupy the Congo, turned to the United Nations for assistance. On July 14 the UN Security Council persuaded the Belgian troops to withdraw and dispatched several thousand peacekeeping troops to the Congo.

When the UN troops refused to help him end the Katanga secession, Lumumba turned to the Soviet Union for military assistance. Kasavubu, seeking continued support from the West, dismissed Lumumba and his government and appointed General Mobutu as commander in chief of the army. Lumumba refused to accept his dismissal and accused Kasavubu of high treason. Parliament refused to act. On December 31, 1960, General Mobutu assumed power and demanded the departure of Soviet diplomatic and military personnel. Because Mobutu was unable at this time to establish a unified government, the centralized state all but dissolved. In the chaos that followed, Lumumba was arrested and murdered. In February 1961, the Security Council resolved to give the UN forces the power to bring the Congo together under a single government. Under UN auspices, a parliament was convened and a broad coalition government, headed by Cyrille Adoula (1921–1978), was formed. Tshombe refused to cooperate, and mercenary troops in the employ of foreign copper companies in Katanga clashed with UN troops. When UN forces gained the military advantage, Tshombe requested aid from the United States. The United States brokered a deal that eventually ended the Katangese succession, brought about the departure of the mercenaries, and sent Tshombe into exile.

Tshombe did, however, maintain an army of Katangese police in neighboring Angola while he was in exile. In mid-1963 the national parliament became deadlocked over the draft of a new constitution. Kasavubu declared a state of emergency for six months, which sparked rebellions in Kuilu and Kivu in early 1964. When in the following months rebellions broke out in other northeastern provinces, Tshombe was asked by Kasavubu to return to the Congo and form a transitional government. Utilizing soldiers who had returned with him from exile, Tshombe recaptured rebel strongholds. These successes and his victory in the parliamentary elections of March 1965 made Tshombe a strong contender for the presidency. Therefore, on October 13, 1965, Kasavubu dismissed Tshombe as prime minister. But, because Tshombe's party held the majority of seats, the new prime minister could not form a government. An impasse resulted. The deadlock was ended when, on November 24, 1965, General Mobutu once again took control of the state and forbade all political activity. Over time, power was increasingly concentrated into Mobutu's hands. Mobutu, who was able to stabilize the situation with U.S. support, became a ruthless, corrupt, patrimonial ruler. On October 27, 1971, Mobutu changed the name of the Congo to Zaire. Other place names were Africanized, and Mobutu changed his own name to Mobutu Sésé Sekou Kulu Ngbendu wa Zabango. Over a three-month period, foreign-owned plantations and businesses were expropriated and given to Zairens, mostly party loyalists, army officers, and civil servants. In 1974 Mobutu Sésé Sekou instituted a new constitution that gave the president control over all organs of the state. Mobutu was reelected president in December 1977 and again in July 1984.

Mobutu Sésé Sekou ruled Zaire until 1997, when his regime was overthrown in a rebellion led by Laurent Kabila, which began in the eastern provinces, primarily among Tutsis, and spread to other ethnic groups. Mobutu survived in power for 30 years because certain European states and the United States needed him. With the end of the Cold War, however, the United States no longer needed Mobutu to support Jonas Sivimbi, the U.S.-backed anticommunist client in neighboring Angola who refused to accept its democratically elected government because of its socialist programs and support by Cuba and the Soviet Union. With the end of the Cold War the United States lost interest in Angola and Savimbi. Moreover, Mobutu's regional alliances unraveled. The white regime in South Africa was replaced and, more significantly, the genocidal Hutu regime in Rwanda, which Mobutu supported, was overthrown by a Tutsi and moderate Hutu force. The rebellion in Rwanda created a refugee crisis, sending nearly two million Hutu refugees across the border into Zaire, where they were exploited by Mobutu and the remainder of the Hutu government. Mobutu temporarily garnered renewed recognition and support from the United States, and from European states that needed his support, to supply the refugees with humanitarian aid and avoid widespread starvation and disease.

He supported the remainder of the radical Hutu military, which used the refugee camps to regroup for an eventual reinvasion of Rwanda, to attack the Tutsi population in Zaire, and to repress political opposition. He also controlled the war economy in eastern Zaire, making a fortune for himself and his cohorts by selling arms and controlling oil supplies in the region.

The new Rwandan government invaded eastern Zaire and attacked the remainder of the Hutu army. In doing so they joined forces with Kabila in order to overthrow Mobutu. Other regional forces backed Kabila, and, somewhat surprisingly, Kabila's forces spread through the country easily. During the final takeover of the state, Kabila refused mediation from the United States or Europe; instead, the final negotiations were made possible by African leaders, most notably Nelson Mandela of South Africa.

Summary

The often turbulent ethnic politics, patrimonialism, and militarization of many postcolonial states are neither the result of neocolonialism nor the failure to modernize, that is, to live up to "modern" standards. Some non-European states, Japan most notably, have become powerful states in the current world order. All nonEuropean states, whether formally colonized or subjected to less formal pressures to conform to the interests of the United States and European states, faced distinctive limits to their sovereignty. These limits were imposed by the historical legacy of colonialism and by continued efforts to regulate their sovereignty so that it conforms to the norms and interests of the states system and world economy.

12

CHALLENGES TO THE STATE

THE PRESENT STATE OF STATES

We have shown that the modern, territorial state is a unique historical creation of relatively recent vintage. It is not eternal, and no form of it is universal. Moreover, it now exists within a world order in which managerial states seem to dominate; indeed, most people live in states whose sovereignty is regulated and disciplined by norms of the international system and by the organizations of the global capitalist economy. Military, economic, and social forces are calling into question the state's territorial imperative, as well as the modern state's insistence on a politics of control from the center. The ability to represent the state as territorially sovereign is diminished by the latest phase of warfare, the globalization of capitalism, the proliferation of international managerial institutions, and the tremendous mobility of peoples around the globe. Present developments not only seem to be challenging the current forms of the state, but are also questioning the possibilities of territorialized, sovereign power. This is not to argue that the nation-state is disappearing, but that the state is in transition, although it is still unclear what its future form will be. Territorial states have always had to confront forces that overflow the representation of a sharp boundary between sovereignty inside—that is, the realm in which states claimed to be "in control" and in which the subject population was pacified—and sovereignty outside, that is, the state's independence in a system of juridically independent states in a world of perpetual violence and war. In this chapter we examine three forces that challenge nation-state sovereignty: (1) post-territorial warfare; (2) the globalization of civil society; and (3) the fracturing of political identity.

POST-TERRITORIAL WARFARE

Although the reliance on sharply defined borders that could be defended by the rational use of violence has constituted modern states, the territoriality of the modern state has always been unstable. The ability of states to defend their borders, and the ways in which resources were extracted and organized to do so, gave particular form to states and was important to their survival as sovereign entities. The idea that violence was a tool that states used rationally to protect themselves, and the specific ways in which they did so, marked their self-identity as states. Since the Peace of Westphalia in 1648, the state system has been constructed around the imaginary of "hard-shelled" and impenetrable territorially sovereign states capable of defending their subject populations from rival states. As one student of the state put it, "The large-area state came to occupy the place that the castle or fortified town had previously held as a unit of impenetrability."

But reimagining spatial boundaries as impenetrable borders of a territorial state instead of the boundaries of the town had enormous significance. Constructing and defending borders involved more than physical defenses. Not only did borders have to be established through such signs as border crossings, flags, and military uniforms, but the people living within them had to be convinced to accept them and had to be made to identify their needs and interests as primarily enclosed within the state's borders. The twentieth century has witnessed a dramatic overriding of the territorial boundaries of the state by military technologies. Here we focus on how the transformation of warfare, in both its normative and technological aspects, has outstripped the state's ability to use war as a rational strategy to defend its territorial borders.

In major part, the military overriding of territorial boundaries was the result of the industrialization of warfare. With the advent of industrialized warfare, the distinctions between civilian and soldier, between socioeconomic infrastructure and military resources, were blurred by technologies that compressed space and time. Industrial weapons rendered warfare more mobile, and more able to penetrate the "hard shell" of the territorial state's imagined borders. Industrialization ushered in what is generally considered the age of total war. This term refers to the way that war with machine weapons targets the entire social and economic fabric of states, not only killing thousands or even millions of people (military and civilian; men and women; young and old), but destroying the infrastructure on which social and economic life in industrial states depends. Total war also refers to the fact that to make war with machine weapons, the state must mobilize the entire industrial and social capabilities of the state. In total war, the distinctions between military and civilian, and between war and peace, essentially dissolve. The new conditions of total war reorganized the internal structure of warmaking by rendering it increasingly dependent on science and technology, which require formal and informal connections between the military and weapons industries.

What the U.S. president Dwight D. Eisenhower (1890–1969) called in 1957 the "Military-Industrial Complex" has been maintained in the United States despite the end of the Cold War. Paradoxically, industrial warfare also created new attitudes and social organizations to promote peace and to limit the destructiveness of war. Beginning in the 1890s, international conferences were convened to codify and expand the laws of war. These international laws of war regulated both when it was just and legal for states to go to war, called jus ad bellum or "justice of war," and how wars should be conducted, called jus in bello or "justice in war." Perhaps most important were attempts to limit or prohibit the use of "cruel and unusual" weapons and prohibitions against targeting civilians. Industrial warfare also generated an international social movement for peace, including the creation of nongovernmental, international organizations the aim of which was to promote peace.

Industrialization also changed the rationale for war, creating a "peace interest" in states. States became more inclined to seek peace and avoid war not out of ethical considerations or concerns for humanity, which animated the international peace movements, but because some sectors of the industrial economy considered peace as necessary to promote industrialization and economic growth. Of course, many other industrialists, especially those directly involved in producing and supplying weapons, recognized how war could be a driving force for an industrial economy and therefore promoted more aggressive foreign policies. The most important sectors of the industrial state that supported peace policies were those whose profit derived in some significant way from trade, especially finance capitalists, who put up the money for industrial enterprises engaged in trade. Industrial warfare, by allowing mass killing at extremely long range (distances beyond the senses or comprehension of the soldier), also fundamentally altered social attitudes toward the meaning of war and, more generally, toward violence and killing.

World War I, for example, generated in England a remarkable body of writing, especially letters and poetry, by soldiers who attempted to come to grips with the implications of industrial war for human life. 4 Contemplate the following two excerpts from very different U.S. writers and times, the first a reflection on the implications of World War I, the second a reflection by a contemporary Native American writer on the implications of modern war: We were in a garden at Mons. Young Buckley came in with his patrol from across the river. The first German I saw climbed up over the garden wall. We waited till he got one leg over and then potted him. He had so much equipment on and looked awfully surprised and fell down into the garden. Then three more came over further down the wall. We shot them. They all came just like that. "You were with the others," he said, "the ones who went to the white people's war?"

Tayo nodded. . . . He didn't know how to explain what had happened. He did not know how to tell him that he had not killed any enemy or that he did not think that he had. But that he had done things far worse, and the effects were everywhere in the cloudless sky, on the dry brown hills, shrinking skin and hide taut over sharp bone . . . But the old man shook his head slowly and made a low humming sound in his throat. In the old way of warfare, you couldn't kill another human being in battle without knowing it, without seeing the result, because even a wounded deer that got up and ran again left great clots of lung blood or spilled guts on the ground. That way the hunter knew it would die. Human beings were no different. But the old man would not have believed white warfare—killing across great distances without knowing who or how many had died. It was all too alien to comprehend, the mortars and big guns; and even if he could have taken the old man to see the target areas, even if he could have led him through the fallen jungle trees and muddy craters of torn earth to show him the dead, the old man would not have believed anything so monstrous.

Ku'oosh would have looked at the dismembered corpses and the atomic heat-flash outlines, where human bodies had evaporated, and the old man would have said something close and terrible had killed these people. Not even oldtime witches killed like that. 6 Representations of industrialized, machine warfare in which soldiers are transformed into machines that kill without human feeling, in which the enemy has become nothing more than an object to be routinely, coldly, and rationally annihilated, have become staples of modern culture. The efficiency and rationality of this form of destruction, rather than being seen as a virtue, are represented as irrational and inhuman, either too efficient or otherworldly and supernatural. Such representations captured and helped to form powerful critiques of not only particular wars but of warfare in general. Important normative frictions between the institution of war as a rational tool of the state and the actual practices of war predate industrialization, however. In general, the industrialization of war intensified a dynamic that European states had to obscure in order to legitimate and secure themselves—that is, the dynamic of conquest that in part stemmed from the Crusades, perhaps with deeper roots in Roman militarism and the invasions of Rome by Germanic tribes, as well as expansion by Charlemagne and his successors. Historically, the practice of European war involved penetrating boundaries, occupying territory, and vanquishing the enemy on its own ground.

Thus, borders, where they existed, were not secure markers of political space but contingent objects to be overcome, manipulated, rearranged, or ignored. Initially, this idea of war had little or nothing to do with protecting or defending sovereign territory. Such war was about conquering peoples and plundering their wealth. Conquest continues to constitute the discourse of war. Warfare in the eighteenth century was essentially a contest limited to relatively small, mostly mercenary armies that engaged each other in formal, set-piece battles. These duel-like battles did not much directly involve civilians. A clear line of demarcation was drawn between combatants and noncombatants. Thus, this late-medieval and early modern idea of war as a series of formal battles, which recognized the distinction between civilians and soldiers and which confined fighting to the battlefield so as to do the least damage to infrastructure, was a counterpractice, in a sense, to the idea of war as conquest. In a similar way, the idea of war as a defense of territorial borders was a counterpractice to war as conquest. 8 The republican tradition of the citizen-soldier, which has been so important to constituting political identity in sovereign states, was by no means fully consistent with the modern state's identity as a rational user of war for territorial defense.

On the one hand, the idea of the citizen-soldier, developed by Renaissance republicans such as Machiavelli, was important to the constituting of the modern state by limiting the soldiery to those within the territory and by eliminating foreign mercenaries and private armies within the state. The practice and the idea of the citizen-soldier also helped refashion the identity of the person so that his first loyalty was to the state. But this made the subject population itself into a legitimate target in war, if not directly then indirectly through economic blockades and psychological warfare. Although they were developed to defend territory, modern industrial weapons render the very borders of the state increasingly vulnerable. The most significant developments appear, interestingly, at opposite ends of the spectrum of weapons: large-scale nuclear weapons on one end, and small-scale, even miniaturized weapons on the other, such as portable, easily concealable bombs, and guns and missiles that can be broken down into their component parts and easily smuggled across borders. Air warfare and nuclear warfare have affected the territorial impenetrability of nation-states most radically, however.

With the development of tactical air warfare during World War I, the perfection of strategic bombing with conventional and nuclear bombs in World War II, and the development of intercontinental ballistic missiles (ICBMs) during the Cold War, the hard shell of the nation-state was decisively blasted away. The development of long-range strategic bombers during World War II made it possible for air forces to fly over the outer defenses of enemy states and directly attack their "soft" hinterlands. Cities, factories, roads, bridges, and civilians came under direct attack. Often the purpose of strategic bombing was not to destroy military targets but to terrorize civilians so that they would refuse to fight or support the war. The normative discourses of war discussed above made such attacks appear morally defensible. The scale of nuclear destruction, however, challenges the very idea that nuclear weapons are "weapons" like other weapons that can "win" wars and achieve political goals. The blast from a nuclear weapon can leave deep craters in the earth of more than a mile in diameter within which everything is instantly vaporized. Nuclear weapons generate tremendous heat, which causes "firestorms" that instantly incinerate buildings, trees, roads, and people within a wide radius of ground zero. They also produce radioactivity that slowly kills thousands more and adversely affects future generations. The scope of their destructive force makes most, if not all, nuclear weapons unusable on the battlefield, although attempts have been made to design tactical nuclear weapons that would confine the effects of blast, heat, and radioactivity. The inability of technology to achieve what many strategic planners consider acceptable limits, along with the concern of military commanders that, in the "heat" and uncertainty of battle, escalation is inevitable, has led many military and civilian strategists to conclude that nuclear weapons are unusable as rational weapons of war.

That is, their use serves no strategic purpose in protecting armies and territory or in winning battles. Nuclear weapons, thus, challenge state sovereignty not only because of the scale and scope of their destructive power but also because of the ways they are delivered to enemy territory. The first form of delivery was, of course, the intercontinental bomber that dropped the first atomic weapons as gravity bombs on the Japanese cities of Hiroshima and Nagasaki in World

War II. Aircraft have remained an important delivery vehicle for weapons, although current technology allows them to avoid flying directly over their targets. Instead they release missiles, called cruise missiles, which use computerized maps to guide themselves to their targets within enemy territory. In order to ensure a retaliatory nuclear capability that could survive any first strike by an enemy nuclear attack, U.S. strategic planners have developed two additional delivery vehicles for nuclear weapons: land-based and submarine-launched ICBMs. Using computerized guidance systems, ICBMs, launched from hardened land-based silos or from submarines, fly outside the earth's immediate atmosphere across several continents to their targets in enemy territory. Both Russia and the United States continue to maintain all three delivery systems, and other nuclear powers, such as England, France, and China, maintain one or two.

All three delivery technologies allow the weapons to jump over, as it were, the territorial borders of an enemy state. Moreover, advanced guidance systems, or "stealth" technology, which makes bombers less detectable by enemy radar, and the sheer speed of ICBMs, which can fly halfway around the globe in less than 30 minutes, have made these weapons impossible to detect with sufficient certainty to ensure a reliable defense against them. Therefore, air warfare and nuclear weapons have made the territorial sovereignty of even the most powerful nation-states increasingly anachronistic. Even one or two medium-sized nuclear weapons could devastate large swaths of a state's territory. Nuclear weapons especially have put an end to the ability of the nationstate to guarantee the security of the subject population because there is no realistic defense against nuclear-armed ICBMs. Such weapons make it impossible for states that possess them to go to war against each other without the risk of mutual suicide. In the words of one scholar: "Nuclear weapons . . . [have] finally put an end to the nation-state's ability to guarantee the security of its citizens . . . There is simply no defense against nuclear weapons." Nuclear weapons have been subject to the rationality of industrialization as much as to strategic considerations. Improvements in them have been subject to the dynamic drive for greater productivity of the large corporations that produce them. In a sense, they are as much the result of the modern penchant for instrumental, means-end rationality as is the zip-lock sandwich bag or double-entry bookkeeping.

Improvements are also the result of the modern attitudes toward scientific progress that feed the advanced capitalist economy: if an object (tool, machine, procedure, human behavior) can be improved (i.e., made more powerful and efficient), it should be, according to what is technically possible. The social and political consequences of such technical improvements are seen as exogenous; therefore, technological improvements take on a life of their own. Moreover, the development of miniaturized electronics used to upgrade ICBMs, such as advanced guidance systems that allow multiple, independently targetable warheads to be placed on a single missile, have "improved" conventional weapons as well as making them more powerful, mobile, and concealable. With the development of miniaturized electronics and the advent of new, more portable means of violence, the global order has become generally militarized. This new technology is not separable from the global context of militarization during the Cold War, which has created both the means and the economic impulses to "microtize" weapons further, and to spread them to private and nonstate groups.

During the Cold War, nuclear weapons produced an uneasy peace that was based on the production of nuclear weapons, which everyone agreed could never be used rationally. State territory came to be defended not by national armies and navies but by the fear of mutual destruction. The deaths of hundreds of millions of civilians and the complete destruction of the enemy state's capacity to function as a viable industrial society was sufficient to keep the peace, at least among the European nuclear powers. Outside of Europe, however, war was frequent, and in almost all cases, warring factions and states were supplied with advanced weapons by the nuclear powers, although neither transferred nuclear weapons to their client states. Most often, this made the client states dependent on the military-industrial complex of their patron, most often the United States or the Soviet Union. Several other European states, such as Britain, France, and Czechoslovakia, became major arms suppliers as well, because client states lacked the industrial and scientific base to produce and maintain modern weapons.

Also, wars outside of Europe in which the superpowers directly participated—the U.S. war in Vietnam (1964–1975) and the Soviet war in Afghanistan (1979–1985) being the most important—spread enormous quantities of surplus weapons throughout the world, such as automatic rifles, tanks and antitank missiles, artillery pieces, antipersonnel mines, and plastic explosives. Finally, arms production became an important industry in many advanced economies as well as in some newly industrializing non-European states such as Brazil, Argentina, and Israel. These non-European states have generated, along with the "leftover" weapons from the proxy wars of the superpowers, a network of arms markets throughout the world in which weapons of all types can be purchased by private persons, movements, or states that cannot produce them themselves. 14 Such military developments have created a severe challenge to the state's ability to use military force to defend its territory, and have led many observers to the conclusion that the continuance of a politics based on allegiance to a territorially based state is neither warranted by the empirical realities of postmodern warfare nor ethically defensible.

GLOBALIZATION OF CIVIL SOCIETY

The state is also challenged by the globalization of civil society. Globalization has expanded not only the scope of economic activity, but also the ways in which the increasing connections between people across state borders have induced changes in people's perceptions of social space and its boundaries. Social relations that nation-states assume to take place inside their borders—family connections, voluntary associations, economic communities, friendships—are increasingly constitutive of networks of social interaction across national borders. Civil society at the end of the twentieth century, in important respects, moves rather freely across and through the territorial boundaries of states. This has rendered national civil societies less easy to manage by states and made the imagining of sovereignty less central to people's identities and more difficult for states to sustain.

Much of the challenge of global civil society stems from the globalization of the capitalist economy. Globalization refers to "the complex of economic, technological, ecological, and cultural structures that are emerging on a global scale which ignore or deny the relevance of any state's territory." Globalization challenges the effectiveness of the territorial state as a guarantor of the economic well-being and the national identity of its subject population. States can still intervene in their national economies, often with considerable impact. However, in many important economic areas, states either have chosen not to constrain globalization, by supporting free trade and refusing to restrict capital flows and labor markets, or have felt too restricted by global financial markets or the international division of labor to make any active attempts at managing the economy. The industrial capitalist system has always been a global system. Historically, capitalism has relied on the nation-state and at the same time challenged its sovereignty by undermining the ability of the state to enclose civil society within territorial boundaries. The industrial capitalist system increased the importance of trade in local economies and made long-distance trade economical.

It also created a new system of global inequality based on the uneven deployment of industrial technologies. Regions that supplied the raw materials of industrial production, both within states and in relations between states, gained less of the profit from industrial production than did those regions or states that supplied the manufactured goods or provided the financing for manufacturing and trade. Steam-powered trains and ships, which became large and fast during the nineteenth century, compressed time and space. Steam power resulted in more goods being traded over greater distances more quickly than ever before. This had the effect of spreading the industrial system to all parts of the world, often destroying indigenous economies because imported manufactured goods could be sold more cheaply than locally produced goods.

The British created and dominated the emerging global industrial capitalist system through much of the eighteenth century. By the 1870s Germany and the United States rivaled Britain in industrial power. In the last half of the nineteenth century the Japanese would also embark on the rapid industrialization of their economy. Industrialization became a global phenomenon. A core of states with industrial economies came to dominate the world economy by spreading advanced technologies over which they maintained control, promoting norms of free trade, and recolonizing other states through the control of their raw materials and markets. After the World War II, the United States created a globally managed free-trade system, as part of the Fordist social economy, in which goods and investment flowed freely across national borders. The main beneficiary of the system was the large transnational corporation (TNC). These corporations maintained headquarters in their home states but invested directly in other states, where they built factories and bought and otherwise established foreign subsidiaries in order to penetrate foreign markets.

They began to organize themselves transnationally in the sense that their "bottom lines" were calculated to include the multinational markets in which they operated. This system has led during the past 40 years to a tremendous concentration of wealth that is organized internationally and is highly mobile across borders. According to one estimate, the largest 300 TNCs, many of which boast sales greater than the gross national product of most nation-states, control nearly a quarter of the world's productive assets. During the 1980s and 1990s those large corporations that dominate the world economy maintain multinational operations and a network of subsidiaries, many of which are becoming global. These "global corporations are the first secular institutions run by men (and a handful of women) who think and plan on a global scale." They develop products—of which Coca-Cola and the Sony Walkman are two significant examples—that, with minor modifications, can be sold in any country in the world, and they plan their production and distribution to fit a global market. For example, McDonald's adjusts its menus to fit local sensitivities and religious practices. In Israel Big Macs are served without cheese; in India mutton-based Maharaja Macs and Vegetable McNuggets are served; in Turkey cold yogurt drinks are available; in Italy espresso coffee and cold pasta can be purchased; in Japan teriyaki burgers are available; in Norway grilled salmon sandwiches; in Germany frankfurters and beer; and in Uruguay egg hamburgers.

Such globalization has been made possible by improvements in transportation (bigger trucks, jet-powered air freighters, containerized cargo, superhighways) and spectacular advances in computing and telecommunications (digital systems, satellites, fiber optics) technology. These improvements and advances have (1) reduced transaction and communication costs, making goods and services globally tradable that were not before, such as perishable, seasonal items (e.g., flowers, grapes, oranges), fashions, back-office accounts, and design work; (2) made it possible for corporations to coordinate effectively and efficiently on a global scale their production, planning, and financial operations; (3) made information, such as films, compact discs, tapes, software, television news, and programs, tradable; and (4) allowed capital to become highly mobile, which has created a global market for currencies and securities.

These developments have made representing the state as securer and manager of an economy inside its territorial boundaries more difficult to sustain. Also, it is more difficult to paint the international and global aspects of economic life as fully outside the territorial state when, for example, subtle changes in interest rates in one state can severely affect jobs in others and when multinational corporations rapidly and frequently shift jobs to lowwage states, producing unemployment and lower wages in other states. Globalization has, paradoxically, disciplined all states to become more or less managerial; at the same time, management of the economy by the state is increasingly problematic, and has become so in a number of ways. First, the amount of profit-seeking, financial capital flowing electronically around the world far exceeds the amount that any state can marshal from its reserves in order to control the value of its currency. Second, a substantial amount of trade is now intra-industry, rather than international, owing to the specialization of TNCs; therefore, the state can no longer easily distinguish national exports from foreign imports for trade policy purposes.

This means that states have lost much of their ability to protect their domestic markets with tariffs. Third, many TNCs have dissociated themselves from their states of origin and seek to locate their operations where wages and taxes are lower and regulations fewer. For example, the Boeing Corporation, a major aircraft manufacturer located in Seattle, Washington, has recently declared publicly that it no longer considers itself a U.S. company but a global one. In 1996, Coca-Cola Corporation, located in Atlanta, Georgia, eliminated the distinction between its domestic and international operations. This means that states have much less control over what happens economically within their territories.

States now compete with one another to provide an attractive business environment, such as good infrastructure, deregulated markets, a trained and docile workforce, and financial stability, in order to attract and retain more capital and investment from TNCs. Thus, the global market has increasingly taken on the role of a regulator of sovereignty, creating institutions and generating norms and discourses that make it appear necessary and inevitable that states both adopt free market economic policies and proffer interpretations of the national interests that conform to the norms of global competitiveness. This is especially true of the poorest states, whose economies are heavily influenced by international regulatory agencies such as the International Monetary Fund (IMF) and the International Bank for Reconstruction and Development (IBRD), also known as the World Bank, through the conditions they impose on states seeking to obtain new loans from international sources or to renegotiate old ones. In effect, the IMF and the World Bank set monetary and fiscal policy for indebted states. Despite claims that economic globalization is beneficial for all, the distribution of winners and losers in the global economy does not neatly respect territorial borders. It has created intractable mass unemployment in some states and high levels of unemployment in most states. In others it has led to resource depletion, pollution, and ecological damage. As two analysts of the global economy put it:

The most disturbing aspect of this system is that the formidable power and mobility of global corporations are undermining the effectiveness of national governments to carry out essential policies on behalf of their people. Leaders of nation-states are losing much of the control over their own territory they once had. More and more, they must conform to the demands of the outside world because the outsiders are already inside the gates. Business enterprises that routinely operate across borders are linking far-flung pieces of territory into a new world economy that bypasses all sorts of established political arrangements and conventions.

Tax laws intended for another age, traditional ways to control capital flows and interest rates, full-employment policies, and old approaches to resource development and environmental protection are becoming obsolete, unenforceable, or irrelevant.

Deeper challenges to the state, moreover, stem from the limited possibilities for generating identities bound to territorial sovereignty in the context of a globalized civil society. Two factors are most significant: (1) the density of nonterritorial-based networks of social relations, and (2) the speed and frequency of movements of people, images, and ideas across borders. To these we now turn.

THE FRACTURING OF IDENTITY

Nation and state have rarely coincided in the history of nation-states. State boundaries have rarely conformed to a particular linguistic, religious, and/or cultural community. Therefore, the persistence of representations of the state as a homogeneous national community has had tremendous costs for those marginalized by the national community. Such representations have brought to bear on these peoples powers of self-discipline (e.g., to make oneself assimilate to the dominant national ideal) as well as overt force and covert surveillance, because those outside the dominant nationality are, in principle, suspect and seen as potential threats. Even those who fit the dominant national representation are forced at times to demonstrate their "true national identity"—their Americanness, Frenchness, Indianness, and so on. Almost all nation-states contain significant minority ethnic groups, many of which are claiming the internationally recognized "right of self-determination of peoples" found in Article I, Section I, of the charter of the United Nations.

Many ethnic groups, such as the Basques and Catalans in Spain, Corsicans and Bretons in France, Kurds in Turkey and Iraq, Chechens in Russia, Tibetans in China, Tamils in Sri Lanka, Chiapas Indians in Mexico, Québécois in Canada, Kashmiris in India, Ibos in Nigeria, Eritrians in Ethiopia, and Native Americans in the United States, to mention only a few, have demanded autonomy within the state or outright independence from it. Many ethnic groups have come to imagine themselves as a nation and to seek statehood for the following reasons:

(1) a sense that the identity of the group is being eroded by strong assimilationist policies of the majority ethnic group that controls the state;

(2) a belief that cultural identity and economic prosperity can be maintained and/or achieved only by breaking away from the existing state; and

(3) the belief that nationalist aspirations cannot be completely achieved without full, independent statehood.

Such fissiparous forces have begun to transform the present state system by producing new states from existing ones. The collapse of the Soviet Union yielded twelve new independent states, and the collapse of Yugoslavia produced five more. According to one observer, the number of new ethnically based states could go as high as 150. 26 Another observer indicates that the number of potential ethnically pure states could be as high as 8,000! No matter the number, there is little doubt that we have entered an age of violent nation-state reconstitution. The boundaries imposed by the European states during the age of imperialism are being redrawn by the local ethnic groups who were disregarded in the process of creating the present global system of states. These new states have also begun to transform the global Westphalian state system, which rests on European principles, regarding the separation of the spiritual and the secular. Increasingly the imagined nationhood of these new states appeals to religion both as an important source of challenge to European hegemony and as an important form of social solidarity and common will. The paradigmatic identity as a sovereign identity has also fractured along gender lines. The state as representation of a sovereign nation continues to marginalize women as a subordinate group. Traditional representations of territorial sovereignty have privileged the ideas of military engagement and soldiering as the most important social role in the state.

These roles were tied to the protection of the domestic life of the members of the state and drew symbolically on gendered discourses of public and private. Women and children constituted the private sphere, which male soldiers protected. Modern concepts of responsibility within sovereign, territorial states have clearly drawn on such ontological assumptions of a split between public and private and the representation of women and children as the ones to be protected. In states in which women have traditionally played important roles in local communities, especially in the agricultural sector, the creation of territorial state sovereignty and nationhood has resulted in a diminution of their position and left them prey to multiple forms of oppression. This is especially the case in the context of globalization, where many states promote export industries and mass industrialization by transforming the local environment in the name of economic development. In such cases, the idea of the sovereign state becomes identified with economic and social trends that destroy the traditional forms of women's (and indigenous men's) authority. Native American women in South and Central America, for example, have organized to protect the environment by promoting representations of identity in which people are presented not as sovereign agents standing outside the environment in order to use it for state development but rather as integral parts of the environment.

An internationalist consciousness among many women's organizations and feminist groups has taken hold; either it challenges the sovereign nation-state or it seeks to reimagine sovereignty in ways more inclusive of not only gender difference, but all sorts of differences that affect the position of women, such as local versus national development, and environmental protection versus economic development. By seeking to reintegrate strong conceptions of liberalism and tolerance into representations of a national community, some women's groups have sought to reimagine sovereignty to be more inclusive of the particular differences of persons. Others have sought new forms of empowerment that often leave the nation-state, and representations of sovereignty, behind, forging alliances with transnational organizations and social movements across national borders. Because membership in a nation-state can no longer reasonably assure employment, security from poverty and destitution, or a meaningful family and social life, membership in a political community becomes a fleeting and constantly moving horizon for many people rather than a secure, permanent, and lifelong identity.

The imagining of politics as located in some central representation of unified, territorially based power (i.e., the state) is difficult to conjure in the minds of ever more nomadic people. Many of the world's poor—and not so poor working class—are left to move in and out of states and to seek new political identities that might secure them a livelihood.

In today's global system, one is neither assured of being born into a nation-state nor likely to be able to create one out of some collective will as was assumed by the idea of popular sovereignty. For many in the current global order, one takes whatever nation-state one can find, often at great cost to one's sense of cultural identity. Economic elites in the global economy are also losing a sense of national political identity. Loyalty to the company—increasingly transnational and global—has supplanted allegiance to a nation-state for managers of major corporations. The pursuit of wealth as a human good and valuable human achievement for the capitalist elite is no longer bound up with the health and well-being of the nation-state into which they were born. This has always been true for many from non-European states, who would leave their home states to be educated and to seek opportunities in advanced capitalist states.

But even many of these would eventually return to their home state; this is less the case in the current global economy. Refugees (political and economic, if they can really be meaningfully distinguished in the current world of drastic inequality), guest workers (who together with their descendants perform a significant amount of the less skilled work in many managerial states), migrants, and dispossessed peoples, among others, are also ripe for appeals of alternative political identities to those of the nation-state.

The nation-state promises prosperity and security within secure boundaries, which it can no longer deliver or is not any longer willing to deliver, to the poor as well as much of the working population. Therefore, although many still seek the security, prosperity, and popular sovereignty of nation-states, at the same time they seek out other identities, often ethnic, which require ethnic "cleansing," or religious, which require the elimination of the "infidel" or "heretic." As one analyst describes the current predicament: "Where there is no nation, there is no community; where there are no territorial boundaries, there is a search for origins. If you do not define yourself by the place where you live, tell me where you come from." Identity in the current world order is becoming increasingly ambiguous, a situation with the potential for a multiplicity of possible futures, some including and some ignoring the nation-state.

Summary

The ability to represent the state as territorial sovereign has been diminished by the emerging global context of politics. The twentieth century has witnessed a dramatic overriding of territorial boundaries by military technologies and global capitalism. Peoples within states as well as those migrating across state boundaries are being forced to renegotiate their identities. The expansion of global corporations and organizations has extended, and privatized, managerial and bureaucratic control. In this context, popular sovereignty has diminished. The organs of the state have become less subject to popular input and accountability. Having lost a relatively secure relation to territory, the state has ceased to be able to secure itself as the representation of a distinct people. The globalist and neoliberal ideologies that inform the international organizations and modes of cooperation states enter into in order to manage global capitalism have freed the bureaucratic and managerial powers of the state from their anchors in ideas of "the people" or the "body politic." Hence, state power has grown and politics has become increasingly trivial. In the final chapter we turn to this paradoxical condition.

13

THE FUTURE OF THE STATE

The state is created and sovereignty instituted under specific conditions at specific times and places. We have traced the evolution of the state as it precipitated out after the collapse of the Roman Empire, as it emerged as a territorial state in early modern Europe, and as it forcefully divided the world into a system of sovereign states linked through global networks of political, economic, and cultural organization. In the previous chapter, we examined several challenges to the modern state by recent events and changes. We conclude by discussing the politics that flow from this condition.

THE END OF MODERNITY?

One of the central attributes of what is known as modernity is the historically created configuration of political space in the form of the sovereign territorial state. Modernity and the territorial state are synonymous. Remember that politics before the rise of the state was based on alternative ways of spatially organizing rule. Among the Germanic tribal peoples who filled in the geographical space of the collapsed Roman Empire, for example, the spatial dimension of rule was demarcated by nonterritorial ties of kinship. This was also the case in many places outside of Europe.

In Africa, the Americas, the Middle East, and Asia a variety of complex political organizations existed, from empires to federal and protodemocratic forms, some based on kinship groups, some on tribe, some on geographical contiguity and diplomatic settlement, some on patriarchalism, or a combination of these. Remember also that in the feudal "states" that grew out of the Germanic kingdoms, rule was fragmented, personalized, and parcelized among a multiplicity of overlapping and competing jurisdictions. There were no clearly demarcated and mutually recognized boundaries between feudal "states," only indistinct frontiers. As we saw, during the Middle Ages the territorially indistinct feudal "state" began to be transformed into the territorially exclusive, centralized medieval state. During the Middle Ages the fragmented, decentralized, personalistic rule of the feudal state was remade into direct, territorially defined centralized rule over an exclusive geographical space. Political space came to be defined as it appeared from the perspective of an indivisible sovereign, and the rule of that space came to be about maintaining public order and territorial security.

After the Peace of Westphalia, reciprocal territorial sovereignty became a fundamental principle of global order. Eventually, no space on the planet, except the open oceans, was left free from the control of a sovereign state, and even the oceans were regulated by international organizations created by sovereign states.

The geopolitics of the modern age is grounded in relations among territorially exclusive states and has been powerfully reinforced by nationalism. The story of modernity's triumph, viewed from the perspective of the territorial state, is less one of the victory of reason, science, individualism, law, and rationality (although it is that in part) and more one of conquest and imposition, of military force and coercion.

Modernity is, of course, a complex, multifarious order, and the state does not exhaust it. Moreover, the state participates in and has helped to foster aspects of modernity—developments of science, technology, and law—that have brought significant benefits. But the same developments have also had enormous negative effects. Considerable debate has emerged in current social theory about whether modernity has come to an end and is being replaced by something called "postmodernity."

Two overlapping questions have been asked in this regard: first, is modernity being replaced by a postmodern condition, and second, should modernity be replaced? In the case of the state, the question of modernity is not easily answered. State power has widened and increased in significant ways in the context of globalization, even as some of the state's traditional functions and powers have appeared to weaken.

The state remains powerful, and territorial identities, although no longer having quite the monopoly on political identity they once did, are still strong. Nevertheless, arguments about the decline of state power and sovereignty seem plausible. Underlying this paradox is the decline of territoriality as the spatiotemporal frame for politics. Having lost a relatively secure relation to territory, the state has ceased to be able readily to secure itself as a representation of a distinct people. In this concluding chapter we address two results that flow from this state of affairs:

(1) the apparent turn throughout the current world order to a "new" type of neoliberal state, on the one hand; and

(2) the emergence of a variety of deterritorialized political and social movements on the other.

The Neoliberal State?

During the 1970s Margaret Thatcher's conservative government in Britain attacked basic presumptions of the Fordist class compromise and the welfare state. Thatcher argued that these were too expensive, too collectivist, and too paternalistic. The welfare state was responsible, so went the argument of her party (the Tories), for the combined stagnation, unemployment, and inflation that plagued Britain and much of the world economy at the time, as well as a decline in patriotism and, in general, the traditional moral values of the national community.

The answer the Tories offered was a "revolution" that would install neoliberal economic policies, such as tight money to reduce budget deficits, an end to state subsidies or ownership of industry, and free trade, along with a neoconservative politico-moral agenda to restore traditional national values. The latter consisted of promoting individual self-reliance against welfare "handouts" by the state and of increasing its police powers.

The neoliberal agenda spread to the United States with the election of President Ronald Reagan in 1980. To the Tory critiques of the welfare state, U.S. neoconservatives added their antipathy to the rise of the New Left, the anti–Vietnam War movement, the radicalization of the civil rights movement, and, later, the rise of a feminist movement within mainstream political organizations.

According to American neoconservatives, these movements had added too much democracy to the political process by reforming the selection of candidates by major parties to give grass-roots members more influence than party professionals and elites, promoting too much equality by instituting affirmative action programs, and, in general, making people more willing to challenge authority in both public and private. During the 1990s the neoliberal agenda has become widely accepted by major political parties in core European states and has spread to the world order itself. In so-called newly industrializing states such as Singapore, South Korea, and Chile, similar programs of neoliberal economics and often harsh and repressive neoconservative social agendas have been promoted as the way to develop the state economically.

The economic success of the former and the appeal to "traditional cultures" and cultural autonomy of the latter have justified restrictions on and often harsh repression of worker and democracy movements. Neoliberal economic programs have been promoted more generally as a way for poorer states to get out from under their enormous debts to Western banks and the IMF. Neoliberalism as the hegemonic ideology in international managerial organizations gained credibility after the collapse of the Soviet Union, as did the acceptance of "shock therapy" to turn post-Soviet Russia and other Eastern European states quickly into advanced capitalist ones.

We do not here evaluate the validity or accuracy of the neoliberal assessment of the crisis of the 1970s. 4 We do, however, question whether the advent of neoliberalism marks a fundamental transformation of the state into a new form. We suggest that, in fact, neoliberalism retools the managerial state in response to the accelerating globalization of capitalism since the 1970s. In our view, rather than fundamentally overturning the managerial state, as the proponents of deregulation argue, the neoliberal agenda, in fact, actually strengthens key aspects of state power.

Most significant is the diffusion and deterritorialization of power. Neoliberalism delegates managerial functions to international organizations and privatizes "public" power to an even greater degree than did postwar Keynesian economic policies. The language of a strictly separate private and public realm is, in fact, reinvigorated by the neoliberal state, for its legitimacy rests on representing the economy as private (meaning outside of government regulation), and the family as private so that it can be deployed as the space in which individual responsibility, patriotism, and traditional "family" values can be nurtured.

Let us take each of these points, the delegation of power to international organization and the world market and the diffusion of state power through privatization, in turn. It is important to remember that international managerial organizations have been adjunct to the managerial state from its beginnings in the late nineteenth century. During much of the twentieth century, sovereignty was instituted by means of the sharp division between inside and outside. Economies were represented as national economies with national firms as basic units that operated largely within the confines of the sovereign territorial state.

The attempt to represent the state as economically sovereign within its territory, of course, has always included "international" aspects—international organizations, trade, foreign investment, currency exchange rate mechanisms, and so forth—but the state's territorial sovereignty presented these as outside the state.

Market theories of the economy supplemented this presentation by situating global aspects of the economy in a cosmopolitan future. As Adam Smith and others argued, the market was the result of a universal human nature, and when all peoples were brought into the system, realizing their basic nature so to speak, they would create a single, harmonious world order based on the universal principles of the market. The strategies used by states for containing the global and international dimensions of capitalism—externalizing them as being outside the primary national economy, and legitimizing them as representing a harmonious future—are no longer very successful.

The markers of the outside increasingly appear inside, and what used to be inside increasingly appears outside. In this context, neoliberalism has flourished as an ideology able to reintegrate the modern managerial state into a condition of globalization that problematizes territoriality. From the middle to late nineteenth century, the power of the state (its systems of rational management and its ability to monitor social problems and deploy expert knowledge) began to grow into a system of international unions and organizations designed to manage the expansion of the capitalist industrial system beyond the confines of the territorial state. The number of such organizations already existing by the turn of the nineteenth century is surprising, given the image of the nineteenth century as an age of realpolitik and the emergence of nationalism.

One scholar of international organizations cites 33 such organizations operating in 1914. These covered such specific areas as infrastructure (e.g., the Universal Postal Union [1874] and the Universal Radiotelegraph Union [1906]); industrial standards (e.g., International Bureau of Weights and Measures [1875]); managing social conflicts (e.g., International Labor Office [1901]; International Council for the Study of the Sea [1901]); and public health (e.g., International Association of Public Baths and Cleanliness). 6 Connected with state sovereignty, then, were a set of international organizations that, while not part of any particular state, generalized discrete functions of the state in the global order in which nation-states existed. The distinction between international and domestic, then, was an effect of managerialism, or of the limits of managerialism: managerialism constituted politics as an attribute of functional organization and management, and those functions that could not be organized by the individual states, because of politics, technological limits of surveillance, and so forth, were spatially located outside, in a new space of international organization.

This space was territorial because it was dominated by specific states that controlled its personnel, set its dominant ideology, and policed its norms of operation; it was at the same time deterritorialized because its organization depended on generating networks of forces and relations that could not be confined within any particular national space. Neoliberalism presents the late modern condition as a deterritorialized world—as a natural system of absolute free trade in which state boundaries do not act as barriers to the flow of goods and services around the globe. If they want to ensure prosperity, all states are constrained by "competitiveness" in the global capitalist economy. Perceiving the new technological revolution, TNCs, and international financial markets as inevitable givens of the late modern world system—rather than historical creations of power and the result of decisions by certain states—states must cede some of their sovereignty to international institutions and organizations (e.g., the European Union, the G-7) that will safeguard and manage the new global competitive capitalism efficiently. (The United Nations could be one such institution, but only if it is reorganized to be more efficient and managerial.) Sovereignty is hence reinstituted according to a regime of economic and technological necessity.

Lost in this reconfiguration is the idea of popular sovereignty, the sense that the central political organs of the state represent a people to which it is accountable. The ideology of neoliberalism, in which liberalism is reduced to market economics, 8 suggests that states are simply passive vehicles in a globalizing world economy whose momentum they are powerless to stop or control. Downward pressures on wages worldwide and the mobility of firms, which has created unemployment and depressed local economies, are the result of inevitable, natural market forces, so the argument goes. The best states can do is get out of the way. What this picture hides, of course, are the ways that states supplement the global capitalist economy. This is impossible for neoliberals to see because their ideology focuses rhetorically on preserving the distinction between state and civil society and state and economy, which their own policies in practice deny. This ideological move was common to the managerial state that neoliberals argue they have supplanted. In many non-European states, such as Indonesia, South Korea, the Philippines, Mexico, and China, wages are kept low by state repression of labor organizations and by restrictions of democratic political activity. In richer European states, market and capital investments are actively promoted over productive capital investments by depressing wages through tight monetary policy as well as by state intervention in labor disputes to break unions or to limit their ability to strike or organize unorganized workers.

European states continue to invest heavily in military industries, reinstituting military Keynesianism, although now with greater emphasis on military exports, which creates a false choice between either increasing state budget deficits or reducing spending on education, health care, and welfare programs. The emerging model of global managerial politics organized through international organizations does not eliminate the power of bureaucracies, as those neoliberals who fulminate against "big government" would like, but, rather, privatizes bureaucratic power. It does this internationally, by delegating power to a network of international organizations; this insulates power from any form of popular sovereignty and generates the space for a liberalism (reduced to economic liberalism) to emerge and appear as legitimate. People, regardless of nationality or political identity, are subject to the discipline imposed by the World Trade Organization (WTO), IMF, IBRD, TNCs, and global financial markets, but they have only very restricted recourse through the political (i.e., electoral) process to hold these entities accountable. In the words of one scholar, "In the current global order Anglo-American ideological presumptions have been transcribed into formal rules of the game, to which individual states must commit themselves or risk becoming economic pariahs."

The privatization of the social service responsibilities of the managerial state—health care and welfare most prominently—promotes the neoconservative social agenda, which attempts to reinscribe national sovereignty by means of promoting traditional values. Witness, for example, recent programs in the United States for retooling welfare programs that replace grants-in-aid with "workfare." Although workfare programs in the United States vary somewhat by state, they involve grants or subsidies to private employers who then hire low-skilled workers, most often at below minimum wage, from the welfare rolls. Benefits are limited to a maximum of five years during a person's lifetime and are given under the condition that recipients work. Work is seen as "its own reward." In other words, the jobs are not stable jobs that will give recipients a living wage but are training grounds of the soul; that is, their aim is to make recipients into moral, self-disciplined, and acquisitive subjects who will make their way indepe..dently in the new competitive economies. Recipients are subjected to a regime of work (rather than to direct regulation by state agencies and officials) that aims to make them into "productive" members of society. The state is still involved and responsible for the overall regulation of these programs, and without subsidies to employers and administrative rules and laws that permit the payment of wages below the minimum wage, these programs would not work. Although the practices and institutions that do the work of reforming welfare recipients are no longer state agencies, state employees still strictly surveille welfare recipients by monitoring their presence at work.

The Politics of Disaffection

One result of the neoliberal ascendancy in the managerial state is a politics of disaffection. The neoliberal view of the relation of territoriality to the "new reality" of global competition, which we have seen renders traditional liberal politics more or less obsolete, has led to widespread disaffection. For many people, it no longer appears feasible and effective to use the electoral system to further and protect their interests because the state appears more responsive to the forces of global capitalism, by presenting itself to the people as having no choice but to make sacrifices to the global reality. Some have sought to save an element of political liberalism at the edges of neoliberalism by promoting "communitarianism," which argues that individual interests are always framed by shared values. Communitarianism argues that the traditional managerial state has mistakenly overemphasized individualism at the expense of the community.

The technocratic and consumer orientation of citizens is seen as a product of a decline in moral values, which are understood as the cement of communities, and states are taken as communities writ large. Revive traditional values, especially traditional family values, whatever these might be, and citizenship will again flourish as it is assumed that it did in some idealized past. Liberal political values for communitarians are depoliticized; that is, they have become shared values that are to be taught by parents to children in a national setting, and promoted primarily through voluntary acts rather than through political organization and struggle. Whether communitarianism can successfully revive citizenship in the managerial state remains to be seen. What is clear is that an alternative response, equally depoliticizing, has taken hold. What little political liberalism the managerial state retains has been the primary victim of the deterritorialized politics of the late twentieth century. As we have seen, managerial states limited political liberalism and democracy through the industrialization and consumerization of the citizen, that is, the transformation of the citizen into a consumer whose normal stance toward the political world is as passive observer, not active participant. Neoliberalism has extended and deepened this transformation by shifting the domain of the political from the electoral system to the privatized bureaucratic systems of the global economy.

This shift does not eliminate bureaucratic and managerial power, however. It only insulates that power from any system of political accountability to the people who are its subjects. In the managerial state that dominates the late-twentieth-century states system, and in the global system of deterritorialized transnational organizations, politics has become increasingly trivial. That is, there has been a reduction of the significance of the electoral process as a means of deciding public policy and holding the state's decisionmakers accountable.

The evolution of the European state toward greater degrees of rationality has produced the managerial state, which, through its administrative apparatus, dominates and regulates an ever-widening number of aspects of social life. In such states, the bureaucratic sphere has increasingly become the site where real political struggles take place and the political sphere less so. At the same time, the political sphere has increasingly become an arena in which political struggles are represented as consumables for a passive, spectator citizenry. The various ministries, departments, bureaus, and regulatory agencies of the managerial state's administrative apparatus have become "self-regarding and selfreferential." They are staffed by a self-confident body of bureaucrats who have tenure, pensions, and autonomy of professional judgment in deciding matters of public significance. For the knowledge to make policy, they are dependent on the private lobbyists with the financial and organizational ability to control the information presented as relevant to policy debates.

Thus, the linkage between the political sphere and actual policymaking has been greatly weakened, if not broken. Shifts in the electoral support of opposing parties and changes in office holders only marginally modify the regulatory activities of the managerial state. As the site of real political struggles has shifted to the administrative arena—much of which is now situated transnationally, not within particular territories—political parties have lost much of their original reason for being. Political parties have become weak and less capable of presenting to the voters coherent policy alternatives. The traditional dichotomy between "left" and "right," which in the past reflected different ideological views about distributive justice and the role of the state, is disappearing. Old parties of the left and right are being swept away or have adopted policy positions that are scarcely distinguishable. Because political parties are no longer seen as relevant to actual political struggles, the electorate is increasingly turning away from them and declaring its independence. Party loyalty and identification have declined dramatically in most managerial states. Voters are more and more supporting one party over another not because of its policy stance but, rather, because through it they can obtain some personal benefit—a government job, a position on the board of a public entity, a more favorable disposition of an application for a subsidy, tax breaks, or a positive decision about regulation by a high-ranking government official.

Access to such a privatized government—but one not necessarily smaller or less regulatory—is reserved to primarily wealthy organizations and individuals who can buy the information and skills necessary to organize it into self-serving representations. Mostly, citizens in managerial states are bored and disaffected from a political process in which the state continues to organize their political identity but in which real decisions are taken in the bureaucracies of the state and through the transnational managerial networks of global capitalism. Turnout in elections has declined markedly in all managerial states, and the number of voters who identify strongly with a political party has fallen. People are turning away from politics to entertainment, and to representations of political struggles as forms of entertainment, such as the 1996 conventions of the Democratic and Republican parties in the United States, in order to relieve the boredom that results from the triviality of politics in the managerial state. Such disaffection, however, feeds the very forces of privatization and the decline of public accountability against which it reacts.

Deterritorialized Politics

The politics of disaffection is countered by various political movements both within and across neoliberal managerial states. In some areas, defined not only as states but subcommunities within states, nationalism continues to appeal, currently most notably in the former Yugoslavia, among Palestinians and Israelis, among the Tamils and the Kurds, and among some fundamentalist Christians in the United States. Significantly, each of these nationalistic movements contains undercurrents or supplements of internationalism within them. Fundamentalist Christians, for example, also seek to spread their religious beliefs to Latin America, Africa, and Asia. But these are not the only responses to trivalized politics, or even the primary ones. Disaffection and revivals of nationalism are increasingly contested by forms of cosmopolitanism and deterritorialized politics. It is not surprising in the current context of globalization that renewed interest in cosmopolitanism has emerged. Cosmopolitanism (from the ancient Greek kosmopolites, "citizen of the cosmos," or world) arose among European liberal intellectuals of the eighteenth century who traveled widely and developed relationships with intellectuals in other states.

They considered their rationalist and scientific orientation as a general creed of life, defining their allegiances to universal principles and humanistic solidarities against the parochial allegiances, especially of nationality and religion, which they held responsible for ignorance, prejudice, violence, and war. They considered human beings, or at least men, to be individuals first, with a universal psychological and moral makeup, which created a basis of solidarity, and even community, prior to the division of the human world into states. Therefore, cosmopolitan intellectuals considered themselves citizens of the world first and citizens of particular states second. Liberal cosmopolitanism was not necessarily antithetical to the principle of state sovereignty. In fact, it developed as an argument against more exclusionist versions of state sovereignty. It did not attempt to reconstruct the political world without sovereignty. It was not interested in engaging in political activity and organization in order to directly create a global or universal society.

For example, in what has become the most famous statement of a cosmopolitan politics, Immanuel Kant's essay Perpetual Peace (1795), Kant proposed a system in which all states would adopt republican constitutions based on the rule of law. Peace would then follow as these states worked out cooperative, juridical, and diplomatic relations among themselves. He did not propose a world government that would supersede the authority of particular nationstates, although he did enumerate universal principles that he believed engender world peace. Other proponents of cosmopolitanism, such as Charles Louis Montesquieu (1689–1755) in L'Esprit des Lois (1748), promoted various models of federalism among states.

For the early cosmopolitans, universal principles were realized in states, and the state took on an ethical character. There has been in the current world a revival of liberal cosmopolitanism of various forms. There are a range of "new federalists" and an interesting variety of proposals for "cosmopolitan democracy" in which principles of liberal representative democracy are transferred from the context of European nation-states to transnational and global institutions. In addition, there has been a revival of neo-Kantian "democratic peace" arguments, that is, arguments that democratic states are less likely to make war on other democratic states, which means that the universalization of principles of liberal representative democracy will produce a peaceful world order.

Perhaps the most striking recent development has been the revival of a liberal cosmopolitanism among business elites, technocrats in international organizations, legal professionals, and advocates of global capitalism. These elites regularly travel and function in a global context, creating personal and professional friendships and solidarity networks. They consider themselves members of a global community composed of others of their class or profession regardless of their state of origin or residence. Imbued with a vision of an unrestricted global capitalism, these cosmopolitans act politically to secure government policies favorable to their own global economic projects. Indeed, many such cosmopolitans provide crucial support, both financial and ideological, for neoliberalism. None of these revivals of liberal cosmopolitanism fundamentally challenge the principles of state sovereignty, however.

Even if an undercurrent of antistatism runs through the economic cosmopolitanism of the global capitalist business class, its understanding of politics does not challenge the political organization of the world around nation-states, even as its ideology presents the nation-state as more or less irrelevant to global capitalism. It is important to remember that in spite of the tremendous increase in the movement of people across borders, ordinary people continue to be members of their state of origin, which continues to determine their identities.

Moreover, when they do travel, most people do so as tourists, not for political or economic reasons. If, as we have argued in this book, the state is an ensemble of practices, institutions, and structures that includes the construction of identity, then the state will certainly continue to persist even as rival ways of organizing political space take hold. However, more-global forms of politics have emerged among people whose presence in the community of the globalized world is of a different sort from that of the cosmopolitan business class. Political organizations, such as Amnesty International, Doctors Without Borders, and Greenpeace, as well as more general social movements such as those concerned with the environment, women, and human rights, have emerged. These groups self-consciously adopt antistatist and global identities.

Recent United Nations– sponsored conferences on the environment and women gave official status to a multitude of nongovernmental organizations composed of individuals rather than representatives of states and governments. For the most part, these organizations and movements are democratic in a deterritorialized sense; that is, the norms, institutions, and practices of the kind of global society they promote are seen to emerge out of the political activity of ordinary individuals in the course of struggles against particular acts of injustice, inequality, violence, and ecological deterioration. A deterritorialized or postmodern democratic politics that might emerge out of the agglomeration of such organizations and activities—such a politics eschews blueprints of what a future world might look like—raises important questions: Does the alleviation of suffering and injustice, and the promotion of human rights and equality, including the defining of what these can mean in a multiculturally saturated environment, have to be tied to the territorial state? Is politics without sovereignty possible? Modernity's answer has been that progressive possibilities can only be entertained under the watchful eye of the sovereign state: that a prosperous, valuable human life is only possible if people first and foremost form communities based on allegiances to a territorial state. This answer has not yet been rejected by most, but is being challenged by many others.

Bibliography

Albert, David H. (ed.), *Tell the American People: Perspectives on the Iranian Revolution*, Movement for a New Society, Philadelphia, 1980.

Albert, Michael, *What Is to Be Undone: A Modern Revolutionary Discussion of Classical Left Ideologies*, Porter Sargent, Cambridge, Massachusetts, 1974.

Anweiler, Oskar, *The Soviets: The Russian Workers, Peasants, and Soldiers Councils, 1905-1921*, Pantheon, New York, 1974.

Chomsky, Noam and Herman, Edward S., *The Political Economy of Human Rights - Volume I: The Washington Connection and Third World Fascism*, South End Press, Boston, 1979.

Enloe, Cynthia, *Does Khaki Become You? The Militarisation of Women's Lives*, Pluto, London, 1983.

King-Hall, Stephen, *Defence in the Nuclear Age*, Victor Gollancz, London, 1958.

Lakey, George, *Strategy for a Living Revolution*, Grossman, New York, 1974.

Liebknecht, Karl, *Militarism*, B. W. Huebsch, New York, 1917.

Martin, Brian, *Social Defence, Social Change,* Freedom Press, London, 1993.

Oppenheimer, Martin, *The Urban Guerilla*, Quadrangle, Chicago, 1969.

Radine, Lawrence B., *The Taming of the Troops: Social Control in the United States Army*, Greenwood, Westport, Connecticut, 1977.

Randle, Michael, *People Power: The Building of a New European Home*, Hawthorn Press, London, 1991.

Rigby, Andrew, *Living the Intifada*, Zed Books, London, 1991.

Semelin, Jacques, *Unarmed Against Hitler: Civilian Resistance in Europe 1939-1943*, Praeger, Westport, Connecticut, 1993.

Sharp, Gene, *The Politics of Nonviolent Action*, Porter Sargent, Boston, 1973.

Shaw, Martin, *Socialism and Militarism: Remaking a Tradition*, Bertrand Russell Peace Foundation, Nottingham, 1981.

Weinstein, Deena, *Bureaucratic Opposition*, Pergamon, New York, 1979.

INDEX

□□□